AF755604

KHUSHWANT SINGH

The Man and the Writer

KHUSHWANT SINGH

The Man and the Writer

edited by

R.K.DHAWAN

PRESTIGE

Published by
PRESTIGE BOOKS
3/28, East Patel Nagar
New Delhi 110 008
e-mail: prestigebooks@greatindian.com

© Editor 2001

All rights reserved. No part of this publication may be reproduced or transmitted in any form or by any means, electronic or mechanical including photocopying, recording or any information storage or retrieval system, without prior permission in writing from the editor

ISBN: 81-7551-028-5

Composed by Vivek Mathur, Delhi 110 006 Ph. 3981867
Printed at Chaman Offset Press, New Delhi 110 002

Contents

The Company of Women

Khushwant Singh: The Man and the Writer

R.K. DHAWAN

Khushwant Singh is one of the most significant authors in the field of contemporary Indian English novel. He was born in 1915 at Hadali in West Punjab, now in Pakistan. He attended St. Stephen's College, University of Delhi, and later on King's College, London. For a while, he worked as a professor of Hindu Law at the Lahore Law College where he trained people to become inspectors, lawyers, and judges. Then he felt a sudden urge to throw away his law books and Partition helped.

In 1947, Khushwant Singh was appointed information officer of the government of India. Stints at various embassies, including the one in London which was marked by a tempestuous and contemptuous relationship with the volatile Krishna Menon saw him also writing his first novel *Train to Pakistan* which became a bestseller.

Both Indian and Western traditions shaped his mind. Though deeply rooted in the soil and in his own culture, he was moulded by the Western education that he received in India and in England. "I am the product of both the East and the West," he declares. "I am, if I may coin the word, an Orio-Occidental." His writings reveal a happy blending of scientific rationalism and liberal humanism.

Khushwant Singh's life is indeed coloured by several factors, the most important of these being his having been associated with the world of journalism. From the first journalistic assignment—a series of articles on the 1965 war for *The New York*

Times—to full time journalism as Editor of *The Illustrated Weekly of India* was a long step. Apart from this weekly, he has successfully pioneered the growth of at least three major publications in India, namely *Yojna, New Delhi,* and *The Hindustan Times.*

II

The first major breakthrough in Khushwant Singh's literary career came in the year 1950 when he published his remarkable collection *The Mark of Vishnu and Other Stories.* Almost all these were based on real experiences or those related by his colleagues and friends. During his years in London and Ottawa, several of his stories appeared in English, Canadian and American magazines. These stories at once reveal Khushwant Singh's extraordinary craftsmanship and his mastery in fusing theme and plot. In 1967, he published another short story collection entitled *A Bride for the Sahib.*

However, it was with the publication of his first novel *Train to Pakistan* (1956) that the critics declared the 'arrival of Khushwant Singh' on the contemporary literary scene. The novel *Train to Pakistan*, first entitled *Mano Majra,* brought Khushwant Singh recognition and wide acclaim. This novel won for him the Grove Press India Fiction Prize for the year 1956.

Interestingly, Khushwant Singh did not become a full-time writer by choice; he had no such intention. The decision to write came to him only when he had found something compelling to write about. This was at the time of Partition; he was greatly moved by the harrowing events during those turbulent days. His outlook towards life underwent a drastic change. He felt thoroughly disillusioned with the contemporary situation. As it was, his faith in the intrinsic nobility of mankind was completely shaken:

> The beliefs that I had cherished all my life were shattered. I had believed in the innate goodness of the common man. But the division of India had been accompanied by the most savage massacres known in the history of the country.

> . . . I had believed that we Indians were peace loving and non-violent; that we were more concerned with matters of the spirit, while the rest of the world was involved in the pursuit of material things. After the experience of autumn of 1947, I could no longer subscribe to these views. I became . . . an angry middle-aged man, who wanted to shout his disenchantment with the world. . . . I decided to try my hand at writing.

Khushwant Singh was a witness to the holocaust that followed in the wake of the partition of the country. It was indeed one of the bloodiest upheavals of history that claimed innumerable innocent lives and loss of property. The traumatic experience made Khushwant Singh restive and in order to give vent to his feelings, he took to writing and hence *Train to Pakistan*. "The partition theme," writes Khushwant Singh, "was born out of a sense of guilt that I had done nothing to save the lives of innocent people and behaved like a coward." (36) He reminds us of Joseph Conrad who as a young boy quit Poland, which was then under the oppressive rule of Russia, and who later on always carried a feeling of guilt having betrayed his country, by not coming to the rescue of his fellow-countrymen.

Mano Majra, a tiny village in the Punjab, serves as the fictional setting of *Train to Pakistan*. It is situated on the India-Pakistan border, half a mile away from the river Sutlej. Though the frontier between India and Pakistan has become a scene of rioting and bloodshed, life in Mano Majra continues to be peaceful. The village is portrayed as epitome of India; it has Sikhs, Muslims and Hindus living in harmony and amity. Partition does not yet mean much to them: "no one in Mano Majra even knows that the British have left and the country is divided into Pakistan and Hindustan." (20)

The tragic love story of a Sikh boy and a Muslim girl, interwoven with a catastrophic event, seeks to bridge the wide gulf of communal hatred. Jugga's love is indeed a positive and dynamic force of the novel. The love affair between the burly Sikh and the pretty Muslim girl cuts across religious barriers. Khushwant Singh depicts not only the emotional ties between the two, but also gives a graphic description of physical love: "Juggat Singh's . . . hand strayed from the girl's face to her breast and her waist. . . . His hand wandered again and brushed against her breasts as if by mistake." And again, he "slipped his hand inside her shirt and felt the contours of her unguarded breasts. They became taut. The nipples became hard and leathery. His rough hands gently moved up and down from her breasts to her navel." (112) By depicting such scenes, Khushwant Singh wants to shock and provoke existing norms of Victorian morality, which have always discomforted him.

Khushwant Singh's second novel, *I Shall Not Hear the Nightingale,* published in 1959, again has a historical backdrop. The action of the novel takes place during the war years, from April 1942 to April 1943. In terms of Indian history, it is about five years before the country's attainment of freedom. The astounding success of the Japanese in South-East Asia in the early forties had unnerved the British government. And now with the Japanese at the gate of India, the British faced the imminent collapse of the Indian Empire. Meanwhile the Indian patriots, sensing the end of the raj, sought emancipation from the clutches of the British through revolutionary means.

Whileas *Train to Pakistan* is a powerful exposition of one of the most moving and violent events of contemporary Indian history, *I Shall Not Hear the Nightingale* treats Indian nationalism in a most detached and critical manner. In the second novel, the sexual theme is as important, if not more, as the political. The portraiture of Sher Singh's wife, the tempestuous, sex-hungry Champak is remarkable. She offers a sharp contrast to the moral values embodied in Sabhrai, her mother-in-law.

Khushwant Singh's third novel *Delhi* created great waves when it appeared in 1990. It was hailed as a great piece of history-fiction and stayed as bestseller for several months. Some critics considered it as a bold expression of love and sex and labelled it even porno. A significant feature of the novel was the portrayal of a *hijra* as the central character—this was both innovative and relevant. No other writer, except Kamala Das in her story "The Hijra," has dealt with the portrayal of a eunuch in such an elaborate and candid fashion.

Khushwant Singh quotes Ghalib, the well-known Urdu poet, in the epigraph of the novel:

> I asked my soul: What is Delhi?
> She replied: The world is the body and Delhi its soul.

This couplet sets the tone and temper of the novel. As Anita Singh says, Delhi may be taken as a site/text/persona that assumes multiple identities. The novel draws on history as its raw material. It celebrates the past of Delhi, the city with a long and chequered history. The central character of the novel is Bhagmati, a *hijra*, who represents the city Delhi. She can be seen as a metaphor for Delhi and history simultaneously. While the narrator is a mask for the author, the *hijra* is a multiple symbol of Delhi, of Indian society and culture. In an interview, Khushwant Singh gives reasons for making a *hijra* the symbol of Delhi. Says he:

> The *hijra* stands for a symbol of sterility. It can never conceive and I thought this was a wonderful symbol for a city in which so much has happened like a sexual intercourse that repeats itself. All that has happened to Delhi—by way of violence, and in the way dynasties have changed, it has still not produced anything as great as one would have expected it.

Both Delhi and the *hijra* are sterile and have lots of fun together. For *hijra* represents Indian society in some ways, trampled repeatedly by invaders, but it represents the best in Indian tradition, especially the universal love. She is the embodiment of certain basic characteristics of Indian society and politics

A favourite subject of Khushwant Singh in his writing is love and sex. He has dealt at length with the emotions of love and passion. What exactly is this phenomenon called love? The basic cause which makes us seek the love of another person is extreme loneliness. He describes it as inner solitude—the feeling of being all alone in this world. It is rare to find people who fall in love only once in their lifetime. Most of them are forever falling in love with other people and hoping that the new involvement will prove more rewarding than the last one. He lays great emphasis on the spiritual love, but is bold enough to declare that physical love is no less important. "The good Lord," says Khushwant Singh, "has understood that, without physical intimacy, there could never be any intimacy of the soul." His latest novel *The Company of Women* (1999) is centred on the individual's search for the truth of existence within society. Mohan Kumar, a thriving businessman, is overcome by the boredom of socially respectable Delhi and embarks on an experiment with short-time companions for he is of the view that lust is true foundation of man-woman relationships "because, unlike love, lust is neither elusive, nor open to different interpretations."

The novel belongs to the tradition of the critique-of-society novels. It is focused on the modernised, westernised urban men and women. The book makes an uninhibited erotic celebration of love, sex and passion. No wonder, it has aroused extreme reactions and a mixed response from the reading public. Khushwant Singh presents a protagonist for whom body is more important than the spirit. Sex is the principal driving force in the life of Mohan Kumar inasmuch as that the book is an account of his relationship with various women. This is very well indicated not only by the title of the book but even the chapter names—Dhanno, Sarojini, Jessica Browne, Yasmine and others.

In certain ways, *The Company of Women* shares its theme with J.M. Coetzee's Booker Prize winner novel *Disgrace*. Like Mohan Kumar, David Lurie, Coetzee's protagonist has instinctive weakness for opposite sex. In the very opening scene of the novel, we meet the central character. For a man of his age, fifty-two, divorced, he has, to his mind, solved the problem of sex rather well. On Thursday afternoons, he visits Soraya who entertains him: "he strokes her honey-brown body, unmarked by the sun, he stretches her out, kisses her breasts; they make love."

The story of *The Company of Women* is similarly based on

the protagonist Mohan Kumar's varied acrobatic sexual exploits with a number of such women who are as different as possible from one another. But while as Coetzee is suggestive and just broaches on the sexual experience, Khushwant Singh is candid and frank. He is in his true element and gives free rein to his fantasies while discussing female body, "above, around, between, below." Again, at the end of each story, the personality of the hero degenerates with passage of time. David Lurie, a professor-scholar, resigns his job and retreats to an isolated farmhouse owned by his daughter Lucy; Mohan Kumar declines from a pure youth to a sexual debauch and catches the fatal disease AIDS.

III

Besides the four novels, Khushwant Singh has a considerable body of writings, both creative as well as critical, to his credit. At present, he is perhaps India's most controversial and widely read journalist. Even when he has retired from active association with any particular paper or periodical, his columns continue to appear in several of them. His son Rahul Singh has edited some of his newspaper writings under a title which perhaps offers a clue to the imagination of Khushwant Singh. He calls one such collection *Khushwant Singh's India*. As this suggests, Khushwant Singh has a specific point of view about the Indian culture. This is corroborated by his *History of Sikhs*, a massive work in the field of Sikh history and biography. His full-length portrait of Ranjit Singh vividly brings out the leader, the ruler and the man.

Khushwant Singh has had a hectic life and met and interacted with a large number of people. Some of the people he has met have left a lasting impression on his mind. In his celebrated book *Women and Men in My Life*, he gives a lively account of some of these. He is able to portray the personality of the concerned persons in such a fashion that they come to us alive and kicking as three-dimensional characters. One of such portrayals is that of Devyani Chaubal who became his friend when he shifted to Bombay, as editor of *The Illustrated Weekly of India*, in 1969. Since she was a film critic, and a gossipmonger at that, Khushwant Singh enjoyed her company and attended several film parties in her company. If he talks about the mind of Devyani, the mention of the body cannot be far behind: "There are some women whose beauty lies in their bulk, Devyani was one of them. No sooner they lose weight, they lose much of their charm." (9) The graphic image of Devyani Chaubal finds an apt description in an aphrodisiac sentence: "fat, full of life, malicious gossip, mimicry and zest for life." (10)

Certain people Khushwant Singh met only a few times but he could depict their personalities with such a finish that the reader has a complete satiety. This is the case of Amrita Shergil whom he had met no more than twice. Talking about her sexual exploits, he says: "She is said to have given appointments to her lovers with two-hour intervals—at times six to seven times a day before she retired for the night. Sex was what mattered to her." (78) Not only a men's seductress, she was also a lesbian. More than that, she was least shy of exposing her body to the male friends. One evening after having dinner with Badruddin Tyabji, says Khushwant Singh, "Amrita simply took her clothes off and lay stark naked on the carpet."

Khushwant Singh projects the picture of the popular film personality Chetan Anand in rather dark colours, someone who was "quite a character." (101) Chetan, like Bhisham Sahni and B.R. Chopra, was his class-fellow at Government College, Lahore, and once spent a summer in his apartment. When Khushwant Singh shifted to Bombay, he expected Chetan to return his hospitality and invite him sometimes to his place. But Chetan never did so. Much later when he met Chetan at a party, he bluntly told the latter: "You are a besharam matlabee (shameless self-seeker). It never occurred to you to return the months of my hospitality you enjoyed." (103)

IV

Khushwant Singh does not believe in the traditional religion. Like Bernard Shaw, he wishes to evolve a religion of his own. His parents were traditional orthodox Sikhs. All religious rituals were observed in their home. As a child of five, Khushwant Singh was initiated into reading the scriptures and at seventeen he underwent a baptismal ceremony which symbolized that he had joined the Khalsa fraternity. At St. Stephen's College, he attended the Bible classes where he was greatly drawn to *Old Testament* and *Book of Job*. And when he was working on the translations of the Sikh scriptures, he found so may references to the Vedas, Upanishads and the epics, the *Ramayana* and the *Mahabharata.* Thus, he became fully acquainted with various religions and developed a cosmopolitan outlook. By the time he was forty, he was equidistant from all religions as none of these evoked any enthusiasm in him. He does not have any soft corner for religions that preach outdated concepts and encourage fanaticism. "What I feel is required today," says he, "is what is basic and rational in the religion of one's birth after removing from it the accretions of dead wood that have accumulated" over the years.

V

If Khushwant Singh is a great writer of Indian English, he is an ardent lover of Urdu language. He is indeed among the very few who, unmoved by the linguistic claptrap, has introduced the richness and bewildering variety of Urdu to English-speaking readers. He is best known for his translation of Mirza Ruswa's *Umrao Jan Ada* which is supposed to be not only the first significant novel in Urdu language but also the first feminist fiction in Indian literature. He has skilfully translated Iqbal's *Shikwa and Jawab-i-Shikwa,* written in 1909 and 1912, and Rajinder Singh Bedi's novel *Ek Chadar Maili Si* as *I Take This Woman* (1996).

The fact that Khushwant Singh has deep love for Urdu and that he comes from West Punjab (now in Pakistan) has a great deal to do with his constant support to the cause of Indo-Pakistan relations. He generally believes that literary and cultural exchange between the two countries can be of utmost use to the betterment of Indo-Pakistan ties. Again, he strongly upholds the Lahore-Delhi bus service, launched by Prime Minister Atal Behari Vajpayee. Says he, in the *Indian Express Magazine* of 14 May 2000:

> Yes. People come and go, they meet each other. And I feel this is a good thing. At least it is doing good for relatives and friends who have been separated after Partition.
>
> It may do little or nothing for both the countries but it definitely serves as a lifeline for people whose relatives live on both sides of the border. I am even hopeful that there can be some sort of trade between the two countries in future though it may not be possible right now.

Khushwant Singh's periodic visits to Pakistan have been instrumental in bridging the cultural gap and cementing the political frictions between the two countries. With his excellent command on Urdu language and poetry, and his easy acceptability as a scholar and elder man, he has been a great draw in Pakistan. He has his own style of winning over the people he meets. In his column "Malice towards One and All" in *The Hindustan Times* of 13 May 2000, he shares with the readers the approach he adopted during his recent visit to Pakistan.

> I begin my speech as I always do before Muslim audiences with the elaborate greeting wishing them peace and prosperity: *Assalaamu Valaikum Va Rehmatullah Va barakat Ho*. They respond warmly to my paigham-i-mohabbat (message of love) from India to Pakistan. They become receptive to all I have to say about Indo-Pak relations, palatable and unpalatable.
>
> My short oration goes down well. Fellow Indians are happy with me: Pakistanis esctatic. I am on cloud nine. I am mobbed by well-wishers, dozens of cameramen follow me wherever I go. I could be a Dilip Kumar or an Amitabh Bachchan. But I am a shabby old Sardar with a yellow *patka* on my head and an *awamee* suit. Everyone addresses me as *Dada*—grandpa. It is the most invigorating ego-massage I've had in my life.

Khushwant Singh is one with Salman Rushdie on his views on writing in Indian languages. If Rushdie's pronouncements on the state of Indian literatures, published in *The New Yorker*, raised heat and controversy, no less pungent are Khushwant Singh's views on the literatures written in various Indian languages. In the writing of creative works, Khushwant Singh finds any Indian language a poor substitute for English. He wonders if any Indian language dares match the vocabulary of the English language. English, he argues, is a hybrid language, enriched by every language it came into contact with, including some ten thousand words from Indian languages. Indian languages, Singh points out, do not distinguish between "a mouse and a rat or between yesterday and tomorrow." (*India Today*, 16.8.1999) They essentially lack a technical, political and commercial lexicon too. Singh does not favour a blind bondage to the English language. He advocates a free adoption of this language for our own purposes. He questions, "What is the harm in taking English over and mauling it as we wish and pronouncing it as we want?" This not merely suits the Indian conditions but will be quite worthwhile doing it in terms of the international importance of the language. Remarks as these are bound to become controversial, given the Indian situation and the chauvinists of the regional literatures. Such bold assertions, notwithstanding the onslaught of the detractors, can be made only by a Khushwant Singh.

VI

Though in his mid-eighties, Khushwant Singh has not lost his zest and fervour for life. He is neither cynical nor disillusioned. He is a rationalist at heart and carries a strong conviction for each statement that he makes. There is not a thing on earth he is not interested in. His approach towards life in all matters is essentially liberal. He is tolerant, eclectic and intellectually committed to pluralism and multiculturalism. Khushwant Singh's contribution to India's multicultural ethos is so significant that one cannot but agree with the renowned historical Mushirul Hasan when he says: "Some people may have complaints about

Khushwant Singh. Yet, they would find it difficult to deny that this man has done so much to enrich our cultural and intellectual life for well over three decades. As an outsider to the capital of India, it is hard for me to think of Delhi without him." One wonders if one can think of an India without Khushwant Singh!

Works Cited

Coetzee, J.M. *Disgrace*. London: Secker & Warburg, 1999.

Hasan, Mushirul. "The Importance of being Khushwant Singh: A Tolerant Iconoclast." *The Indian Express*, 26 January 2000, p. 8.

Singh, Khushwant. *Train to Pakistan*. London: Chatto and Windus, 1956.

______. *I Shall Not Hear the Nightingale*. London: John Calder, 1959.

______. Transcript of a talk for the Australian Broadcasting Commission *Guest of Honour* programme, broadcast on 5th April 1964.

______. *Delhi*. New Delhi: Penguin, 1990.

______. *Men and Women in My Life*. New Delhi: UBSPD, 1995.

______. *The Company of Women*. New Delhi: Viking Penguin India, 1999.

Compulsions to Write

KHUSHWANT SINGH

The decision to write comes at the same time as when one has found something compelling to write about. I can best illustrate this theme from my own career as a writer.

I had no intention to becoming a writer nor indeed had any illusions about my capacity to handle words. I was trained to be a lawyer. Not many cases came my way and I had plenty of time to read and gossip in coffee houses. The first few cases that came my way as counsel appointed by the court were to defend people on trial for murder who could not afford lawyers (I received Rs. 16/- per day to do so). I made it a point to visit sites where the murder had taken place, interview the person in his or her prison cell and talk to their relatives. All this gave me some insight into the lives of the Punjab peasantry and exposure to the countryside. This was new to me as it was to the company I kept. I related my experiences to my drinking companions and became a bit of raconteur. I was pleasantly surprised to discover that I was able to hold the attention of my listeners. And many times someone or the other tossed the suggestion: "You should write about them."

My poor academic career daunted me from taking up my pen. Writing was for people who had topped their classes in literature or English essay and not for the likes of me who barely scraped through their exams. It took me several years to get over this sense of inferiority. And that only after I had heard stories read out by men with great academic distinctions and read Indian novelists who had made good: Mulk Raj Anand, Raja Rao and

R.K. Narayan. I came to the conclusion that one did not have to be a good student to be a good storyteller. I also said to myself, "If these fellows can write and be published, so can I."

My first collection of short stories *The Mark of Vishnu* (Saturn Press, London) was largely the product of my briefless days as a lawyer in Lahore. Almost all of them were based on real experiences or those related by friends. I took minimum liberties with the facts and this only to give them some punch.

The Mark of Vishnu did not bring me much money and was only a *success d'estime* eliciting good reviews in the British and the Indian press. I was launched on my new career. Partition of the country had rescued me from the legal profession. I was working as a press officer in London but my mind was set on having a go at the profession of writing.

The years in London and Ottawa gave me the necessary contacts. Several of my stories appeared in English, Canadian and American magazines. All I needed was the courage to kick diplomatic life and launch my bark on unchartered seas of literature. The decision was made for me by Krishna Menon under whom I was serving. At the end of four years with him I could not take his eccentricities any more and put in my resignation. "Nothing venture, nothing have," I kept repeating to myself. I had two books in my system which I wanted to get out. One was on the partition; the other on my own community. The partition theme was born out of a sense of guilt that I had done nothing to save the lives of innocent people and behaved like a coward. Writing on the Sikhs was a calculated move. I felt that in a highly competitive field my best chance was to specialise on a subject on which very little had been written. No Sikh had published a book on the Sikhs either in England or the United States.

The gestation period of these two books were the most anxious years of my writing life. I was beset with doubts of my own ability, the scoffing of friends and relatives (*Dekho ji ye bhi apney aap ko* writer *samajhta hai*) was very wounding. For six months I lived alone in England working on these books. *The Sikhs*, a thoroughly bad book, full of errors and omissions, was accepted and published by Messers Allen & Unwin and brought me some very good notices. *Train to Pakistan* (first entitled *Mano Majra*) was completed on my return to India at Bhopal. It won me the Grove Press Award from which I was able to buy a Mercedes Benz and restore my lost prestige in my family. I never looked back thereafter.

I have flitted from job to job but continued churning out books at the rate of one every six months. A Rockefeller Foundation grant gave me the opportunity to make amends for the shoddy work I had done earlier on my community. I did so by two sizable volumes (published by Princeton and Oxford), a biography of Maharajah Ranjit Singh (Allen & Unwin) and an anthology of the sacred writings of the Sikhs (UNESCO). I felt I had justified my existence and ended my Sikh history with the Latin *Opus Exegii*—my life's work is done.

A writer's work is never done till he dies. If there is anything in what he wrote, it lives after him. What drives a writer to write, I do not know except that it is a pain in the ass to do so. If he stops writing, he feels frustrated and often finds his pen has rusted and he is unable to wield it for quite some time. If he writes too much (as I do) he runs out of the ink of ideas. All the jobs I took were taken at times when my inkpot was dry; I threw them up when it was refilled by some mysterious hand. When my mind went blank I turned to translating other people's works: Iqbal, Zakir Hussain, Azad, Prem Chand, Bedi, Amrita Pritam—just about anyone whose work took my fancy.

It has been a rewarding life in more senses than one. I made quite a lot of money; I travelled to all parts of the world (at least twice a year round the globe) with travel and five-star hospitality taken care of by my hosts. But most rewarding of all was to be recognised by strangers. To this day when a pretty girl comes up to ask for an autograph, my skies are spanned with rainbows. What more can one ask of one's life?

An Interview with Khushwant Singh

MALASHRI LAL and VIJAY K. SHARMA

Khushwant Singh (b. 1915) is a well-known fiction writer, Sikh historian, and journalist. His reputation as a writer rests on the Partition novel, *Train to Pakistan* (first published in 1956 as *Mano Majra*, named after the novel's fictional border town near the North West frontier), a harrowing narrative of events resulting in ruthless mass destruction marking the division of India in the autumn of 1947. In the words of Warren French, "Singh's terse fable suggests a profound disillusionment with the power of law, reason, and intellect in the face of elemental human passions. . . . Singh is a brilliant, sardonic observer of a world undergoing convulsive changes; and his novels provide a unique insight into one of the major political catastrophies of this century." His novel *I Shall Not Hear the Nightingale* (1959) is about British abetted terrorism in pre-Independence days; according to French, it "takes a much dimmer view of human capacity for compassion and self-sacrifice than *Train to Pakistan*" (820). In many of his short stories, Singh exposes so-called religious and superstitious beliefs, expressing disillusionment about man's rationality.

Trained as a lawyer in England, Singh worked as Press Attache in Indian Foreign Services in Ottawa and London, taught at Oxford, Princeton, and various other universities. He has been a journalist of long standing and repute, writing columns for a number of national and international publications. He is also a well-known translator.

What follows are extracts from a wide-ranging interview, which took place at Singh's home on a pleasant afternoon, 5 October 1997.

Lal: How did you start writing?

KS: Interestingly, I started my career as a writer in Canada in 1947-48, when I was posted in Ottawa, in the Indian High Commission. My first story was "Portrait of a Lady," which was published in *Canadian Forum*. Then I wrote for *Saturday Post* (Toronto) and then published some stories in the American Magazine *Harper's*.

Lal: In a recent article, you said that during Partition you "lost faith not only in humanity but also . . . in religion" and that you have been "an agnostic ever since." (5) How is this reflected in your literary works?

KS: I continued to write stories that are anti-belief and that mock superstition. I have a story called "Agnostic," and my much anthologized story "The Mark of Vishnu" is rather well-known since it appears in a number of school textbooks.

VS: Yes, you are known for that kind of stance, but whenever the subject of Operation Blue Star[1] is discussed, you seem to express strong sentiments against it and tend to favour the Sikh religion.

KS: That's not quite true. Operation Blue Star has now been acknowledged as a blunder. I had made several statements about the Punjab situation to Mrs. Indira Gandhi and also in Parliament. I told Mrs. Gandhi: "You don't know my community. It is like a nest of hornets." She said that there was no intention to send in the army but then she did. I am not a believer, but I have a sense of belonging and am concerned about what happens to my community. I do not have religious belief in God and scriptures. On this account, I have often been called a hypocrite, a person who observes symbols of Sikhism. But, despite these outward symbols, I have never compromised my position. I have written on Sikh history and translated the scriptures. The more I read about religion, the more I was convinced that I should be a non-believer.

VS: You have expressed your sentiments about India's Partition and how the trauma affected various communities. Your novel *Train to Pakistan* brings out the tragedy so effectively.

Lal: And now your novel has been turned into a film. What changes did this entail in terms of dramatizing the characters and replacing English with a robust Punjabi?

KS: I think it is a well-made film. The censors have objected to the use of Punjabi abuses, but how is it possible to convey that atmosphere without *ma behan ki gali* (abusive language involving mother and sister). When the two Punjabi jats talk to one another, it comes naturally. The case is still pending in the court and the judgment is awaited. I passed the script (of the film) but had nothing to do with the casting of actors.

VS: The action in the novel evolves gradually and is very convincing, but in the film it seems rather rapid and sudden.

KS: Yes, I was surprised by the beginning of the film. In the novel, I had made this character Jugga, the son of a dacoit. In the film, his father is shown being hanged. But then that is a valid change, otherwise how could they show it on the screen? However, I have two regrets about the film: more of the pastoral life was not shown and the climax did not get the attention it deserves.

VS: Were you aware of any other creative work about Partition when you wrote *Train to Pakistan*?

KS: I believe mine was the first Partition novel. Later there were several. Saadat Hasan Manto's story "Toba Tek Singh" got a lot of attention, but it is utterly contrived. The story is about people in a lunatic asylum being divided between India and Pakistan on the basis of their religion. It tells the story of Partition in a tragi-comic way.

VS: Some other well-known ones are, for example, "Tamas". . .

KS: I saw the film *Tamas* but have not read the book. Yes there have been quite a few on this theme of Partition, much in the vernacular, which did not make the impact it deserved. For example, K.A. Abbas's "Sardarji" was not adequately translated. Initially it was misunderstood because it captured the stereotype—*Joon* (lice) in their long hair, their madness at noon—but it was a powerful story.

Lal: What is your assessment of the literature about the Partition written by later writers, say, Mukul Kesavan, Bapsi Sidhwa, and others?

KS: Mukul Kesavan, I like his writing. Bapsi Sidhwa is good, but she makes a bloomer in *Ice-Candy-Man*. The novel is based in Lahore, of course. When I met Bapsi, I told her that she had mentioned only seven Sikh gurus. You see, she had misunderstood Satguru ("Sadguru": guru who leads one to truth) as seven gurus. So I told her: *Tum hamare teen guru kha gai* (You swallowed our three gurus).

VS: Do you think she made this mistake because she lives in North America and is not familiar with . . . ?

KS: No. A Pakistani had no business not to know the basics and since she lives in America she should have done her homework better. *Ice-Candy-Man* will probably be made into a film. Yes. It has wonderful visual qualities.

VS: One wonders how Partition has been viewed in Pakistan. In India, for example, the idealists never favoured it but they had to give in. In Pakistan, people were looking forward to the birth of an entirely new nation.

KS: On the subject of Partition, the Pakistani writer is full of compassion. Yes, it was a new nation but there was a sense of tragedy about how it took place. Most of the writing is in Urdu. There is rich Urdu poetry about Partition. And then there is Punjabi writing as in the work of Ustad Daman from Lahore.

VS: This brings us to Rushdie's recent remarks on Indian literature (that prose writing—both fiction and non-fiction—by Indian writers working "in English" is proving to be a stronger and more important body of work than most of what has been produced in the 16 "official languages" of India, the so-called "vernacular languages" [x]) and the controversy generated thereafter.

KS: Rushdie was a little rash in making the statement, but I tend to agree with him generally. Vocabulary in all Indian languages is comparatively limited; English is a richer language and has a larger market. It is true that we have very good writers in Amitav Ghosh, Vikram Seth, Githa Hariharan, and this young woman Arundhati Roy. It is surprising that all this good writing in English has been during the last two decades. At one time, we used to read the Latin American writers and now all the good writing is coming from this part of the world.

VS: Do you think what Rushdie said about literatures in Indian languages has something to do with the lack of availability of good translations?

KS: No. I have seen a lot of translations. My own analysis is that it is the poverty of vocabulary. Tagore's novels are disappointing; his poetry reads better. I have read William Radice's translations. I am not familiar with Mahasweta Devi, but Satyajit Ray's stories are more readable than Gurudev's, though it is blasphemy to say so. Regional writing is limited . . .

Lal: Who have been the literary influences in your life and for what reasons?

KS: The incentive came from bad Indian writing in English. I did extensive reading of the older writers—Aldous Huxley and Evelyn Waugh. I enjoyed the wit, irony, and malice. Then there were prose writers like (Malcolm) Muggeridge.

VS: But Huxley is not known much for fiction.

KS: I like his essays, but he wrote some good fiction as well. I like the handling of language by English writers rather than the Americans such as Philip Roth.

VS: A fine story of yours, "Bottom Pincher," published long time back in *London Magazine*, reads like a piece of writing by an Englishman.

KS: I am half a Brit! I tell writers that you cannot write English unless you've made love to an English woman.

Lal: What would you tell female writers?

KS: The same!

VS: Do you think a writer has any role to play in situations such as after the demolition of Babri Masjid? Can a writer help in bringing about cultural understanding among communities?

KS: I am concerned about the resurgence of fundamentalism—the phenomena of Bhindrawale, Hindu fundamentalism, Sangh Parivar, Muslim fundamentalism. This is a theme in my (newspaper) columns and in my other writings. I write two syndicated columns a week (in *The Hindustan Times* [New

Delhi] and *The Tribune* [Chandigarh]) and they are translated and carried in different papers and magazines. . . . Sometimes when I am in a small town, a policewoman would ask me about something that I had written.

VS: It means that your views are able to reach the masses. Now that we are celebrating the 50th anniversary of India's independence, do you think there is enough to celebrate? Is it right the way we are doing it?

KS: As I have said in my columns, there is not much to celebrate. All this fanfare and razzmatazz is not justified. We have a long way to go and a lot of hard work to do.

NOTE

1. Operation Blue Star is the military action ordered by Mrs. Indira Gandhi in early June 1984 to combat the Punjab terrorists hiding in the sacred shrine, the Golden Temple, in Amritsar. Khushwant Singh as well-known intellectual and nominated member of the Rajya Sabha (Upper House of the Indian Parliament) was very critical of the action. He returned the decoration *Padma Bhushan* in protest.

Works Cited

French, Warren. "Khushwant Singh." *Contemporary Novelists*, ed. Lesley Henderson (Chicago: St. James Press, 1991), 818-20.

Rushdie, Salman, and Elizabeth West, ed., *The Vintage Book of Indian Writing 1947-1997* (London: Vintage, 1997).

Singh, Khushwant. "I Thought the Nation Was Coming to an End," *Sunday Magazine, The Hindustan Times*, 28 Sept. 1997, 5.

The above interview was first published in *Ariel*, vol. 29:1, January 1998.

Attitudes to Political Commitment in Three Indian Novels: Raja Rao's *Kanthapura*, Khushwant Singh's *Train to Pakistan* and Nayantara Sahgal's *Rich Like Us*

GILLIAN DOOLEY

Politics, and the way major events shape individual lives, and how individuals react to these events, have always been of interest to the literary imagination, since the Greek and Roman epics and *The Mahabharata* and, no doubt, beforehand. Orwell wrote, "There is no such thing as genuinely non-political literature."[1] Interpreting the word "political" broadly, this is probably true. But some writing focuses more specifically on politics in the sense of government and social organization, and my intention is to look at three such novels set in twentieth century India, and try to assess the writers' messages, particularly their attitudes to commitment to political ideals, shown through the action or sometimes inaction of the characters in the face of large-scale events which will change lives. Each of the three novels presents an insight into a particular period in Indian history: Raja Rao's *Kanthapura* deals with the independence movement; Khushwant Singh's *Train to Pakistan* with the partition of India and Pakistan; and Nayantara Sahgal's *Rich Like Us* with the Emergency of 1976. Each writer has an idiosyncratic way of revealing his or her own ideals and opinions, and from each novel we can learn something about the underlying attitudes the author holds to the difficult question of the individual's place in history, and whether loyalty to a particular ideal or system of political thought is desirable or useful

In *Kanthapura*, the idealism of Gandhi's independence movement touches the whole village, with a few exceptions. Despite the village's eventual destruction, the villagers live on with the strong hope of better times to come: "They say Rangamma is all for the Mahatma. We are all for the Mahatma. . . . They say there are men in Bombay and men in Punjab, and men and women in Bombay and Bengal and Punjab, who are all for the Mahatma. They say the Mahatma will go to the Redman's country and he will get us Swaraj. He will bring us Swaraj, the Mahatma. And we shall all be happy."[2] This passage sets the tone for the last paragraph, which describes the village of Kanthapura in a desolate state, with "neither man nor mosquito." (190) All the villager's land has been auctioned and their homes destroyed as a result of their participation in Gandhi's Satyagraha, but there is no implication that the sacrifice had been futile: self-government will be achieved. The qualities that stand out in Moorthy, the most idealistic and politically active character in the novel, are very much those of the heroes of Hindu legend, expounded in the verses 16:1-3 of the *Bhagavad Gita*. "Nonviolence, truth, freedom from anger, renunciation, serenity, aversion to fault-finding, sympathy for all beings, peace from greedy cravings, gentleness, modesty, steadiness."[3] From the narrator's first mention of him, he is almost idolized: "Moorthy, who had gone through life like a noble cow, quiet, generous, serene, deferent and brahminic, a very prince, I tell you." (5) Some allowance needs to be made for the partiality of the narrator, a Brahmin widow old enough to be his mother, towards the hero of her community, but there is no doubt that Raja Rao is basically in sympathy with her opinion. There are times when the details to which she is privy are rather implausible. On an impartial examination, we must either allow her some artistic licence, or assume that the author has enough confidence in the aura of authenticity he has created to allow the reader to accept that a middle-aged widow can know young man's innermost thoughts about a young woman, for example. It is important for us to know, after all, that during his three-day fast, "when Ratna came to see him, he felt there was something different in his feelings toward her. Her smile did not seem to touch his heart with delicate satisfaction as it did before. She seemed something soft and feminine and distant, and the idea that he could ever think of her other than as a sister shocked him and sent a shiver down his spine." (68)

This purity of thought is an important step in Moorthy's development as a good Hindu warrior, and thence as a good Gandhiman. The notion of idealistic commitment to the cause is tied at every point to Hindu ethics. Moorthy uses Hindu rites and festivals to awake political consciousness among the villagers, but he is not cynical in this. He himself believes that "If I, alone, could love Bade Khan, I am sure our cause would win." (69) But there is another side to his political activities which takes him out of the orbit of an orthodox Hindu: his dealings with the pariahs. He finds it very difficult at first to drink the milk offered by the pariah woman, and will not enter the Brahmin Rangamma's house afterwards without bathing. (77) His association with the pariahs, and the family's consequent excommunication, drives his mother to suicide. There is no mention of his reaction to his mother's death, except that he leaves Kanthapura that very night, and perhaps performs the obsequial ceremonies while he is away, "but nobody thinks of it now and nobody talks of it." (46) The good Hindu believes, of course, that he should be "free from the chain of attachments" and that "the eternal in man cannot die,"[4] and perhaps we are to accept that these beliefs carry Moorthy through his grief at his mother's death with no effect on his determination to carry on his political struggle. He is not entirely free from attachments, however. During the wedding of Venkamma's daughter, which involved the whole village, he "wandered by the river all day long, and when dusk fell and evening came he stole back home . . . and laid himself down, thinking. How, how is one an outcaste?" (84) Looking beneath the idealized Moorthy usually presented by the narrator, we can sense a human being who struggles with himself to maintain his commitment to the cause. He develops through the novel, and at the end we see him changing his allegiance to Nehru, in the hope of a better future. His political commitment is mature enough to be influenced by new ideas, while the older villagers, with Rangamma, the educated woman who had been one of the leaders in the struggle, continue to be "with the Mahatma."

(189) Ratna, the young widow inspired by Moorthy to religious and political awareness, after an unpromising beginning—"She was but fifteen. Praying seemed merely to fall flat before the gods in worship" (68)—is at the end of the novel joining Moorthy in Bombay to help in the freedom movement. Her development from flighty, sharp-tongued child-widow to independent, mature freedom fighter provides insight into the changing morality of the village itself. At first she is criticized for going "about the sheets alone like a boy," (32) but in the end she leaves the community for Bombay alone, seemingly with the blessing of the villagers. As the novel progresses, the worthy characters care less and less about worldly possessions and outward appearances, and give themselves whole-heartedly to the cause. It is surely the message of *Kanthapura* that commitment to political ideals is not only worthy in itself, but is the best means to secure a better future.

By the time of *Train to Pakistan*, most of the hopes of Kanthapura had been betrayed. Far from Swaraj providing widespread happiness, it had only been achieved by the abandonment of the notion of a united India, and the partition brought disaster to many individuals and communities. In *Train to Pakistan*, the question is not so much how to bring about a desired result as how to prevent, or at least minimise the carnage and destruction caused by events beyond the character's control. The only character who expresses, or is even fully aware of political ideas, is weak, cowardly and self-serving. Iqbal, the communist social worker from the city, is admired by the villagers of Mano Majra as "the England-returned,"[5] but it is clear to the reader, and suspected by the magistrate Hukum Chand and the sub-inspector of police, that he is not an admirable character, and he rationalizes his decision to take no action by his belief that his sacrifice will be useless if none is present to see and appreciate it. Bravery for its own sake, or for the greater good, is of no value. Iqbal has none of the Sikh virtues, and indulges in some of their vices: he drinks whisky and cuts his hair, and does not fight for *dharma* as a Sikh warrior should.

Juggut Singh is not a perfect Sikh, either, and he certainly has no notions of any political ideologies. His creed is simple:

he and authority are on different sides of the law. He is a *bud-mash* and proud of it. He is a simple man of violent, strong emotions, and although he believes in God—"No one can escape from God," he says vehemently—he breaks many of the Gurus' injunctions, in particular those to do with lust, anger, pride, attachment and thieving. However, despite these failings, he is the only character who will risk his life to save innocent people. Ironically, his motive is his illicit love for Nooran, the Muslim girl, and it is to save her life that he gives his own. Thus he is not even in his death fighting solely for *dharma,* although he is mindful of his religion when he decides to act: he requests Meet Singh to read him a verse of the Guru's word before he goes:

> . . . the elect his court adorn,
> And God himself their actions honors.
> There are sorted deeds that were done and bore fruit,
> From those that to action could never ripen. (174)

Juggut, with his simple, naive passions, is surely one of the elect, while Iqbal's good intentions will never ripen and bear fruit. Another irony implicit in the ending of the novel is that by dying to save her life, Jugga may be condemning Nooran to a worse fate, the fate she anticipates when talking to his mother: "I have Jugga's child inside me. If I go to Pakistan, they will kill it when they know it has a Sikh father." (131) Also, by dying, he eliminates any hope that he will come for her and marry her. Nevertheless, he saves her life and many others, and it is a noble act and makes a satisfying climax to the narrative.

Of course, Jugga could not have performed his noble sacrifice if he had not been released from gaol in time on the orders of Hukum Chand. Hukum Chand is a kindly, worldly man who has little time for any ideology. "The right and wrong of his instructions did not weigh too heavily on him. He was a magistrate, not a missionary. It was the daytime problems to which he had to find answers. He had no need to equate them to some unknown absolute standard." (100) He is not a Sikh, nor is his Hinduism apparent in anything except his name. He drinks, sleeps with Muslim women, and has a completely pragmatic view of life. He is almost reduced to helplessness by the force of events: "The whole world has gone mad. Let it go mad! What does it matter if another thousand get killed." (155) However, in his case as well as Jugga's, it is his personal feeling for a Muslim woman which urges him to action. It is when he learns that Haseena will be on the train to Pakistan that he conceives the idea of releasing Iqbal and Jugga in the hope that one or both of them will prevent the massacre that has been planned. His action is indirect and requires no personal bravery, and he is not even confident of its success: "He had released the budmash and the social worker without knowing much about them. They probably had no more nerve than he." And of Jugga, he thinks: "His type never risked their necks for women." (175) The impression the novel makes towards the end is that anyone who tries to use reason, or who has any intellectual ideas of morality at all, is virtually paralyzed by events. The Sikh villagers, in their attempts to do the right thing by not touching their Muslim neighbours' property, in effect surrender it to Malli and his gang. Iqbal talks himself into the impossibility and ineffectiveness of any action. Hukum Chand is almost ready to give up, but he, like Jugga, is stirred to action by personal feelings for a woman, rather than political ideals or notions of *dharma.* It is difficult not to draw a humanist moral from this result, and conclude that religious ethics may have almost as little efficacy in the face of overwhelming events as political ideals.

By the 1970s, when *Rich Like Us* is set, the hopes of the freedom fighters had been all but forgotten. This complex novel, with its plurality of narrative voices and puzzling ending is not as amenable to straightforward interpretations as the other two I have considered. Jasbir Jain writes, "*Rich Like Us* offers no easy solutions to mankind's problems, on the contrary it challenges all known solutions . . . finally *Rich Like Us* is about the complex nature of reality."[6] Once again, however, there seems to be an implication that personal feelings for others on a human level can lead to redemption of a kind. There is certainly no sense of poetic justice in the novel. It is not on the plane of rewarding virtue and punishing vice, but on that of exemplifying the courageous and good, and attributing to them a kind of redemptive power even in death, that the narrative expresses its morality.

As in *Train to Pakistan*, the politically committed figure is unable to carry through his Marxist ideals when faced with the real world. Ravi Kachru, at Oxford, was a committed communist. Sonali, the western educated part-narrator, says, "Even when we did not agree with him, he was the inspiration of all us radicals, and we never did understand why instead of throwing in his lot with the communists after Oxford he changed his mind and joined the civil service, as I, in search of another kind of involvement, had already decided to do."[7] Within a few years, Ravi is making his way up the hierarchy, and when the Emergency comes, he is one of Mrs Gandhi's favourites; the "higher up" (176) it makes sense to ask for favours. By the end of the novel, he has fallen from political grace but has finally attained the maturity to be honest on a personal level. After Ravi's admission to her of his continuing love, Sonali finds: "this admission of waste, of years gone and opportunity lost, filled me with a sweet relief. Isolated from all that had happened outside our private creation it had the wonder for me of broken ends mending, of Kachru becoming Ravi again, of friendship resuming, of love having been really love and not a mistake he had been trying to forget." (261) Thus the hot-headed political commitment of the young man is finally seen as merely one of the stages to be experienced on the path to full maturity.

Sonali herself has a system of ideals which are severely shaken by the events of 1976. Her Marxist commitment had been different to Ravi's: "Our hearts beat quite differently over our discovery of it [Marxism], his for humanity, mine for small actual conscience-pricking images, giving me a scratchy inner lining of anxiety." (110) Already Sonali's commitment is closer to reality, and she refuses to be carried away by ideology. Later she sees that "only the cloudless commitment, like the perfect relationship, could be knocked sideways with a feather. It was doubts and uncertainties that kept things alive and kicking." (261) Her strong sense of service receives a blow when she is demoted from her responsible position in the civil service because she refuses permission for a "preposterous proposal, requiring the import of more or less an entire factory," (29) when the proposal, unknown to her, had the blessing of her superiors. In spite of her feeling that she was "pretending the Empress's new clothes were beautiful,"[30] there is the implication that she would have acted in the same way even if she had known that the proposal had high political backing. It would have been impossible for her to continue to work in such a corrupt environment, in any case: "The emergency had finished my career, but suddenly I didn't want a career in the crumbling unprofessionalism that bowed and scraped to a bogus emergency." (36) Her father dies rather than "compromise with dictatorship," which she regards as "him at his strong and positive best," (175) in spite of her grief at his death. Her ideas about the virtue of taking action against tyranny are further illuminated when she reads the story of her great-grandmother's death by *sati*, and her son's desperate struggle to avenge her: "I saw a world revealed, but strangely enough it was not the evil in it I saw. . . . Not all of us are passive before cruelty and depravity. . . . And I fell asleep to dream of heroisms whose company I was scarcely fit to keep." (152) The message here is clear: individual acts of bravery, to save one's loved ones or even oneself from death, degradation or disaster, are always worth doing, whether the ends are achieved or not.

Rose, the London-born second wife of a rich businessman, could be seen as epitomizing this ideal of redemption through personal courage. Firstly, she takes a huge risk in marrying Ram and coming with him to India, even though she knows he is already married. She saves Mona, Ram's first wife, from suicide, and in spite of their initial antagonism, befriends her. And she helps the crippled beggar, who is shunned by the rest of the family. But her principal bravery is her outspokenness. It is this Cockney bluntness that makes her particularly unpalatable to her stepson Dev when he is making deals with the new regime, and secretly importing car parts for Mrs Gandhi's son under cover of his soft-drink factory. Rose is a brave woman, but she is doomed by her honesty and her invidious position in Dev's household after her husband is incapacitated by illness. Her position as a virtual widow leads to her death, arranged, as *sati* usually is, by her husband's relatives and partly motivated by the same economic reasons. Sonali, following Rose's example—she had always seen her as a friend and mentor—takes the beggar with her to safety after he has witnessed Rose's murder. And Kishori Lal, who is at first prepared to renounce his political allegiances to obtain his release from prison, finally refuses to be released and leave his young cell-mate behind. The brave, the incorrupt, the outspoken in face of evil, are admirable and inspiring, although they may not be rewarded either in this life or any other. Certainly there is no religious orthodoxy propounded in *Rich Like Us*. Mona's Hindu rites are seen as overdramatic and somewhat ridiculous, and Sonali's grandfather rejects Hinduism because it cannot explain evil. Sahgal said in an interview that "morality is ingrained deeply in everyone of us, though it may vary in details."[8] The idea of individual morality seems to underpin her writing in *Rich Like Us*.

Historically, one could perhaps trace the development of Indian political beliefs in a simple way through these three novels. Firstly, in *Kanthapura*, there is the highly committed communal movement, strongly linked with traditional religious beliefs and deeply optimistic for the future. Then comes the chaos and destruction resulting from independence and the partition in *Train to Pakistan*, where individual bravery and sacrifice seem the only appropriate response to events. Finally, in *Rich Like Us*, Sahgal describes "the decline and despair and the gathering clouds after freedom, the build-up of the totalitarianism which . . . led to the climax of the emergency,"[9] a world in which personal integrity and bravery may lead to death or failure, but are still important in themselves. All three novels imply that the individual's role in shaping history is important, but only in the early, optimistic *Kanthapura* is political commitment seen as convincing and useful. In the later novels, political commitment is rarely genuine, especially when it involves dogma or ideology, and many of those who subscribe to a particular creed are immature and self-serving. A system of ingrained morality, however, and the courage to act according to one's conscience whatever the consequences, is important in all three novels.

NOTES

1. George Orwell, "The Prevention of Literature" in *The Orwell Reader* (New York: Harcourt Brace Jovanovich, 1956), p. 373.
2. Raja Rao, *Kanthapura* (Delhi: Oxford University Press, 1989), p. 189.
3. *Bhagavad Gita*, trans. Juna Mascaro (Harmondsworth: Penguin, 1974), p. 109.
4. *Ibid.*, pp. 98 and 50.
5. Khushwant Singh, *Train to Pakistan* (New York: Grove Weidenfeld, 1990), p. 166.
6. Jasbir Jain, "The Emporer's New Clothes: The Emergency and Sahgal's *Rich Like Us*," *The New Indian Novel in English: A Study of the 1980s* (New Delhi: Allied, 1990), p. 34.
7. Nayantara Sahgal, *Rich Like Us* (London: Heinemann, 1993), p. 113.
8. Nayantara Sahgal, "Writer at Work," *Literary Criterion*, 25, 1, (1990), p. 64.
9. *Ibid*, p. 63.

Theme of Partition and Freedom in Khushwant Singh's *Train to Pakistan* and Amitav Ghosh's *The Shadow Lines*

D.K. PABBY

As the plot of Khushwant Singh's novel *Train to Pakistan* progresses towards its concluding part, one of the main characters viz. Hukum Chand, the magistrate of Chundunnugger, is a disillusioned man as he feels the sting of his helplessness to do much to stop the communal violence that had erupted in the wake of the partition of the country. Political freedom had been achieved apparently through 'non-violent' means but Hindu-Muslim riots had erupted in several parts of India and also in the newly-created Pakistan. Hukum Chand's words of self-introspective rumination quietly proclaim the futility of this political freedom without proper orientation of the people: "What were the people in Delhi doing? Making fine speeches in the assembly! Loud speakers magnifying their egos; lovely-looking foreign women in the visitors' galleries in breathless admiration: 'He is great man, this Mr. Nehru of yours. I do think he is the greatest man in the world today. And how handsome!' Wasn't that a wonderful thing to say? 'Long ago we made a tryst with destiny and now the time comes when we shall redeem our pledge, not wholly or in full measure but very substantially.' Yes, Mr. Prime Minister, you made your tryst. So did many others."[1] The two novels, Khushwant Singh's *Train to Pakistan* (1956) and Amitav Ghosh's *The Shadow Lines* (1988) attempt to grapple *inter alia* with this question of 'the tryst of others' i.e. 'the tryst of the common people' caught between the greed of self-seeking politicians, fanatic religious leaders and their cohorts, power-wielding corrupt bureaucrats and anti-social elements always looking for opportunities to exploit any situation to their own advantage; and the unseemly haste with which the labour government in Britain decided to transfer power. It is on record that Lord Mountbatten, the then Viceroy of India and later the first Governor General of free India, got his reforms commissioner, Mr. V.P. Menon, to draw up the plan for the transfer of power and the division of India in just a few hours. With this plan, he himself flew to London and got Mr. Atlee the Prime Minister of England and his cabinet to accept it in exactly five minutes. The subsequent hasty implementation of this plan without much foresight, farsightedness and the much-needed preparedness at several levels, led to an unprecedented holocaust of communal frenzy. Before the people could realize the political and social implications of the partition, they were swept off their feet by a wave of violence that swiftly became a tide. Hundreds of people were killed, raped and butchered on either side of the border, and for those who survived the catastrophe, the experience was so traumatic that the memories of those grief-stricken days haunted them for years to come. For millions of people, the independence of the country brought terrible but avoidable suffering and humiliation, a loss of human dignity and a frustrating sense of being uprooted. This is not what they had aspired for in the name of freedom—the partition was a dirty trick.

In *Train to Pakistan*, Khushwant Singh brings to the centre stage the fact of the partition of the Punjab and the question of the subsequent violence on both sides of the border in a very effective, vivid and graphic manner. In a brief preface to the novel, Arthur Lall aptly comments: "Its intrinsic qualities as a novel grip the reader. Throughout, the action sweeps one along. The characters are vivid and highly credible, and Khushwant Singh keeps them going magnificently on two levels: in their quotidian matrix compounded of their passions of love and revenge, their tremendous sense of belonging to a village community, and their insolence and heroism; and then again on the wide stage set by the tornado that breaks on their lives in the shape of the cataclysmic events of the partition of India in 1947." In fact, the novel opens with forebodings of ill omen: "The summer of 1947 was not like other Indian summers. Even the weather had a different feel in India that year. It was hotter than usual, and drier and dustier. And the summer was longer. No one could remember when the monsoon had been so late. For weeks, the sparse clouds cast only shadows. There was no rain. People began to say that God was punishing them for their sins." (1)

Khushwant Singh goes on to describe how the feeling of guilt arose from the maddening violence by the Hindus and the Muslims precipitated by reports of the proposed division of the country into 'a Hindu India and a Muslim Pakistan.' The riots had first broken out in Calcutta and then spread north and east and west engulfing a vast segment of population. Though the novelist does hold the Britishers and the political leaders responsible for the avoidable communal riots, he does not take any sides: "Muslims said the Hindus had planned and started the killing. According to the Hindus, the Muslims were to blame. The fact is, both sides killed. Both shot and stabbed and speared and clubbed. Both tortured. Both raped. . . . The riots had become a rout. By the summer of 1947, when the creation of the new state of Pakistan was formally announced, ten million people—Muslims and Hindus and Sikhs—were in flight. By the time the monsoon broke, almost a million of them were dead, and all of northern India was in arms, in terror or in hiding." (1-2) The massacres and brutalities unleashed by the partition are then juxtaposed against the harmonious bonds of friendship, brotherhood and good-neighbourliness in an obscure, sleepy and tiny village Mano Majra situated near the border and inhabited by only seventy families out of which "Lala Ram Lal's is the only Hindu family. The others are Sikhs or Muslims, about equal in number." (2) Simplicity and calmness of the lives of the Mano Majrans can be gauged from the fact that all the activities of villagers are closely related to and measured in terms of the arrival and departure of various trains from early morning till late in the evening. The shattering of the peace and harmony of this small helmet with the brutal murder of the village moneylender Lala Ram Lal and the daring dacoity at his house by the gang of

Malli and his men, is a kind of foregrounding of the communal violence and the anarchic chaos that was to be let loose later. "Ram Lal uttered a loud yell and collapsed on the floor with blood spurting from his belly. The dacoits jumped off the roof to the lane below. They yelled defiance to the world as they went out towards the river. 'Come' they yelled. 'Come out, if you have the courage! Come out, if you want your mothers and sisters raped, Come out! brave men!'" (10)

A close reading of the novel clearly reveals that the dacoity at his house and murder of the moneylender are not merely accidental—these are a prelude to the swelling acts of murder and violence across the frontier which do not remain unretaliated. Though the conversation between the police sub-inspector and the District Magistrate of Chundunnugger about the communal situation in the district town, in the border village of Mano Majra, and the general situation on both sides of the border, is subsumed with gentle irony, it does articulate the general mindset as is clear from the following:

> "Do you know," continued the magistrate, "the Sikhs retaliated by attacking a Muslim refugee train and sending it across the border with over a thousand corpses? They wrote on the engine 'Gift to Pakistan'!"
>
> The subinspector looked down thoughtfully and answered: "They say that is the only way to stop killings on the other side. Man for man, woman for woman, child for child. . . . Here we are on the border with Muslims living in Sikh villages as if nothing had happened. Every morning and evening the muezzin calls for prayer in the heart of a village like Mano Majra. You ask the Sikhs why they allow it and they answer that the Muslims are their brothers." (19-20)

But the calmness of the atmosphere in this 'oasis of peace' gets shattered when the 'ghost trains' start arriving in Mano Majra. The tense situation is evocatively articulated by the novelist in the opening paragraph of the chapter titled *Kalyug*: "Early in

September, the time in Mano Majra started going wrong. Trains became less punctual than ever before and many more started to run through at night. . . . children did not know when to be hungry. . . . Goods trains had stopped running altogether, so there was no lullaby to lull them to sleep. Instead, ghost trains went past at odd hours between midnight and dawn, disturbing the dreams of Mano Majra." (77) And as days passed by, there were more news as well as rumours about the brutalities by the Muslims and Sikhs against each other on this and that side of the border. These obviously led to suspicions between the two communities which had lived together as family members for decades. "Quite suddenly every Sikh in Mano Majra became a stranger with an evil intent. His long hair and beard appeared barbarous, his kirpan menacingly anti-Muslim. For first time, the name Pakistan came to mean something to them—a haven of refuge where there were no Sikhs." (120-21) And the Sikhs too became sullen and angry and some of them started saying "Never trust a Mussulman." The young were particularly unhappy and agitated especially after the arrival of some 'refugees' from across the border. Yet the feeling and spirit of mutual welfare and brotherhood endured and after a long meeting Imam Baksh said: "What have we to do with Pakistan? We were born here. So were our ancestors. We have lived amongst you as brothers." (126) But when the Muslims feel compelled by the circumstances to leave for Pakistan in spite of all the good intentions of the local Sikhs, another aspect of partition/freedom is revealed. Infamous Malli and his gang who had looted the village moneylender and murdered him in defiance of the law, not only now align themselves with the instigators but are also officially appointed 'custodians' of the Muslim property left behind and proceed to loot in broad daylight. On the instigation of the young Sikh boys, quite a few of the Mano Majran Sikhs volunteer to aid and abet the destruction of the train stealthily at night so that the Muslims of Chundunnugger and Mano Majra among others, would not go alive and safely to Pakistan. The young Sikh, ironically of course, swears by the Gurus and inflames the fellow Sikhs of Mano Majra with the words "By the Grace of God/We bear the world nothing but good will" (152) on his lips. It is, however, the sagacity of the shrewd and wily but good-intentioned District Commissioner who heaps all kinds of abuses on the new political bosses for creating the traumatic situation, that saves the Muslim passengers from being butchered not with the help of the police but with the help of the village Budmash Jugga who was released from the jail and who was told that his beloved Nooran was also travelling by the same train. Jugga, though a dus-numbri (a proclaimed offender) had his mind and heart fired with the noble sentiment of love for Nooran. No sooner is he released than he rushes to cut the thick rope stretched and tied tightly across the railway bridge, after seeking Guru's word from Bhai Meet Singh even without understanding the meaning of that word. In the process of ensuring safe passage of the train to Pakistan, he has to make the supreme sacrifice of his own life: "He went at it with the knife, and then with his teeth. The engine was almost on him. There was a volley of shots, the man shivered and collapsed. The rope snapped in the centre as he fell. The train went over him, and went on to Pakistan." (181) Though some critics have labelled this ending of the novel as 'somewhat melodramatic' due to the lack of sufficient foregrounding of Jugga from a budmash, an anti-hero, into a hero, Jugga's sacrifice can be probably viewed as a form of wish fulfilment for the writer to achieve in fiction what on his own admission, he could not achieve in real life at the time of partition. Referring to the questions raised at the Press Conference after the screening of the film version of *Train to Pakistan* directed by Pamela Rooks at the recently concluded International Film Festival in New Delhi (11-20 January 1998), Khushwant Singh made the following comments which seem to be very pertinent even today i.e. fifty years after the unfortunate tragedy of Partition took place:

> Should the partition be forgotten? Has it any relevance to us today? My answer to both the questions is an emphatic yes. We must not forget the partition because it is relevant today. We must remember that it did in fact happen and

> can happen again. That is why I keep reminding people who clamour for an independent Kashmir, Khalistan or Nagaland to remember what happened to Muslims when some of them asked for a separate Muslim state. I keep telling my fellow Sikhs that the worst enemies of Khalsa Panth are Khalistanis, and of the Nagas those who ask for an independent Nagaland. Reminding ourselves of what happened in 1947 and realizing the possibilities of its recurring, we should resolve that we will never let it happen again.[2]

In *The Shadow Lines* the development and growth of Tha'mma's character encapsulates the futility and meaninglessness of political freedom which was otherwise supposed to usher in an era of peace and prosperity for all. During the days of her childhood and youth, she had her sympathies with all those who were fighting for the cause of freedom. In fact, she too wanted to earn small portion of the glory enjoyed by some of her classmate 'terrorists' by running secret errands for them or even cooking for them and washing their clothes. The aim was to be associated with such a group of persons, actively involved in fighting for a 'pious cause.' In response to a question by the narrator, "Do you really mean Tha'mma, that you would have killed him?"[3] we are told thus:

> She put her hands on my shoulders and holding me in front of her, looking directly at me, her eyes steady, forthright, unwavering: 'I would have been frightened. . . . But I would have prayed for strength, and God willing, yes, I would have killed him [the English Magistrate.] It was for our freedom: I would have done anything to be free.' (39)

Her formative years have taught her the need, necessity and desirability of political freedom which is a sort of pre-requisite for economic, social, cultural and intellectual freedom and development. As Novy Kapadia points out, the theme of the novel encompasses all these experiences: "By exploring connections, distinctions and possibilities, Amitav Ghosh shows that in a changing world, different strands of nationalism and ideology will exist and even compete. The force of nationalism in the quest for freedom or ideology is often a source of violence. . . . So the 'shadow line' between people and nations is often mere illusion. The force and appeal of nationalism cannot be wished away (so easily), just as death by a communal mob in the bye-lanes of old Dhaka."[4] Dhaka has been Tha'mma's place of birth, but her nationality is Indian. As a young girl, she had thought of fighting for freedom in East Bengal. But those very same people for whom she had been willing to lay down her life are enemies now in 1964. Feelings of nationalism had after all motivated the fight against the British in Khulna. But in 1964, the group of Indians travelling in the embassy car are the enemies to be hunted down and killed.

However, Tha'mma's disillusionment increases when she has to mention her birthplace on the passport-form during her visit to Dhaka. Home ought to be the place where one was born and brought up, sealed by an emotional bond, where one can claim one's right without a thought and without any hesitation. And if there was a basic confusion on this score—about the very roots of one's origin—an individual's identity would be in question. Leaving Dhaka during the Partition had obviously meant severing old roots and groping for a new kind of stability and identity. Therefore, years later, on her visit to Dhaka, she is distressed to write 'Dhaka' as her place of birth: "She liked things to be neat and in place—and at that moment she had not been able to quite understand how her place of birth had come to be so messily at odds with her nationality." (152)

Finally, the fact that "The border isn't on the frontier: it's right inside the airport" (151) puzzles Tha'mma all the more and she feels that her sacrifice has been in vain: "But if there aren't any trenches or anything, how are people to know? I mean, where's the difference then? And if there's no difference both sides will be the same; it'll be just like it used to be before, when we used to catch a train in Dhaka and get off in Calcutta the next day without anybody stopping us. What was it all for then—partition and all the killing and everything—if there isn't something in between?" (151) Tridib's death bewilders her further. She finds her idealism fast turning into helplessness as the anarchic tendencies within and without her gather force. There is obviously need for an order, a new order, but what kind of an order, remains an unanswered question. Tha'mma lies in bed, weak and helpless. Even as she realizes that war, partition and violence are meaningless if they create no visible borders between two countries; she never accepts and understands Ila's desperate urge to settle in England. Her orientation may be apparently that of a 'war-mongering fascist' as Ila terms it, it is nevertheless a harsh truth or at least a harsh partial truth that marks the psyche of the modern nation-states. The likes of Tridib have to die so that a comprehensive view of real freedom may find favour and flourish with the help of personal relationships. Ultimately, the responsibility of achieving and sustaining real freedom rests with every individual as it lies with every nation too within the larger framework. In fact, *The Shadow Lines* questions prevailing precepts and ethics which man inherits blindly. The value of political zeal and social freedom is no longer stable, exclusive, permanent and immutable as Tha'mma and Ila had believed. The apparent stability which is offered by such ideas often proves to be illusory. With Tridib, however, the novel emphasizes the relevance and significance of human relationships. This alone can lead to an attainment of genuine freedom. Man is free to decide on a course of action which is found to affect a whole group of people, a nation, mankind. Every individual shares the responsibility of establishing a code of values which would ensure peace and solidarity for mankind. As Sartre said: "Every one of our acts has at its stake, the meaning of the world and place of man in the universe. Through each of them, whether we wish it or not, we set up a scale of values which is universal."[5]

It has to be remembered that freedom is not just the absence of external pressure, it is also the presence of something else. The struggle for freedom is not without its darker side. If the fight for political freedom aims at ensuring peace for a particular community, it may also arouse and mobilize diabolical forces in man—forces which one would have believed to be non-existent, or at least to have died out long ago. If social and moral freedom is unlimited, it may unleash the numerous problems of excess and the lack of restraint. Taking all this into account, the question that arises is whether there is such a condition as complete freedom? Are freedom for the individual and for the society linked to and compatible with each other? And is absolute freedom a possibility for an individual, a community or for a nation? Should there be sufficient essential preparation, orientation and education of the individuals and of the society to enable them to digest their freedom, realize its full potential and cope with this freedom with dignity and with rationality? Fortunately both the novels *Train to Pakistan* and *The Shadow Lines* raise these significant questions in all their various dimensions and the narratives of the two obliquely explore and subtly answer these questions with the much needed flexibility of interpretation especially with reference to the pluralistic, multilingual, multicultural, multireligious and multiethnic character of the vastly-spread society of India in its widespread regions and teeming with paradoxes and contradictions at several levels.

In conclusion, it can be said that the partition of the Indian sub-continent was the single most traumatic experience in our recent history. The violence it unleashed by the hooligan actions of a few fanatics, the vengeance that the ordinary Hindus, Muslims and Sikhs wreaked on each other worsened our social sense, distorted our political judgements and deranged our understanding of moral righteousness.

The real sorrow of the partition, however, as portrayed in the two novels under review, was that it brought to an abrupt end a long and communally shared history and cultural heritage. The relations between the Hindus and the Muslims were not, of course, always free from suspicions, distrust or the angry rejection by one group of the habits and practices of the other; but such moments of active malevolence and communal frenzy were a rare and transient exception to the common bonds of mutual goodwill and warm feelings of close brotherhood. Even if there were some disruptions on some rare occasions, the rich hetero-

ligious identities. Organizations which nurtured violent hatred towards each other and incited communal passions did exist, but at the very margins of the solidly and healthily functioning social and cultural order. It is the unthoughtful decision of partition and hollow love of 'nationalism' that let the mischief off and out.

NOTES

1. Khushwant Singh, *Train to Pakistan* (1956; New Delhi: Time Books International, 1989), p. 176.
2. Khushwant Singh, "A Forgetful Nation" in "With Malice towards One and All," *The Hindustan Times*, January 31, 1998, p. 13.
3. Amitav Ghosh, *The Shadow Lines* (Delhi: Ravi Dayal Publishers, 1988), p. 39.
4. Novy Kapadia, "Imagination and Politics in Amitav Ghosh's *The Shadow Lines*," ed. Viney Kirpal, *The New Indian Novel in English: A Study of the 1980s* (New Delhi: Allied, 1996), p. 205.
5. Sartre, *Le Sursis*, qtd. Henry Peyre, *French Novelists of Today* (New York: Oxford University Press, 1967), p. 267.

The Doomed Hero in the Novels of Khushwant Singh and Manohar Malgonkar

HAYDN MOORE WILLIAMS

The hero as once understood in classical literature has virtually disappeared from modern literature, conspicuously so from the literature which has dominated the world since the first world war. Perhaps when James Joyce made Ulysses into a 'mean sensual man' wandering round a distinctly unheroic Dublin Town in 1904, he signalled the end of that old type of hero and ushered in the new, a kind of shuffling Chaplin figures in baggy pants. The Penelope of this new Ulysses was equally unheroic and unchaste, rather the slightly decrepit ex-singer of operatic areas who lay abed unwashed in slightly soiled knickers waiting to 'entertain' a faintly ridiculous lover called Blazes Boylan. Interestingly enough, even this apotheosis of the non-heroic was a deliberate reflection of the heroic, if only in parody and irony; hence the Homeric parallels.

Insofar as Indian literature in English was related to this wider English literature, it too seems to have begun with the unheroic. Mulk Raj Anand's novels *Untouchable* and *Coolie* were very much part of the naturalism which called for fiction that explored the lives of the poor and the outcast and sought to embrace tragedy in the Thomas Hardy mode of the 'Humble Victim' crushed by the relentless immobility of rigid class structures and imperial feudalism. This does not mean that there is no heroism in Anand or in such a novel of village India as Raja Rao's *Kanthapura* which also appeared in the 1930s. Heroism there is—in the sense of the heroism of the group, the masses, the downtrodden millions. It was heroism linked not only with the theoretically based realism of the Socialist art of Russia sometimes imitated by American writers like Dreiser and Steinbeck but with the cinema of the time with its specialised ability to depict the movement of masses and crowds in revolution and war or gripped by the savagery of Nature in famine and flood. What was absent from Anand and others was the romantic hero, the military hero, the 'Great Man' in the Carlylean view of history, and the epic hero of Homer, Virgil and the Indian epics. Since the novel itself had emerged in Europe as in Fielding's ingenious insight, mock-heroic—'a comic epic in prose'—it was very difficult for the typical novelist to return to the heroism of the true epic unless, like Joyce, he should hold up the distorted mirror of a Leopold and Molly Bloom. To substitute for the hero the heroic masses was to seek a way of compromise doomed to failure. The realism of the socialists and the realism of "little men and women" as envisioned by Steinbeck in *The Grapes of Wrath* leaves the hunger for romanticism unsatisfied. In America *The Grapes of Wrath* could not compete in popularity with the romantic and nostalgic *Gone with the Wind.* In England, there was a similar hunger after the second world war and the hunger was satisfied at least for a while by Tolkien's *Lord of the Rings.*

> The romantic hero has in fact returned to Indian literature in English also, in the novels of Khushwant Singh and Manohar Malgonkar. I will suggest that with these writers too, nostalgia and revolt against realism have played not insignificant roles. But a more obvious role in the revival of romantic heroism (however fitfully and ironically) has been taken by history. The revival is the product of three historical moments: World War II in which Indians were involved as combatants on the side of both Allies and Axix; the arrival of Independence and the assassination of Mahatma Gandhi; and lastly the series of wars that India has fought against Pakistan and China. Involved in the first two of these was of course the struggle for liberation from English rule. However this too was treated very singularly indeed by Khushwant Singh and Manohar Malgonkar and not at all

in the way it had been treated by Anand, Raja Rao and R.K. Narayan, the three most distinguished of Indo-British writers before 1947.

My next point is the intrusion of the adjective "doomed" to stand next to "hero." There is nothing unusual about the collocation. Nearly all the heroes of classical epic were doomed to die, or at least to suffer, for their people—including Rama and Sita and the Pandava heroes of the *Mahabharata* no less than Achilles, Hector, Beowulf, Siegfried, Roland and Oliver, King Arthur and Lancelot du Lac. Doom is something that appeals to our more unheroic and masochistic age. A tragic destiny hangs over modern literature like a miasma from Hardy's Tess and Jude, Conrad's Kurtz, Thomas Mann's Leverkuhn and Aschenbach, and Kafka's Joseph K. to the heroes of Scott Fitzgerald, Faulkner and Hemingway. This existential doom is something peculiar to this age of anxiety which has lost contact with the relative certainties and confidences of a pre-scientific, pre-Freudian, pre-Darwinian age. But doom attended the destiny of heroes of antiquity and the middle ages. Greek heroes and Shakespearean kings were inevitably murdered or died by their own hand. After the heights—the depths. They died in some mysterious way for their people like the archetypes—King Arthur, Oedipus or King Lear. The fallen dictator did not retire to write his memoirs or "get back to power with an increased majority." He might, like Mussolini or Stalin, hope for rehabilitation with some wheel coming full circle—after death, not before. Hamlet's dying wish, Othello's last gasp of terrible self-justification, Macbeth's act of despairing heroism are all related to the inevitability of doom. And it is the doom that in some strange way seals the heroism. It is as if every earthly Christ must die before his body and blood can be available for the soul-nourishment of all the faithful. King Arthur or Sita or Arjuna must all go away the better to be available to us little ones.

The doomed hero then is a mystic archetype totally out of touch with the modern age's scepticism and banality, an age for whom the natural heroes are not kings but pop-singers and footballers. The doomed hero of epic is also at the other end of the pole from the doomed peasant or "little man lost."

In the post-World War II, post-Indian Independence fiction of Khushwant Singh and Malgonkar, heroism is sought in the ranks of the military, the princes, and paradoxically too among bandits and the criminal classes. Khushwant Singh adds an element of ethnological difference—or sectarian difference: his heroes are usually Sikhs. This is not unexpected in an author who is a Sikh and the historian of a community with a remarkable martial tradition, a community that nurtures as a communal and religious virtue. *Train to Pakistan* (1956) is one of the great novels of the Partition and in its tone reflects much of the cynicism and fear of human savagery which was generated as the result of the communal massacres that resulted from the forcible splitting of the sub-continent between India and Pakistan in 1947. In this, Khushwant Singh's first novel, there is a village called Mano Majra which is astride the Pakistan-India border and it is a railway junction. Muslims, Hindus and Sikhs live there in easy comradeship until the Partition. Ironically the only problem until then is from the depredations of the dacoit, a Sikh called Juggut who emerges gradually as the hero of the book. Magistrate and police can just about deal with dacoity which is after all traditional and even intercommunal. They are totally unable to control the communal violence that threatens to erupt when a train arrives full of slaughtered Hindus and Sikhs. The Sikhs vow vengeance. A train of Muslims is to be waylaid and the passengers (refugees on the way to Pakistan) are to be massacred to the last man, woman and child.

With effective satirical irony Singh shows the failure of various key characters to solve the appalling dilemma presented by the Partition crisis. The police are corrupt. The magistrate Hukum Chand is clever, but he is also corrupt and very lecherous (as is the Sikh *budmash* Juggut if it comes to that). Recoiling from the awfulness of the dead Muslim corpses, he buys the favours of a little prostitute and goes to bed to fornicate and get drunk. As for the new rulers of India—Congress politicians—they are universally despised and derided. There are new men on the way—a new political philosophy represented by a newly arrived Sikh intellectual, Iqbal. He is a Communist and therefore shares the villagers' dislike of Congress, yet he too is the victim of the Marxist illusion that class struggle will replace "idiotic" communal friction. All men are brothers. This is the Communist cry—but it was also the motto of the Sikhs in their emergence as a martial community. The paradox of this defeats Iqbal; and in the event he is inadequate and inert. He is even prepared to allow a massacre of the Muslim trainload if it will help in the ultimate class struggle and the victory of Communism. Even worse than this Machiavellianism is the cowardice; he is one of those "milquetoast" intellectuals pilloried in Singh's pages—who can do nothing except theories. His complete antithesis, Juggut, is a passionate man of action, as adept at murdering and thieving as he is at "fetching down a wench's bloomers." Almost comically lecherous, he cross-examines Iqbal about the sexual endowments of European women only to be disappointed by the Sikh Comrade's ignorance on this "most interesting subject." Ironically his lust for his Muslim mistress (turning to love) stimulates Juggut to an act of self-sacrificial heroism. He saves the refugees and falls under the wheels of the train. Juggut is indeed a doomed hero; but he accepts his doom with an astonishing cheerfulness that is the very reverse of the existential anguish. Strongly superstitious, he believes in Fate. The Baluch soldiers of Pakistan will, he says, meet their fate somehow "They cannot escape from God." (66) Like one of Hemingway's "dumb oxen" but without the despair he lives moment to moment, alert to the joy and pain of the physical, and accepts the brutal and the physical whenever it comes, savage and sensual fornication in the fields or a flogging on the buttocks from Hukum Chand's policemen. The casual brutality of nature and simple men—even the policemen who flog and insert red hot chillies into the bums of prisoners—he accepts with goodhumoured resignation. He reserves his contempt for the cowards and hypocrites and *real* sadists—the Baluchis, Hukum Chand, Congress politicians and intellectual Communists like Iqbal.

Train to Pakistan for all its obvious fascination with violence is a tour de force of imaginative storytelling, a profoundly moving and moral work that is perhaps one of most telling refutations of certain types of pacifism to have emerged from the India of Mahatma Gandhi—which is also of course the India of Netaji Bose and the Sikh military orders. Khushwant Singh followed it up with a novel that deals with the lure of violence and the paradox of heroism. *I Shall Not Hear the Nightingale* centres on a middle class Sikh family in the Punjab during World War II. Where *Train to Pakistan* had been all action, passion and a hymn to the heroism of simple peasants and wild bandits, the new novel was a complex and disturbing study of adolescent psychology. Buta Singh is a magistrate attempting the difficult juggling feat of loyalty to the British while keeping on the right side of Indian nationalists who are certain to win at the war's end. His son Sher Singh is a would-be hero fascinated by guns living in arrested childhood subservience in his father's house though married—prematurely—to a nymphomaniac called Champak who deceives him shamelessly. Sher Singh's gun-fever is in obvious Freudian terms presented as a phallic substitute, since he is rather an inadequate lover in ludicrous contrast to the sexually hyperactive Champak. Meanwhile the famous cricketer Madan, Sher Singh's hero, not only cuckolds him with Champak but makes sexual advances to his sister. Sher Singh in compensation becomes the leader of a gang of schoolboy terrorists. When a police spy is murdered, the gang is arrested.

In prison awaiting possible death by hanging Sher Singh proves to be far from a hero. His father abandons him to his fate but his mother insists that he should die rather than betray his friends. The old woman so impresses Taylor the benevolent English Resident that he pardons Sher Singh who luckily gains freedom before having to prove his heroism. It is a deeply ambiguous and cynical ending. But there is heroism in this novel—the heroism of Sher Singh's mother who emerges in strong lines at the end of the book. Yet ironically she does not live to "hear the nightingale" of Indian freedom. She dies in the middle of the celebration of the British honour conferred on Buta Singh for loyal service to the Raj!

Khushwant Singh's interest in sexual behaviour and in the fascination of violence especially to young Indians brought up in the rigid extended family system and under British rule in the exciting atmosphere of the war years is obvious in *I Shall Not Hear the Nightingale.* But as a novel, it is less effective than *Train to Pakistan* by the very fact of its greater complexity and its psychology. Sher Singh's problems are almost entirely psychological and sexual. There is no evidence that he is in any sense a political idealist or a genuine nationalist hero. He flirts with violence and death, lured by the phallic gun and the base corrupt example of Madan. Even in bed with his bride he remains a spoiled child, half-impotent and yet a boaster. The simple violence of a Juggut is transferred to the Eurasian policemen (the Hydes of the British Jekylls) when they casually kick Sher Singh in the testicles, utter fulsome obscenities, and threaten to put some hot chillies "up his arse." The true centre of Sikh traditional heroism lies in the dying mother—a doomed and admirably tragic—one who will not hear the nightingale sing of freedom and peace.

Doomed heroes are the preoccupation—one might even say the obsession—of the novelist ex-soldier, ex-hunter, ex-Right-wing politician, Manohar Malgonkar whose books like Singh's appeared in the 1960s—a great decade for Indian-English writing, incidentally, seeing the publication of Raja Rao's *The Serpent and the Rope* and R.K. Narayan's *The Man-Eater of Malgudi.* Heroism and the importance of action rather than the pale cast of thought become thematic for Malgonkar as for Singh, but in other ways there are great differences. Malgonkar is not primarily interested in the Sikhs or in any other specific national or religious grouping with its traditions and "hang-ups." What intrigues him is the *Kshatriya* prince and soldier with codes of honour which are irrational and historic, or mythic even, but certainly have nothing to do with practical politics or with the modern illusions of either Marxism or parliamentary democracy. More particularly Malgonkar seems to have been immensely influenced in his social thinking by the codes promulgated in the British trained Indian Army. The hero of *Distant Drum* Kiran

Garud is drenched in the rituals and taboos and immemorial traditions of the 4th Satpuras when the officers of that regiment were mainly British. In the colossal mutations of Independence, partition and war, it is these apparently absurd irrationalities that survive and prove productive and living rather than ideas or mundane practicalities.

The "British" Indian Army emerging as a strange but strong plant out of the manure of blood and suffering was founded on the principles originally inculcated in generations of English public schoolboys educated according to the rather extraordinary principles of Dr. Thomas Arnold of Rugby father of the poet and accidental foster-father of the game of rugby. "Arnoldism" was a queer amalgam of "Muscular Christianity" (the reverse of piety) with Roman stoicism and the stiff-lipped ideals coldly asserted in the poetry of Virgil and Horace. It was essentially a "school" code of honour. A boy passed the test by enduring without protest the apparently irrational and sometimes unjust system imposed upon him from on high. He did not sneak, did not complain, took his floggings with buttocks bared, teeth gritted and upper lip stiff. The Army code was like that. It also bred an intense and passionate comradeship that could survive war, nationalism and communal violence in India. It was, Malgonkar suggests in the career of his hero Kiran, one of the few gifts of the British Raj to emergent new India. Its morality has little to do with good versus evil, but a lot to do with loyalty versus disloyalty and action versus inaction. Bravery, endurance, mutual trust, are the virtues which emerge curiously from fatuous Mass rituals and idiotic games.

The story told in *Distant Drum* is indeed an unusual one compared to the average Indian-English novel of the period. Only Singh's tales, of Sikh crooks and "he-men" come near it. Kiran's love-affair with the Army proves to be the strongest impulse of his life—stronger than love of women or even of life itself. Kiran is like Singh's Juggut, essentially simple, passionate and wilful. Tamed but never subdued by the British or their Officer's code, he conceives, with intuition not intellect, that the Indian Army alone stands between India and the chaos of communal division, political corruption and despair. With some hubris reminiscent of Shakespeare's boasting heroes—Coriolanus and Cassius—Kiran asserts his military code of honour against politicians and against nationalism itself. In one remarkable episode he defies orders, and fraternizes with a Pakistani officer in the Christmas of 1949—in other words during a war between India and Pakistan. Bravery, loyalty and folly! Is Kiran doomed? It would seem so. He is in deep trouble with the authorities and the Satpuras may themselves be the sufferers by his hubris. Yet Malgonkar will not allow tragedy to take its course. Too fond of his own character, he redeems him when he is exculpated by an Indian general who "understands." The book told with such zest and with an appealing narrative is easy to misread. Its fundamental subversion of the accepted values of post- Independence India, its virtual (perverse?) ignoring of the pacifist tradition and its deliberate refusal to compromise with the modern world make it one of the most original fictional works of the decade. Kiran is an unlikely character to come across after Anand's Munoo or Narayan's devious self-deceiving protagonists or the capitalists and bohemians of Jhabvala's Delhi scene. He is wrought in the Clark Gable Hollywood tradition—cynical, grinning, a Lady's man cocking an outrageous snook at the Indian establishment whether armchair generals or Congress politicians or hypocritical preachers of *ahimsa* in a country at war, forging its soul in the smithy of blood and fire.

But Malgonkai does not recoil from the doom he sees in wait for some heroes. *The Princes* (1963) turns to the *Kshatriyas* rather than the soldiers to provide the example for a violent conflict that emerges finally into a grand catharsis. There is no attempt to subdue the savage colours in the portrayal of the old Prince, the Maharajah of Begwad, a passionate tiger of a ruler, who tyrannizes over a small princely state that is passing from British overlordship through the fires of World War II to the inevitability of Indian Independence when princely states will be an anachronism. The Maharajah is already an anachronism long before the Congress party politicians plot his downfall. Commanding the loyalty of his peasant subjects and his son Abhay, he is hated by his wife who elopes with a Muslim lover tried of the Prince's egotism and his promiscuous "use" of mistress, concubine and slave, quite in the old manner no longer in fashion. The brave, bad old ruffian fights everybody—his wife, the British, the Congress, loving only his son whom he sends to fight *for* the British "*for* India," and his beloved simple Bhils who share his jungle code of kill or be killed and his demand for loyalty and blind obedience to caste. Malgonkar's second character is the son Abhay who shares his father's physical bravery and simple code while inheriting his mother's more civilized manners. With grief in his heart Abhay, purged in the fires of the war where he has learned much of the truth of his father's *Kshatriya* code, watches his father go out into the jungle to seek death at the hands of the wounded tiger. One wounded tiger hunts another! Abhay turns bitterly on the Congress leader who has broken his father and horsewhips him in a scene oddly reminiscent of Kipling's *Plain Tales from the Hills.* The old Maharajah, a dynosaur in Nehru's India, dies for his people, for the forgotten Bhils and for the spurned ideals and traditions which Malgonkar sees being betrayed by the casteless and the revolutionaries who fail to see that India is more than the new country that came into existence in 1947, that it is the immensely old and delicate fabric of class and class, caste and caste, people and people, painfully and slowly assembled in the crucible of history and myth as the warlike Aryans moved down from the Northern mountains into the Gangetic plains.

Much more complex problems are presented for analysis in *A Bend in the Ganges* (1964), a novel that revolves around two opposite kinds of heroism and of treachery. The time is again Indian Independence and the Partition. Gian Dayal, a peasant, finds himself in prison in the Andamans for murder (justifiable according to the code of family honour) whereby a complex of circumstances he betrays an aristocratic political prisoner (Debi) to the British authorities and gets him a severe flogging.

This curious act of treachery has unforeseen result for both men. Gian sides with the British against the Japanese and then redeems his tarnished honour during Partition by rescuing Debi's sister and father from the Muslims along with a convoy of fleeing Hindus. In this somewhat ambiguous manner Gian becomes a "national hero" after all. Gian is one of Malgonkar's most remarkable characters. For this novelist he is an unusually complex and mysterious figure. Like Singh, Malgonkar thinks peasants function mentally and spiritually on a plane very different indeed from the educated middle-class Indians. Impervious to Gandhi's appeal, Gian is obstinately, even treacherously, nonpolitical, more interested in the land itself than in such abstractions as "nation" or "Empire."

In contrast Gian's victim the intellectual and rich Debi joins the pro-Japanese Indian National Army. At first he is riding high on the Japanese successes, until these turn into defeat by the British India Army and the Americans. A disillusioned and neurotic Debi marries a Muslim prostitute and with her suffers a ghastly death at the hands of Muslim prostitute and with her suffers a ghastly death at the hands of Muslim fanatics in the West Punjab during the Partition crisis. A doomed hero? Yes, but Malgonkar suggests a tragic doom which is the result of a marvellous but obstinate hubris nourished on hatred and a self-destruction. Like an Indian Macbeth or Cariolanus, Debi hastens to the death that his passionate and blind nature invites. The peasant survives and even triumphs because like the Maharajah he is part of a changeless and cryptic mythic India—yet an India of earth, blood and seed. The intellect, the Yeatsian "weasel of politics," like the latter, "killeth."

Singh and Malgonkar are essentially writers of adventure tales of heroes and outcasts embroiled in great events—war, Partition, freedom struggles—that call for heroic action rather than words. Yet in the worlds of their novels, the heroes called upon to deliver the people from the monsters that assail them will suffer and die. Their doom is inevitable. Singh sees the necessity of action, courage, endurance, whether this be in the active heroism of the half-mad budmash Juggut dying in the end because the memory of his Muslim mistress who gave herself to him in the fields is sweeter than life itself lived under the Hukums and

Iqbals of "free" India, or in the stoical piety of a Sikh mother trying to steel her pusillanimous son to a final act of glory. Malgonkar's hero, whether Maharajah or Indian Commanding Officer of an "old" regiment, is likewise a curious anachronism, odd man out in an India that is secular, humanistic and democratic. It is an India in which "the Captains and the Kings" have no real place—at least not until called upon by the enormity of great events that the "smart-assed" politicians cannot cope with. It would be idle to look for subtlety in these novels. Singh has psychological complexity in *I Shall Not Hear the Nightingale* and there is some attempt on Malgonkar's part to suggest ambiguity in the characters of Gian and Debi. But by and large the people of Malgonkar's world are simple, portrayed in broad strokes of characterization and even caricature. Leading men are Hemingway oxen with the faces of Hollywood he-men; heroines are pretty, romantic and desirable while their "fallen" sisters don short skirts, drink gin for gin in the officer's mess and are readily seduced because, after all, aren't they "good sports?" It is not a world that would appeal to E.M. Forster. Everything is brash and overcoloured and there is a crudeness in the characters and ideas which lends itself to broad cinematic effects. Why then do we turn to these writers with relief? Because subtlety can be stifling, and we live in a world that suffers from the failure of nerve that prevents us from action. Like Hamlet, modern man is paralyzed by thinking too precisely on the events. We are all Iqbals or Hukums, poisoned by the intellect or by sweet reasonableness. "Conscience doth make cowards of us all." The drums of Fortinbras bring the breath of a world that we have forgotten still exists wherever men and women are willing to surrender to passion and emotion in the cause of loyalty or a patch of land they call "home." So when the old Maharajah goes out to meet the tiger in *The Princes* he touches some forgotten but moving string that has remained silent too long.

The Sikh Perspective on Partition: A Study of *Train to Pakistan*

JAGDEV SINGH

Rooted in the catholicity of the Sikh faith that was born out of the Hindu-Muslim cultural confluence and set against village locales, the seats of the popular culture of India, the Sikh novels on Partition show the strength of communal harmony in not being palpable during the pre-Partition period but also remaining intact during communal genocide of Partition. True, the Muslims and the Sikhs are shown at daggers drawn during the migration of people across the Radcliffe line. But then, the pattern of communal harmony between the two communities of the same place is never shown to have been vitiated. It is always the marauders from outside who strike much against the wishes of the local residents.

Titled Manomajra in the first edition, Khushwant Singh's *Train to Pakistan*[1] (1956) gets at the pulse of the pulsating rural India when in portraying the changing patterns of communal relations between the Sikhs and the Muslims, it focuses attention on the inseparable bonds of friendship between the two communities in the village where the composite culture of India breathes in all its vitality. Accordingly, when the over-all pattern of pre-Partition communal amity between the Sikhs and the Muslims begins to give way like a ramshackle hutment, the exponents of the Sikh-Muslim brotherhood rise to prop up the crumbling superstructure. If, in the process, their lives are lost, they do not go in vain. They highlight the quintessential unity between the two communities in the inundating sea of blind and reckless fury.

The novel is set against the background of Mano Majra, a tiny village of the Punjab, about two kilometres away from the river Sutlej. The village is portrayed as an epitome of India, for its population consists of the Sikhs, the Muslims and the Hindus, who live in amity and harmony.

Apart from the three brick buildings, one of which is the house of the Hindu money-lender, Ram Lal, and the other two, a *Gurdwara* and a Mosque, other houses in the village are a cluster of flat-roofed mud huts with low-walled courtyards which open on narrow lanes. At the western end of the village is a pond ringed by *Keekar* trees. It is by means of such concrete particulars that the place and its inhabitants lend to Khushwant Singh's thematic concerns a "local habitation and a name": the Muslim *Mullah*, whom the villagers out of respect and love, call *chacha* Imam; Bhai Meet Singh with his long hair tied in a knot held by a wooden comb; the sweepers, "whose religion is uncertain"; the women squatting in the street after their mid-day meal rubbing clarified butter into each other's hair, discussing births, marriages and deaths. Apart from this picture of unruffled rural life, the novelist draws attention to the central point of gravitation in the social and cultural life of this village. It is the three-foot tall 'slab of sandstone' standing upright under a keekar tree beside the pond that all Mano Majrans venerate. It is the local deity, the 'deo' to which all the villagers—Hindu, Muslim, Sikh, Christian—repair whenever they are in special need of blessing. Religious diversities are thus overcome by the centre of pristine and divine power. The novelist seems to suggest that somewhere deep in their psyche the people of the village feel the folly of erecting communal barriers. That the people of Mano Majra feel a sense of unity in their religious attitude to life is a point worth consideration. Partition has generally been understood as a religious schism. The novelist, it appears, disagrees with the hypothesis: He is of the opinion that religion acts as a cohesive force in communal relationships. The people of this village, irrespective of their religious affiliations, show solidarity in the symbolic act of repairing to the 'slab of sandstone' whenever they face hard times.

The pattern of communal harmony evoked here has its roots in the two levels of cognition on which Sikhism and Islam operate. Both the Sikhs and the Muslims share a common cognitive view of the world which concerns the nature of daily life in the local environment. Sociologist Giri Raj Gupta observes: "When the ultimate concerns of human existence are not called into question, people decide a course of action in terms of alternative cultural conceptions, not those expressed in transcendental ideology and tradition."[2] Analytically, when a Sikh in Mano Majra goes to the *Gurdwara* to perform some religious ceremony as a devout Sikh one day and receives "verses from the Koran" written by the village *Mullah* "to wear as charms" and "to swallow as medicine" or he goes to the "slab of sandstone" for blessings, he is operating on two different cognitive levels. The first is general in nature and part of the ideology and tradition of transcendental Sikhism. The second is specific and part of the cultural complex which is shared by the Sikhs and the Muslims alike, having been derived from local beliefs and practices.

The pattern of communal harmony played up in the centrality of the 'slab of sandstone' in the religious life of Mano Majrans is further elaborated in the continuity of "nirgun" life in its various religious manifestations that come alive at the arrival of the morning train. In fact the only thing modern that touches the periphery of this tradition-bound typical Indian village is the train which regulates their daily routine from the break of the dawn till the descent of night. As the mail train bound for Lahore rushes by the village at daybreak, it rumbles past the bridge on the Sutlej and blows two long blasts of whistles. Hearing the sound of the train, the *Mullah* knows it is time to call the faithful to prayer. He has a quick wash, stands facing west towards Mecca and with his fingers in his ears cries in sonorous tones "Allah-o-Akbar." The priest in the *Gurdwara*, who remains in bed till the *Mullah* has called, gets up, draws a bucket of water from the well, pours it over himself and intones prayer. It looks as though the Sikh priest could not do without the *Mullah* offering his prayer. Moreover, the *Gurdwara* is invariably the place, where the Muslims and the Sikhs meet and discuss common problems of the village. Even the tree in the triangular common ground in front of the *Gurdwara* and the Mosque seems to suggest the "Upanishadic oneness of creation," for it gives shelter to all without distinction—Sikh or Muslim.

Thus in recreating Mano Majra for the reader reading carefully selected details, the novelist is unconsciously aware of the Guru's words:

> He is in the temple and He is in the Mosque:
> He is in Hindu worship as He is in Muslim prayer,
> Hindus and Muslims are one.

This unity is a living force in the way the Sikhs make their *Chacha*'s sorrows their own, for, without this, unity is meaningless. When the Muslim weaver's wife and their only son die within a few days of each other, and his eyesight, which was already bad, becomes worse and he is unable to work his loom, reduced to beggary with a baby girl, Nooran, the village folk bring him 'small offerings' of flour, vegetables, food and cast-off clothes. "There is no feeling whatever of their giving and receiving it is an 'offering' for they respect him as much as they love him."[3]

It is as though the people 'doing their little jobs and living in a world of their own somehow wish that politicians would keep themselves out and not disturb the peace of the village. One doubts whether anyone of them has ever heard of Jinnah but some of them know of Gandhi.

As *Chacha* Imam says to Iqbal, the pseudo-intellectual who has come to the village: "All the world respects a religious man. Look at Gandhi! I hear he reads the Koran Shariff and the Unjeel along his Vedas and Shastras." (44) Gandhi, the man of God, impressed the old man, but freedom meant little or nothing to them as the *lambardar* of the village tells Iqbal: "Freedom must be a good thing. But what will we get out of it? Educated people like you, Babu Sahib, will get the jobs the English had. Will we get more lands or more buffaloes?" (43)

The indifference of the Muslim *Mullah, Chacha* Imam Baksh

and the *lambardar* to the freedom struggle and the demand for Pakistan shows the general apathy of the common man to the power struggle between the elites of the two communities and between them and the British. It is this attitude which forms the bedrock of communal amity between the Sikhs and the Muslims in rural Punjab in pre-Partition period.

As the spectre of Partition begins to cast its shadow of imminent bloodshed and communal divide, communal amity in rural India becomes a victim of the internecine power struggle between the power elites of the Hindus and the Muslims in distant cities like Delhi and Lahore. The communal peace of Mano Majra faces its first jolt with the arrival of a train-load of dead bodies of Sikhs and Hindus at Mano Majra railway station. The Sikhs and the Muslims, dazed and stunned, meet in the *Gurdwara*. The novelist touches the hearts and intensifies the terrible impact of the suddenness with which the barriers, which the Sikh Gurus had laboured to cast down have been recreated in this village.

It is against the background of the train-loads of dead bodies of the Hindus and the Sikhs, which are given a common burial, as if they were rubbish heaps, that we look at the Sikhs retaliating and attacking the Muslim refugee train, sending it across the border with a thousand corpses, 'Gift to Pakistan' written on the engine, the second train-load of men, women and children from Pakistan—all buried in a trench dug out by the monster of a bulldozer, "eating chewing up the earth, casting it aside" and then "belching and vomiting it out," the Sutlej whose life-giving waters had nourished both the Muslims and the Hindus defiled by human bodies—"stabbed and speared and clubbed"—thrown into it; the cruel fate of Sundari who had been married only four days and both her arms covered with red lacquer bangles helplessly watching the private parts of her husband Mansa Ram cut and placed in her hands: trains carrying five hundred men, women and children in compartments meant to carry '40 sitting, 12 sleeping,' no shade, only the sun and the sand and no water; the father shooting his baby and his wife unable to bear the agony of their suffering, and trying to kill himself, the revolver misfiring and the horror of having to live after that; and all the untold tales of "gruesome murders" that came trickling across the border from Amritsar, Lahore, Gujranwala and a host of other places to "feel the magnitude of the violence that makes the Punjab a waste land."[4]

It is as if to agitate the troubled hearts of the villagers and break whatever resistance there was left that the Deputy Commissioner, Hukum Chand, wanting to effect the "peaceful evacuation of Muslims," spreads rumours that a gang of Muslim dacoits has murdered the Hindu-money-lender and that a certain Mohd. Iqbal is spying in the village.

Consequently, the police arrives in the village and the "social worker" Iqbal is arrested along with Juggut Singh, "the tallest man in this area," a "confirmed budmash," who is required not to leave his house after sunset and is unable to explain the cause of his absence at the time of Ram Lal's murder.

How the emotions of the people are aroused by the rumours spread by each community about the barbaric deeds of the other, is described by the novelist through the mounting tension between the Sikhs and the Muslims who had hitherto lived in amity in Mano Majra. As the village gets divided—"The head Constable's visit had divided Mano Majra into two halves as neatly as a knife cuts through a pat of butter" (105)—the Muslims and the Sikhs gather in separate groups and talk of inhuman savagery of each other. Muslims brood over the rumours of atrocities committed by the Sikhs:

> They had heard of gentle women having their veils taken off, being stripped and marched down crowded streets to be raped in the market place. Many had eluded their would-be ravishers by killing themselves. They heard of mosques being desecrated by the slaughter of pigs on the premises, and of copies of the holy Koran being torn up by infidels. Quite suddenly every Sikh in Mano Majra became a stranger with an evil intent. His long hair and beard appeared barbarous, his Kirpan menacingly anti-Muslim. For the first time, the name of Pakistan came to mean some-

> thing to them—a haven of refuge where there were no Sikhs. (105-6)

The Sikhs, on the other hand, have 'never trust a Mussulman' attitude:

> The last Guru had warned them that Muslims had no loyalties. He was right. And what had they done to the Sikhs? Executed two of their Gurus, assassinated another and butchered his infant children . . . their temples had been desecrated by the slaughter of kins; the holy Granth had been torn to bits. And Muslims were never the ones to respect women. Sikh refugees had told of women jumping into wells and burning themselves rather than fall into the hands of Muslims. Those who did not commit suicide were paraded naked in the streets, raped in public and then murdered. (206)

The wall of differences raised between the two communities on the basis of rumours and hearsay do not, however, divide the village to such an extent that they should forget their age-old friendship and indulge in mutual genocide. Instead, the pattern of communal harmony remains impregnable. Apprehending danger to their Muslim brethren from outsiders trickling into the village, especially the refugees from Pakistan, the Sikhs of Mano Majra advise the Muslims to leave Mano Majra for Pakistan as long as the storm of communal warfare does not abate.

When Imam Baksh is asked to leave Mano Majra for Pakistan, lest he be tortured by Sikh refugees, he is moved and tears trickle down his eyes:

> Imam Baksh wiped a tear from his eyes and blew his nose in the hem of his shirt. "What have we to do with Pakistan? We were born here. So were our ancestors. We have lived amongst you as brothers." Imam Baksh broke down. Meet Singh clasped him in his arms and began to sob. Several of the people started crying quietly and blowing their noses (110)

After much deliberation, all come to the conclusion that in the interest of the Muslims themselves, it will be better for them to leave the village. Imam Baksh says:

> All right, if we have to go, we'd better pack up our bedding and belongings. It will take us more than one night to clear out of homes it has taken our fathers and grandfathers hundred of years to make . . . (111)

On the eve of the departure of Muslims not many people slept in Mano Majra that night. They went from house to house—talking, crying, swearing love and friendship, assuring each other that this would soon be over. Life, they said, would be as it always had been.

The poor Mano Majrans hope that the Muslims could return after the trouble had subsided, not knowing that the Pakistan military officer is going to pack them off by train to Pakistan never to return and the looting of their scanty belongings by refugees and dacoits that follows—"Malli's gang and the refugees then unyoked the bullocks, looted the carts and drove the cows and buffaloes away" (102)—though Mano Majran Sikhs do not "touch anything." The novelist, therefore, draws attention to the tenacity of the bonds of friendship between the Sikhs and the Muslims of the village in an all-enveloping sea of communal discord. The departure of the Muslims of Mano Majra splits the composite culture of the village as the village is bereaved of an important segment of its population. The novelist portrays this split symbolically in the fate that stares Jugga and Nooran's love.

What strikes us in the love story of Jugga and Nooran is the way human love breaks the barriers man in his ignorance has erected—barriers of caste, sub-caste, religion and nationality and responds to the subtle vibrations of the heart and seeks fulfilment. When we first hear of Jugga and Nooran from the scandalous talk of Malli and his gang, we wouldn't believe that it was the poor Muslim weaver's daughter who had weaned Jugga away from evil company and crime, and accomplished with her 'magic eye' what the Punjab Police and their third-degree methods of torture could not

Jugga, who is arrested on suspicion, is released late in the evening of the day the train carrying evacuated Muslims is to leave for Pakistan. "If we have no faith in God then we are like animals" that was what Chacha Imam Baksh had said. And as Mano Majra's cup of sorrow is filled to the brim, we wonder whether the Guru was not justified on enjoining upon the Sikhs to resort to protect righteousness from inhuman cruelty. Isn't there a single Sikh in the village who could redeem the pledge?

Now the only true Sikh to redeem the *Kirpan* is Jugga and he, therefore, runs to the *Gurdwara*. "Bhai," he whispers, "I want the Guru's word. Will you read me a verse?" (150) Bhai Meet Singh had put the Granth Sahib to rest and believed that the Scripture must not be disturbed but he reads him Guru Nanak's morning prayer. The word of the Guru gives him all the courage he needs and he rushes to the bridge and begins hacking and slashing the rope tied across the bridge to sabotage the Muslim refugee train. Other Sikh rioters who believe that "for each Hindu or Sikh they kill, kill two Mussulmans. For each woman they abduct or rape, abduct two. . . . For each train load of dead they send over, send two across," (129) and now those who have been awaiting the cutting of "many people in two like a knife slicing cucumbers," (157) spot him in the darkness and fire shots at him. Jugga clings to the rope and cuts it to pieces. He falls down dead and the train "went over him, and went on to Pakistan." (158)

The love of Jugga and Nooran is no ordinary love. By adding a metaphorical dimension to this love story, the novelist invests it with a symbolic significance in the context of the enveloping pattern of communal strife and dissension. The love of Jugga and Nooran has a sublimating effect on a hardened criminal like Jugga in whom criminality is deep-seated, for it runs in the family—his father Alam Singh "was hanged two years ago" for murder. However, this change is not abrupt as K.K. Sharma[5] makes it out to be. True, in the initial stages of their intimacy,

Jugga is aware only of the physical aspect of love. But even at that stage, he shows his mettle in his silence about the cause of his absence from his house on the night of the money-lender's murder.

The spiritual elevation in Jugga is marked by his heroic resolution to save Mano Majran Muslims—including his beloved Nooran—from the death-trap. It is this heightened sense of oneness, affected by the love of Nooran that makes him to take the *Kirpan* in defence of the Muslims. Sharma appears to have overlooked the graph of Jugga's gradual development through his love of Nooran.

The heroic spirit of man is revealed in this novel not by men who are considered religious and respectable in the public and supposed to have innate goodness but by a man like Jugga, who is treated as "budmash number ten." When powerful and "potential authority" of the State represented by Hukum Chand, sulks in "indifference and inactivity," religious priests like Bhai Meet Singh "cower in timidity," and the best "political" and "rational ideologies" represented by Iqbal of the novel, recoil in fright, it is Jugga, the deviant, who combats the forces of destruction and sacrifices himself to save innocent lives threatened by the planned Mano Majra massacre.

Jugga's death under the rumbling wheels of the *Train to Pakistan* may suggest the final estrangement of the two communities, but his heroic defence of the Muslims of Mano Majra and his consequent martyrdom attract attention to the inseparableness of the two communities in rural India, the heart of the popular culture of India.

It may, therefore, be concluded that in highlighting the absolute nature of the pre-Partition pattern of communal amity between the Sikhs and the Muslims in Mano Majra, a representative Indian village, and showing its resistance to the pattern of communal discord in the sublime sacrifice of Jugga, Khushwant Singh's *Train to Pakistan* stands out as a shining example of the Sikh novels, wherein the two communities in a particular village are never shown up in arms against each other.

NOTES

1. Khushwant Singh, *Train to Pakistan* (New York: Grove Press, 1956; Bombay: India Book House, 1976).
2. Giri Raj Gupta, *Cohesion and Conflict in Modern India* (New Delhi, 1978), p. 112.
3. M. Tarinayya, "Bhabani Bhattacharya: *So Many Hungers* and Khushwant Singh: *Train to Pakistan*" in C.D. Narasimhaiah, ed., *Indian Literature of the Past Fifty Years* (Mysore: University of Mysore, 1970), p. 194.
4. *Ibid.* p. 196.
5. K.K. Sharma, "The 1947 Upheaval and the Indian-English Novel," R.K. Dhawan, ed., *Explorations in Modern Indo-English Fiction* (New Delhi: Bahri, 1982), p. 45.

Khushwant Singh Writes at Home: A Postcolonial Reading of *Train To Pakistan*

S. RAVINDRANATHAN & R.K. JACOB

> We distinguish . . . between the 'standard' British English inherited from the empire and the english which the language has become in the post-colonial countries.[1]

An attempt is made to distinguish between Indian or Canadian or Australian English with British English, by denoting the English of the commonwealth countries as lower case English (english) while old British English remains capital English. But then, it is interesting to note that of all the Indian English writers, it is Khushwant Singh who has got the courage and conviction to say: "My mother-tongue is English though my mother cannot speak one word of it."[2] In his characteristic way, Khushwant Singh defines "mother tongue" as the language one is most at home with and which one loves. English served us in the past and it does so even today. It was the language of our protest against our rulers. Quite strangely, it is English, more than any other Indian language, which gives us Indianness. Khushwant Singh's plea for retention of English is quite meaningful: "Very rightly we got rid of our English rulers; but must we foolishly also give up the good with the bad? Must we throw out the baby with the bath-water?" (117) Of course, Khushwant Singh's affluent family background, his proximity with English and the English culture during his student days and later his exposure to the language in a variety of diplomatic assignments in the western countries have created in him a passion for English.

One could argue that Khushwant Singh's *Train to Pakistan* is a good Indian English novel. Though Khushwant Singh wrote the novel on the partition theme—a historical event—the characters are imaginary and the story of Jugga and Nooran is a love story—pure and simple. Khushwant Singh was forty when he wrote *Train to Pakistan* (1956). His childhood in the Punjabi villages has acquainted him with its natural surroundings and moods of changing seasons. This, again, gives him an insight into its men and their morals. His British education has relieved him of his narrow parochialism and made him "a cultured humanist," as Shahane would call him. The animalistic savagery of the partition has disillusioned him about human nature. He has acquired precision of style, thanks to his hard journalistic work. The tone of the book is set by the peculiar mixture of sympathy and bitterness in the author's attitude. He is simultaneously inside the action as a participant and outside it as a dispassionate observer. *Train to Pakistan* is at once a grim and pathetic tale of individuals and communities caught in the swirl of partition.

The action of the novel spans a few weeks of the fateful days of August and September in 1947 in Mano Majra, a border village, with a river and a bridge over the river. Though the frontier between India and Pakistan becomes a scene of rioting and bloodshed, everything is quiet and normal in Mano Majra. Hindus, Sikhs and Muslims still live there peacefully together. Partition does not yet mean much to them. The Sub-Inspector of Police, one of the characters in the novel, mentions this to the Deputy Commissioner: "I was sure that no one in Mano Majra even knows that the British have left and the country is divided into Pakistan and Hindustan. Some of them know about Gandhi but I doubt if any one has ever heard of Jinnah."[3] But then, the beginning of the novel strikes the key-note:

> The summer of 1947 was not like other Indian summers. Even the weather had a difficult feel in India that year. It was hotter than usual, and drier and dustier. And the summer was longer. No one could remember when the mon-

> soon had been so late. Four weeks, the sparse clouds cast only shadows. There was no rain. People began to say that God was punishing them for their sins. (11)

While the 'weather' refers to the political weather as well, "Train" has been used as a significant symbol in the novel. Life in Mano Majra is regulated by the passing of trains across the bridge nearby. The village wakes up when the mail train rushes through the bridge before break. The whole village, then, echoes with Mullah's cries of "Allah-o-Akbar" from the mosque and the Sikh priest's prayers from the Gurudwara. By the time 10.30 morning passenger train from Delhi comes in, life in Mano Majra settles down to its dull, daily routine. People stop work and have dinner and the siesta when the mid-day express passes. As the evening passenger from Lahore steams in, everyone gets to work again and by the time the night goods train comes in, Mano Majra gets to sleep with the echoes of the prayers of the Mullah and the Sikh priest.

However, "the train" acquires sinister dimensions when its smooth running in and out of the village is disturbed in the wake of partition. The irregularity of trains is symbolic of disturbance in the smooth and quiet life of Mano Majra. A train which comes from Pakistan at an odd time in the morning with heaps of dead bodies of Hindus and Sikhs, sets in motion the dark forces of violence and revenge. This leads to the attempted massacre of Muslims of Mano Majra leaving for Pakistan by a train from which the novel derives its title. It is to let this train carrying his girl Nooran pass safely through to Pakistan that Jugga sacrifices his life. "Train" thus becomes a crucial symbol in the life of Mano Majra.

The quiet life of the village is suddenly disturbed when a local money lender, Ramlal, is murdered. Juggut Singh—known as a bad man in the village—he is known only as "Badmash 10"—is suspected and arrested for he is absent from his house at the time of the incident and is unable to explain the cause of his absence. At that time, he was with Nooran, but he does not want to betray her. Iqbal, an England-educated communist worker, who has been sent by the People's Party of India—to preach Hindu-Muslim unity—is also arrested. Iqbal is suspected to be a member of the Muslim League.

Meanwhile the condition in Mano Majra deteriorates further and its time schedule starts going wrong because of the sudden irregularities of trains. People whisper about a train which comes from Pakistan in an unusual hour, carrying dead bodies of Sikhs and Hindus. Simultaneously, rumours are heard about Muslims being slaughtered in Patiala, Ambala and Amritsar, mosques being demolished, and the holy *Koran* being torn by infidels.

Soon, the village becomes a battlefield of conflicting loyalties. Though the people of Mano Majra still pledge to protect the Muslims there, they shift them to the refugee camps. As the flooded Sutlej brings the dead bodies of more Hindus and Sikhs, tension rises in the village. The communal fire is fanned by the young Sikh boys who come from outside and incite Mano Majrans to take revenge upon Muslims. They succeed in getting the support of bad characters like Mali and dacoits of his gang who had earlier murdered the money-lender. They conspire to fire at the train taking refugees to Pakistan and tie a rope across the bridge to drag the Muslim down the roof of the running carriage.

Unable to control violence and feeling helpless, police authorities release Jugga and Iqbal of whose innocence they are by now fully convinced. The authorities believe that these two might be able to make the people see reason. While Iqbal keeps himself away from the scene of action, Jugga acts. When he learns of the conspiracy and comes to know that the train is carrying his beloved Nooran and other Muslims of Mano Majra, he climbs over the bridge and diverts the attention of the conspirators by cutting the rope meant for killing Muslims. The train of Muslim refugees passes over safely to Pakistan, Jugga being shot dead.

The novel juxtaposes system against the individual. Khushwant Singh's irony manifests itself here with ruthless bitterness. Jugga, though condemned by a society as a criminal and irreligious person—in brief an anti-hero—succeeds in achieving what the Deputy Commissioner, Iqbal Singh, Meet Singh and others fail to accomplish.

Train to Pakistan is a realistic novel. It transcends the actual history and asserts the value and dignity of the individual and finally expresses the tragic splendour of a man's sacrifice.

Khushwant Singh's language is lucid and simple. His expressions are never obscure. The authorial point of view is effectively communicated without the reader feeling it as intrusion. And through his characters, Khushwant Singh expresses his wrath against religious fanatics. Khushwant Singh has mastered the structure of the novel so well and uses the language with such ease that he can be argued to be an Indian English novelist, using upper case for 'English' though the author of *The Empire Writes Back* makes a subtle distinction between English English and english written by commonwealth writers.

A post-colonial reading of *Train to Pakistan* underscores its "Resistance to History" in a peculiar way. One finds a shift from a mere glorification of the past to an interpretation of the recent colonial regime. In *Train to Pakistan*, a hint at disillusionment regarding post-colonial milieu is made. The horror accompanying the transfer of population as a sequel to the independence and partition of India has been effectively handled by Khushwant Singh. Since partition and independence are inter-dependent, one can understand his reservations against either independence or partition.

Singh presents a situation whereby the fact that common people are unaware of everything about independence: "Freedom must be a good thing. But what will we get out of it? Educated people like you, Babu Sahib, will get the jobs the English had. Will we get more lands or more buffaloes?" (62)

The novel has a parodic dimension and presents cyclic rather than linear time. Common people—Hindus and Muslims—live together peacefully. "Politicizing" religion by a handful of people leads to the destruction of values. "Colonizers" from without have gone back. "Colonizers" from within continue to "colonize." When will this "colonization" end? Should there be another war of Independence? . . .

NOTES

1. Bill Ashcroft, Gareth Griffiths & Helen Tiffin, *The Empire Writes Back* (London: Methuen, 1987), p. 8.
2. Khushwant Singh, *We Indians* (New Delhi: Orient Paperbacks, 1982), p. 85.
3. Khushwant Singh, *Train to Pakistan* (New Delhi: Ravi Dayal Publishers, 1956), p. 117.

Historical Text, Human Context: A Study of *Train to Pakistan*

V.T. GIRDHARI

The novel is the history of human experiences.

Joseph Conrad

Khushwant Singh's picture of Indian society in *Train to Pakistan* is like the state of Eden before and after the Fall. Symbolic Eden is Mano Majra and the date of the Fall is summer of '47: 'When the creation of the new state of Pakistan was formally announced,' it 'was not like other Indian summers. Even the weather had a different feel in India that year. It was hotter than usual. and drier and dustier . . . for weeks, the clouds cast only shadows. There was rain. People began to say that God was punishing them for their sins."[1]

The life in Mano Majra is punctuated by the morning and evening train to and from Lahore when it is time for the mullah at mosque to offer morning prayer facing Mecca towards west with his sonorous notes of "Allah-ho-Akbar" and the Sikh priest responding by his prayer while splashing water over himself from the well in Gurudwara compound. Evening views the same chore after which the life in Mano Majra is stilled. This was the paradoxical state of Mano Majra until the summer of '47. Even the sub-inspector confides to Hukumchand that no one in Mano Majra knew that the British had left India and the country was divided into Pakistan and Hindustan. There are the reports of riots and retaliations from various parts of the country and Hukumchand's subtle question 'how long will it be before it starts here,' strikes the keynote. Sub-inspector throws in the feeler that there were some Muslim families in every Sikh village like Mano Majra. One has to read this novel in a very broad social perspective.

Train to Pakistan is not just a political novel but a social one—a politics-polluted society, played with by the bureaucrats for their personal and private ends, under the pretensions of executing the so-called policies of the so-called Government. After all what are Hukumchands and sub-inspectors?—mere helpless instruments for execution of law. Despite their apparent manipulations and manoeuvrings they are all human beings. Khushwant Singh appears to bless them all and forgive them all with his Christ-like compassion. Love is the only redeeming grace of human life, the only impulse to which one and all respond instinctively. Hukumchand's love for Haseena Begum not only creates moral compunctions in him but makes him change his ways only if to save the train in which Haseena is to leave for Pakistan. He releases Jugga Badmash and Iqbal whose arrest order he himself had signed and had also justified it to himself. The love of Jugga for Nooran is a saga of human sufferings and sacrifice elevated to epic grandeur. Jugga's struggle and ultimate death to save the train in which Nooran is supposed to be travelling to Pakistan is truly Greek in its catastrophic effect.

Khushwant Singh's transcendental views on love as an ultimate expression of life and its truth enable him not to harp upon Juggatsingh as a criminal or Hukumchand as a corrupt bureaucrat. He treats them simply as human beings. Sin is their share of life, hence the suffering. The process of introspection in the mind of Hukumchand, while with Haseena, young enough to be his daughter, shows him a better human being than all the immoralities and corruptions put together can show him as a brute. The stream of his thoughts at the sight of so many dead gives a right comprehension of his consciousness, his broader sense of human values. He suffers like Buddha at the sight of so much pain and suffering, decay and death: "It was everyone's destiny. . . . He had watched young and old brought on crude bamboo stretchers, lamented for, and then burned. Visits to the cremation ground left him with a sense of tranquillity. He had got over the immediate terror of death, but the idea of ultimate dissolution was always present in his mind. It made him kind, charitable and tolerant. It even made him cheerful in adversity." (76)

The departure of Muslims from Mano Majra is another scene symbolic of human solidarity and faith. Two communities had been there together for centuries with their lives in such a well-knit social and personal pattern that the thought of one community leaving brought tears to both. It is so gratifyingly pathetic to see Sikhs greeting Muslims with "Salaam" and Muslims wishing them back with 'Sat Sri Akal.' In spite of all the turmoil around, Sikhs assure Muslims: "As long as we are here nobody will dare touch you." Imam Baksh breaks down—what they had to do with Pakistan? They were born here, so were their ancestors. They had lived amongst Sikhs as brothers. All fell into each others' arms and cried. "This is life . . . this is the way of the world":

Not forever does the bulbul sing
In balmy shades of bowers,
Not forever lasts the spring
Nor ever blossom flowers.
Not forever reigneth day,
Sets the sun on days of bliss,
Friendships not forever last,
They know not life, who know not this. (112)

Most of the people in Mano Majra did not sleep that night. They kept moving from house to house—talking, crying, swearing love and friendship. This is Khushwant Singh's vision of life—comic in thought and tragic in feeling. All the situations and the characters therein embody this vision. Nature, with its whims and vagaries, does not appear just for its aesthetic value but represents the changing situations of human lives regulated by politics-dominated civilization. Rhythmic pattern of this change, in terms of time motion, is symbolized by the train. The train is the hopeful conveyor of the masses from both sides of territorial divisions to their respective heavens of hope. Their roots losing their grip over the native soil, men, women and children on the move in search of a new home, a new harbour, a new identity, is a pathetic process of disintegration of human lives segregated by the decisions not their own. Khushwant Singh observes:

> Early in September the time schedule in Mano Majra started going wrong. Trains became less punctual than ever before and many more started to run through at night. Some days it seemed as though the alarm clock had been set for the 'wrong hour.' On others, it was as if no one had remembered to wind it. Imam Baksh waited for Meet Singh to make the first start. Meet Singh waited for the mullah's call to prayer before getting up. People stayed in bed late without realizing that times had changed and the mail train might not run through at all. Children did not know when to be hungry, and clamoured for food all the time. In the evenings, everyone was indoors before sunset and in bed before the express came by—if it did come by. Good trains had stopped running altogether, so there was no lullaby to lull them to sleep. Instead, ghost trains went past at odd hours between midnight and dawn, disturbing the drams of Mano Majra. (67)

Nature too seems to respond to and sympathize with the plight of human beings:

> The sun behind the bridge, lighting the white clouds which had appeared in the sky with hues of russet, copper and orange. Then shades of gray blended with the glow as evening gave way to twilight and twilight sank into darkness. The station became a black wall. Wearily, the men and women went down to their courtyards, beckoning the others to do the same. They did not want to be alone in missing anything. . . . That evening, for the first time in the memory of Mano Majra, Imam Baksh's sonorous cry did not rise to the heavens to proclaim the glory of God. (73)

Hukumchand, lying lonely in his rest house, brooded over a glass of whisky, watching lizards and moth with their shining black eyes. 'Perhaps that was its destiny,' he thought 'it was everyone's destiny.' He realized that, 'that was life, and it was very depressing.'

There is a comic side too, to Khushwant Singh's view of life. His day-light sun-bright, broad humour, his extra-overtones and robust 'nar-admi' hopefulness and faith in innate goodness of man have its native roots in Punjabi ethos. Jugga is an incorrigible Don Quixote to suffer the physical indignities at the hands of police with a pinch of salt and acceptance but is a serious lover in the next moment ready to lay down his life, for love, without a second thought. He feels it an act of affrontry and stain on his personal honour when Malli, an outsider, commits murder in his village Mano Majra. The Punjabi's code was that truth, honour, financial integrity were 'all right,' but these were placed

> lower down the scale of values than being true to one's salt, to one's friends and fellow villagers. For friends you could lie in court or cheat, and no one would blame you. On the contrary, you became a nar admi—a he-man who had defied authority (magistrates and police) and religion (catch on the scripture) but proved true to friendship. It was the projection of rural society where everyone in the village was relation and loyalty to the village was the supreme test. (37)

Hukumchand accepted gifts and obliged friends when they were in trouble, but he was not corrupt. He even joined parties for dancing and singing—sometimes sex, but he was not immoral. That was the core of his philosophy of life, says Khushwant Singh.

Very typically Indian are the colloquial obscenities like 'sala' and 'susra,' the terms of love and intimacy amongst friends. Every topic of talk leads ultimately to sex, which everyone enjoys with a lot of "giggling and handslapping." Khushwant Singh's literal translations of obscenities related to sister and mother have been used so spontaneously that they seem to have lost their bitterness.

In Khushwant Singh's world of realities, life is not monopolized by either of the two forces—tragic and comic—life is a harmonious fusion of the two.

N O T E

1. Khushwant Singh, *Train to Pakistan* (Pearl Paperback Edition, Bombay: India Book House), p. 1.

Trauma of Partition in *Train to Pakistan*

C.L. KHATRI

Indian freedom movement is so great and gigantic a theme perfectly suitable for a vast epic that it requires if not a Veda Vyasa at least a Tolstoy or a Pasternak to give epic vent to it. Novels relating to the subject are legion: Venu Chitale's *In Transit* (1950), Khwaja Ahmad Abbas's *Inqilab* (1955), B. Rajan's *Dark Dancer* (1959), Khushwant Singh's *Train to Pakistan* (1956), Chaman Nahal's *Azadi* (1975), Malgonkar's *A Bend in the Ganges* (1964), Amrita Pritam's Punjabi novels *Pinjar* and *Doctor Devi*, Attia Hosain's *Sunlight on a Broken Column* (1961), Bapsi Sidhwa's *Ice Candy Man* aim at creditable sampling of the horror and the pity involved in the trauma of partition. But they don't have epic dimension of Tolstoy's *War and Peace* or Pasternak's *Doctor Zhivago*—epics of revolution and reconstruction.

Train to Pakistan differs from most of the novels on partition in respect of canvas and unity of time, place and action. It has greater unity of time and place. Its action centres in the vicinity of Mano Majra and it covers a period of not more than a month. Perhaps this is an important factor that enables Khushwant Singh to transform the horrendous raw theme into a fine fiction that is steeped in human compassion and love

B. Rajan's *Dark Dancer*, Venu Chitale's *In Transit*, Khwaja Ahmad Abbas's *Inqilab* and Malgonkar's *A Bend in the Ganges* have far greater canvas with action spreading into years and decades. In the absence of tri-unity, different strands concerning personal and national perspectives in the novels often stand apart. However, Chaman Nahal's *Azadi* and Khushwant Singh's *Train to Pakistan* are done with rigorous and resolved selectiveness. Nahal concentrates on Lala Kanshi Ram's family and his nightmarish track from Sialkot to Pakistan. *Train to Pakistan* concentrates on the village Mano Majra, the oases of peace and communal harmony and views the winds of communalism and bloody reprisal blowing all over the country and affecting this village too. It shows how peace is disturbed by the fundamentalist forces in connivance with the government machinery and how personal love of Hukum Chand for Haseena and of Jagga for Nooran asserts itself and saves the train to Pakistan from being ambushed.

Khushwant Singh reveals a sound historical sense like Manohar Malgonkar. Both *Train to Pakistan* and Malgonkar's *A Bend in the Ganges* are successful experiments in artistically fusing the personal and historical perspectives in a fictional guise. Singh's two other novels reflect the same taste. Only the time span in each novel increases successively. The first novel *Train to Pakistan* (1956) deals with the period of partition; the second novel *I Shall Not Hear the Nightingale* (1961) covers the period of Quit India movement from April 1942 to April 1943. The third novel *Delhi* presents the history of Delhi, its past and present, rise and fall, grandeur and vulgarity.

Train to Pakistan is a sensitive and realistic picturization of the trauma of partition that gave birth to two political boundaries—India and Pakistan—destined as if they were to live with an air of perpetual suspicion and enmity after a profuse and prolonged bleeding in which ten million people were on flight and around one million lost their lives. "The riots had become a rout. By the summer of 1947, when the creation of the new state of Pakistan was formally announced, ten million people—Muslims and Hindus and Sikhs—were in flight. By the time the monsoon broke, almost a million of them were dead, and all of northern India was in arms, in terror, or in hiding. The only remaining oases of peace were a scatter of little villages lost in the remote reaches of the frontier. One of these villages was Mano Majra."

Characteristically enough. the novel begins with a small paragraph on the unusual weather condition which is exceedingly hot and dry in the month of August and is very much in consonance with the exceptional heat and holocaust of communal riots generated by "reports of the proposed division of the country into a Hindu India and Muslim Pakistan." (1) It is interesting to note that nature in its different moods—summer, monsoon flood, rain—is functional in the novel. As nature's holocaust in the month of monsoon coincides with the holocaust of partition, the two movements are taken together throughout the novel to reinforce the total effect of the events described in the novel.

Monsoon is a constant symbol in the novel that suggests vicissitudes of human destiny. The nature of communal frenzy is like monsoon. "Once it is on, it stays for two months or more. Its advent is greeted with joy. . . . But after a few days the flush of enthusiasm is gone. The earth becomes a big stretch of swamp and mud." (93) It echoes what happened just after independence. The advent of monsoon brings cheer to peasants. But at times it acquires a devastating dimension. This juxtaposition reverberates in the mind of Hukum Chand, the magistrate, when he recounts "the corpses sizzling and smoking" and the rain pattering. "Rain! At long last the rain, thought the magistrate. . . . It smelled good, it sounded good, it looked good—and above all it did good. Ah, but did it?" (94)

The answer to this rhetorical question lies in the contrast between the two situations: the expected cheer at the advent of monsoon and the charred bodies of the victims of partition being burnt at the same time. No doubt, political freedom brought the long awaited moment of joy in the country. But miscalculation and lack of foresight on the part of our leaders turned this glorious moment into the bloodiest chapter of Indian history.

The first two seemingly incongruous paragraphs giving a sketchy glimpse of inferno let loose by the fundamentalist forces tagged with the two-nation theorists in the section on 'Dacoity' have an important function in the novel. They set the tone of the novel and tell us precisely what the novelist is going to say in the novel. The first section of the novel has nothing to do with the theme of partition except its first two paragraphs. Rather it tells us about robbery in the house of Lala Ram Lal, a money-lender, his murder, perfunctory action of the police and inter-religious love affair of Jugga and Nooran. However, they are at least aware of the freedom, partition and 'the winds of destruction' 'blowing across the land.' (49)

Such a beginning is indispensable for showing the cataclysmic change brought about in Indian rural scene with the partition of the country. It is through the pattern of contrast between pre-partition and post-partition scenario, Khushwant Singh best illustrates the tragedy of partition and indirectly suggests the short-sightedness of Indian leadership who failed to foresee the consequences of division and to handle the situation even after Churchill's forecast of blood-bath. Communal discord was not a feature of Indian rural scene but it was engineered first by the British Government under the policy of divide and rule and then by the nationalist leaders, though unintentionally. As Bipin Chandra says: "In the beginning of the 20th century what nationalist thought we had and what was propagated under it, had a Hindu tinge on the major part of it."[2]

The section "Dacoity" shows how calm, placid and indifferent to the greatest political event in a nation's life—independence—is the life at Mano Majra. As the lambardar questions "But what will we get out of it? Educated people like you, Babu Sahib, will get the jobs the English had. Will we get more lands or more buffaloes?" (48) Freedom becomes important for the villagers only when it brings "more land, more buffaloes." Otherwise it hardly appeals to them. As a Muslim says, "we were slaves of the English, now we will be slaves of the educated Indians or the Pakistanis." (48) They cannot welcome freedom at the cost of mass destruction. The lambardar expresses the feelings of the common man when he says: "The only ones who enjoy freedom are thieves, robbers and cut-throats," and goes on to add "We were better off under the British. At least there was security." (49) But Mano Majra retains its integrity and age-old communal harmony and brotherhood:

> Mano Majra is a tiny place. It has only three brick buildings, one of which is the home of the moneylender Lala Ram Lal. The other two are the Sikh temple and the mosque. The three brick buildings enclose a triangular common with a large peepul tree in the middle. The rest of the village is a cluster

> of flat-roofed mud huts and low-walled courtyards, . . . There are only about seventy families in Mano Majra, and Lala Ram Lal's is the only Hindu family. The others are Sikhs or Muslims about equal in number. The Sikhs own all the land around the village; the Muslims are tenants and share the tilling with the owners. There are a few families of sweepers whose religion is uncertain. The Muslims claim them as their own, yet when American missionaries visit Mano Majra the sweepers wear khaki sola topees and join their womenfolk in singing hymns to the accompaniment of a harmonium. Sometimes they visit the Sikh temple, too. But there is one object that all Mano Majrans—even Lala Ram Lal—venerate. This is a three-foot slab of sandstone that stands upright under a keekar tree beside the pond. It is the local deity, the duo to which all the villagers—Hindu, Sikh, Muslim or pseudo-Christian—repair secretly whenever they are in special need of blessing." (2)

So in the beginning, peaceful coexistence and communal harmony prevail in the village. It stands as a replica of unity and integrity in diversity that is the fundamental feature of Indian culture.

Train is another important symbol in the novel that stands for the routine life of Mano Majra before independence and disordered life after independence. Daily life at Mano Majra runs parallel with the systematic arrivals and departures of trains there. "All this has made Mano Majra very conscious of trains. Before daybreak, the mail train rushes through on its way to Lahore, and as it approaches the bridge the driver invariably blows two long blasts of whistle. In an instant, all Mano Majra comes awake. Crows begin to caw. . . . The Mullah at the mosque knows that it is time for the morning prayer. . . . By the time the 10.30 morning passenger train from Delhi comes in, life in Mano Majra has settled down to its dull daily routine. Men are in the fields. . . . As the midday express goes by, Mano Majra stops to rest. . . . When the evening passenger from Lahore comes in everyone gets to work again." (4-6)

All this stands in contrast with the new found situation in

Mano Majra with the succession of national governments which finds a succinct description in the second part of the novel named 'Kalyug.' The first visible effect is in the running of trains that disrupts normal life of the village:

> Early in September the time schedule in Mano Majra started going wrong. Trains became less punctual than even before and many more started to run through at night. Some days it seemed as though the alarm clock had been set for the wrong hour. On others, it was as if no one had remembered to wind it. Imam Baksh waited for Meet Singh to make the first start. Meet Singh waited for the mullah's call to prayer before getting up. People stayed in bed late without realizing that times had changed and the mail train might not run through at all. Children did not know when to be hungry, and clamored for food all the time. In the evenings, everyone was indoors before sunset and in bed before the express came by—if it did come by. Goods trains had stopped running altogether, so there was no lullaby to lull them to sleep. Instead, ghost trains went past at odd hours between midnight and dawn, disturbing the dreams of Mano Majra. (77)

The situation is further vitiated by the arrival of the "Ghost Train" carrying the bodies of thousands of Hindu and Sikh refugees from Pakistan for their common funeral at Mano Majra. With this comes the first taste of nightmare "the killings, flamings, rapings, and pillagings." It creates commotion in the village. Everyone tries to get as much information as they can. This has been a way of life at any village where the people have plenty of leisure. The soldiers collect the fire-wood and kerosene oil from the villagers and cremate the bodies by the station. They are not told anything but they are tense and suspicious. The truth is discovered by the night and this discovery is suggested with colour and smell images:

> The northern horizon, which had turned a bluish gray, showed orange again. The orange turned into copper and

> then into a luminous russet. Red tongues of flame leaped into the black sky. A soft breeze began to blow toward the village. It brought the smell of burning kerosene, then of wood. And then—a faint acrid smell of searing flesh. (24)

When the truth is known they are gripped with "deathly silence." And Imam Baksh who has borne the death of his wife and only son is so shocked that he forgets to do his evening prayer for the first time in his life. The seed of 'religional' suspicion inherent in the heterogeneous social structure of the village shows its head first when the people of Mano Majra come to know the truth behind the 'Ghost Train': "When it was discovered that the train had brought a full load of corpses, a heavy brooding silence descended on the village. Everyone felt his neighbour's hand against him and thought of finding friends and allies." (117)

The partition of India led to the evacuation of the Hindus from Pakistan and the Muslims from India and border crossing of refugees. This also precipitated the communal riots in retaliation of killings of the Hindus in Pakistan and the Muslims in some parts of India. Muslims from Chundunnuger and some other villages were evacuated and shifted to refugee camps. Some of the refugees at Mano Majra raise the cry for reprisals. But the administration plays the final game to cleave it into two halves. Hukum Chand feels it necessary for easy evacuation of the Muslims from Mano Majra. He thinks of a cunning plan and gives instructions to the sub-inspector to set free Mali and his four friends who are arrested in the murder case of Lala Ram Lal and to send for the commandant of the Muslim refugee camp for evacuation of Muslims from Mano Majra. Mali and his friends are the murderers of Ram Lal, and Jugga has once been in their company. Under Hukum Chand's game plan, Jugga and a social worker are kept behind the bars while the real culprits are released in Mano Majra and the villagers are asked about Sultana Budmash and Iqbal Singh. The latter is declared a member of Muslim League and called Mohammed Iqbal by the police. In fact the murder of Ram Lal is given a communal colour. The modus operandi of the police here sheds light on the true face of administration at lower level. The people have no say in the searing decision. But the obnoxious design of the bureaucracy is realized as the narrator says:

> The head constable's visit had divided Mano Majra into two halves as neatly as a knife cuts through a pat of butter.
>
> Muslims sat and moped in their houses. Rumors of atrocities committed by Sikhs on Muslims in Patiala, Ambala and Kapurthala, which they had heard and dismissed, came back to their minds. They had heard of gentlewomen having their veils taken off, being stripped and marched down crowded streets to be raped in the marketplace. . . . Quite suddenly every Sikh in Mano Majra became a stranger with an evil intent. His long hair and beard appeared barbarous, his Kirpan menacingly anti-Muslim. For the first time, the name Pakistan came to mean something to them—a haven of refuge where there were no Sikhs.
>
> The Sikhs were sullen and angry. "Never trust a Mussulman," they said. The last Guru had warned them that Muslims had no loyalties. (120-21)

This is a case of reason giving way to communal emotion and of tolerance breaking its limit. Once negative thinking sets in, the memories recollected also show the same colour. The young generation who obviously has a weaker bond of fellow-feeling gets swayed more easily and reacts offensively in a meeting of the Sikhs at the lambardar's house. The youth are revengeful of what has happened to the Sikhs in Pakistan. One of them says: "Our problem is: what are we to do with all these pigs we have with us? They have been eating our salt for generations and see what they have done! . . . They have behaved like snakes." (123)

On the other hand, Meet Singh who represents the old generation strongly protests: "What have they done to you? Have they ousted you from your lands or occupied your houses? Have they seduced your womenfolk? Tell me. what have they done." (123)

At this critical juncture the lambardar diplomatically handles the situation and convinces both Imam Baksh and the Sikhs of the necessity of evacuation in the wake of in-coming refugees who may wreak their vengeance on the Muslims of the village. "As far as we are concerned, you and your children and your grandchildren can live." (126)

The decision of parting was not easy. It shook the roots of togetherness that was centuries old. It created a mournful numbness and made them weep. Their tremendous sense of belongingness and the trauma of being uprooted from their soil is reflected through their words and tears. One of the young men says: "It is like this, uncle Imam Baksh. As long as we are here nobody will dare to touch you. We die first then you." (125-26) Imam Baksh, Meet Singh and several other people are weeping and sobbing. Imam Baksh says: "What we have to do with Pakistan? We were born here. So were our ancestors. We have lived amongst you as brothers." (126) This reminds one of Toba Tek Singh's protest against his transfer to India in Saadat Hassan Manto's Urdu short story "Toba Tek Singh." When people try to take him to India by force, he fixes himself at the place that is neither India nor Pakistan and dies. In *Train to Pakistan* Imam Baksh, in the interest of the Muslims, decides to take shelter in the refugee camp. The last resistance comes from Nooran, Imam Baksh's daughter, who says, "I cannot leave. Jugga has promised me to marry." (130) Jugga's mother does not allow her to stay there although she consoles her that Jugga will take her back as soon as he is released from the jail. It gives a direly needed relief to Nooran who is pregnant.

Next morning the Muslims of Mano Majra were evacuated by the Pakistani soldiers. The news that they will be taken to Pakistan comes as a surprise to the lambardar and other Sikhs. But the villagers, both Sikhs and Muslims, are helpless. The Muslim officer orders them to leave their cattle, furniture and the goods which cannot be accommodated in the trucks and asks the lambardar to look after their cattle and other property. But lambardar refuses to do so on the plea that property spoils relations. This pious attitude of the lambardar and Meet Singh gets a scornful rebuff from a Sikh officer. "You are quite right, Bhaiji, there is some danger of being misunderstood. One should never touch another's property; one should never look at another's woman. One should just let others take one's goods and sleep with one's sisters. The only way people like you will understand anything is by being sent over to Pakistan; have your sisters and mothers raped in front of you." (135)

It amply displays the general mood prevailing among the soldiers. The whole atmosphere is filled with reactionary and vindictive temperament. The situation is well-echoed in Malgonkar's *A Bend in the Ganges*: "Every citizen was caught up in the holocaust. No one could remain aloof; . . . The administration, the police, even the armed forces were caught up in the blaze of hatred." (325-26) In this situation even an army officer looks for criminals like Mali and his gang, who can do what they cannot do in their uniforms. Mali and his men are given the responsibility of looking after the left-over property of the Muslims of Mano Majra; and subsequently they plunder their property with impunity.

The people of Mano Majra encounter yet another ghastly scene when they see floating corpses of men, women, children on the flood water that has swept away some of the nearby villages. Soon they come to the conclusion that 'they are not drowned. They are murdered.' (143) Khushwant Singh gives a pathetic portrayal of this ghastly scene:

> There were also men and women with their clothes clinging to their bodies; little children sleeping on their bellies with their arms clutching the water and their satiny buttocks dipping in and out. The sky was soon full of kites and vultures. They flew down and landed on the floating carcasses. They pecked till the corpses themselves rolled over and shooed them off with hands. (143)

But this is not the last nightmare in the life of Mano Majra. When the lambardar and his company return to the village to report, they find that the villagers are gripped with the fear of another 'ghost train' that has just arrived at the station. The last line of the passage suggests that it carries some corpses of the Muslims which are buried in the grave the soldiers dug with the bulldozer: "Two soldiers were left to guard the grave from the depredations of jackals and badgers." (145)

In fact the partition plunged India into a blood bath and sparked off civil riots. But all this is given hint of and not directly shown as the sample village Mano Majra has witnessed no communal riots, no act of bloody reprisal. By and large, they are still committed to peace and brotherhood. But this humanity and sanity is regarded as a sign of cowardice by the Sikh youths who come to the gurdwara at night to provoke the fire of reprisal. "Do you know how many trainloads of dead Sikhs and Hindus have come over? Do you know of the massacres in Rawalpindi and Multan, Gujranwala and Sheikhupura? What are you doing about it? You just eat and sleep and call yourselves Sikhs—the brave Sikhs! The martial class!" (148) He continues to whip up emotion with his vituperative speech full of rhetorical questions and punch. "You expect the government to do anything? A government consisting of cowardly bania moneylenders! Do the Mussulmans in Pakistan apply for permission from their government when they rape your sisters? Do they apply for permission when they stop trains and kill everyone, old, young, women and children? You want the government to do something! That is great! Shabash! Bravo!" (149) When the lambardar asks what we can do, he promptly says: "For each Hindu or Sikh they kill, kill two Mussalmans. For each woman they abduct or rape, abduct two. . . . For each trainload of dead they send over, send two across." (149)

Obviously they were guided by the maxim 'tit for tat' in a wrong perspective. The Muslims of Mano Majra, whom they want to avenge for what had been done to the Hindus or the Sikhs in Pakistan, have done no harm to any Hindu or Sikh. But for the fundamentalist forces all Hindus or Muslims are alike. Meet Singh's protest, "What bravery is there in killing unarmed innocent people?" (150) yields little result. In this perversion, a man like Meet Singh is called the curse of this country. (150)

Once again the show is hijacked by Mali and his men who unexpectedly come there to support their move to ambush the train carrying the refugees to Pakistan. Some youths of the village and refugees join them in sending a trainload of corpses. Ironically enough all this is done allegedly in 'the service of the

Guru.' The leader puts forward the plan: "Tomorrow after sunset, when it is dark, we will stretch a rope across the first span of the bridge. It will be a foot above the height of the funnel of the engine. When the train passes under it, it will sweep off all the people sitting on the roof of the train." (153) They plan to kill them with swords and spears and to fire indiscriminately at the windows of the train so that it carries only the dead. To project abject helplessness of administration in the wake of 'universal madness' is an important motif of the novelist. It is well described by Hukum Chand who himself is a rake and his character is an indictment against the bureaucracy. "Yes, Inspector Sahib, you and I are going to get nothing out of this except a bad name. What can we do? Everyone has gone trigger-happy. People empty their rifle magazines into densely packed trains, motor convoys, columns of marching refugees, as if they were squirting red water at the Holi festival; it is a bloody Holi. What sense is there in going to a place where bullets fly? The bullet does not pause and consider 'This is Hukum Chand; I must not touch him.' Nor does a bullet have a name written on it saying 'Sent by So-and-so.'" (156)

When the conspiracy to sabotage the train to Pakistan is revealed to Hukum Chand, he is shocked; and he desperately looks for ways and means to save it. But the sub-inspector informs him that they can do nothing. If they are not taken to Pakistan 'the whole camp may be destroyed' by the 'mobs of twenty to thirty thousand armed villagers thirsting for blood.' (158) If they are taken to Pakistan, there is the danger of inevitable ambush. In such a situation when the magistrate fails, the lover prevails over the situation. It is his indulgence in Haseena, a Muslim prostitute, that brings about the release of Jugga and Iqbal. Srinivasa Iyengar rightly observes that even in this universal madness, humanity or the simple uncalculating love of a man for a woman asserts itself and saves the situation.' (501)

Accordingly they are released and brought to Mano Majra by the fateful evening. The sub-inspector deliberately instigates Jugga against Malli by informing him that Malli has been the cause of the evacuation of the Muslims from Mano Majra and that he has plundered their properties. But it is not the fire of revenge that propels him to save the train at the cost of his life. His immediate concern is the safety of Nooran; and the danger to the train means danger to her life. He manages to get at the rope and slash it away. Though he is shot down he gives a safe passage to the train. The climax is exciting but it looks theatrical like a typical Hindi film with the only difference that the hero here, though victorious, loses his life. However, the dramatic effect is well realized and the reader feels satisfied and relieved:

> The leader raised his rifle to his shoulder and fired. He hit his mark and one of the man's legs came off the rope and dangled in the air. The other was still twined round the rope. He slashed away in frantic haste. The engine was only a few yards off, throwing embers high up in the sky with each blast of the whistle. Somebody fired another shot. The man's body slid off the rope, but he clung to it with his hands and chin. He pulled himself up, caught the rope under his left armpit, and again started hacking with his right hand. The rope had been cut in shreds, only a thin tough strand remained. He went at it with the knife, and then with his teeth. The engine was almost on him. There was a volley of shots. The man shivered and collapsed. The rope snapped in the center as he fell. The train went over him, and went on to Pakistan. (181)

The ultimate optimism of the novelist is shown in the end that shows the victory of virtue and love over vice and hatred even in this utter chaos. Interestingly the crusader is not the politician, not the administrator or the army personnel and not even the social and political worker Iqbal Singh but a robber and self-confessed budmash. The plan to sabotage the train is known to everyone. But only Jugga rises to the occasion. Implicit in this preference is Khushwant Singh's ire against the power-hungry leaders of national movement who could celebrate 'the baptism of freedom' with blood-bath. He leads credibility to his feeling by making Hukum Chand, who is a part of the government and a legacy of the colonial rule, rail against national leaders:

> What were the people in Delhi doing? Making fine speeches in the assembly! Loud-speakers magnifying their egos; lovely looking foreign women in the visitors' galleries in breathless admiration. 'He is a great man, this Mr. Nehru of yours. . . . Wasn't that a wonderful thing to say?: Long ago we made a tryst with destiny and now the time comes when we shall redeem our pledge.' (176)

Malgonkar, Khushwant Singh and Chaman Nahal have taken to task the British rulers and short-sighted national leaders afflicted with sudden blindness and loss of nerve for exploding this horrendous catastrophe. Malgonkar raises a more direct question and puts the whole non-violence movement and the British rule in dock: "Tekchand had never imagined that such happenings could be possible, now, in the middle of the twentieth century after more than a hundred years of the sanity and orderliness of British rule, after thirty years or so of the Mahatma's non-violence. Had Gandhi ever envisaged a freedom that would be accompanied by so much suffering and release so much hatred?" (327)

Train to Pakistan is also a valuable social and political document and a highly readable fiction that keeps the reader engrossed. As Arthur Lal puts it in an introduction to this book. "Its intrinsic qualities as a fine novel grip the reader. Throughout, the action sweeps one along. The characters are vivid and highly credible, and Khushwant Singh keeps them going magnificently on two levels: in their quotidian matrix compounded of their passions of love and revenge, their tremendous sense of belonging to a village community, and their insolence and heroism; and then again on the wide stage set by the tornado that breaks on their lives in the shape of the cataclysmic events of the partition of India in 1947."

As a piece of fiction *Train to Pakistan* is 'cleverly contrived' and articulative of the pity and horror involved in the partition tragedy. The third person omniscient narrative technique helps the novelist dive into the minds of characters and present his candid views with precision and objectivity on the different shades of this tragedy.

NOTES

1. Khushwant Singh, *Train to Pakistan* (New Delhi: Times Books International), pp. 1-2.
2. Bipin Chandra, *Bharata ka Swatantrata Sangharsh* (Delhi: Delhi University, 1993).
3. Manohar Malgonkar, *A Bend in the Ganges* (London: Hamish Hamilton, 1964).
4. K.R. Srinivasa Iyengar, *Indian Writing in English* (New Delhi: 1989).

The Pangs of Partition: A Study of *Train to Pakistan*

K.V. SURENDRAN

Train to Pakistan (1956) is a magnificent novel where Khushwant Singh tells the tragic tale of the partition of India and Pakistan and the events that followed which will be remembered as one of the blackest chapters of human history. On the eve of the partition of the Indian subcontinent thousands fled from both sides of the border seeking refuge and security. The natives were uprooted and it was certainly a ghastly experience for them to give up their belongings and rush to a land which was not theirs. Partition touched the whole country and Singh's attempt in the novel is to see the events from the point of view of the people of Mano Majra, a small village. The peaceful life in Mano Majra suddenly came to a jolt when the village moneylender's house was raided. This and the other events narrated in the novel can only be described as breathtaking. This article is an attempt to look at the novel in some depth and show how Singh effectively depicts the pangs of partition of the Indian subcontinent which was certainly a dark chapter in its history.

The novel begins with a reference to the summer of 1947 which was noted for its scorching heat and rainlessness and marked for hot and dusty atmosphere:

> The summer of 1947 was not like other Indian summers. Even the weather had a different feel in India that year. It was hotter than usual, and drier and dustier. And the summer was longer. No one could remember when the monsoon had been so late. For weeks, the sparse clouds cast

> only shadows. There was no rain. People began to say that God was punishing them for their sins. (9)

The summer before, communal riots, precipitated by reports of the proposed division of the country into a Hindu India and a Muslim Pakistan, had broken out in Calcutta and several thousands had been killed. The Muslims said that the Hindus had planned and started the killing. The Hindus, on the other hand, put the whole blame on the Muslims. the truth was that both sides had killed. People belonging to both the sides were shot, stabbed, speared, tortured and raped.

From Calcutta the riots had spread north and east and west. In Noakhali in East Bengal, Muslims massacred Hindus and in Bihar Hindus massacred Muslims. Mullahs were reported to have roamed the Punjab and the Frontier Province with boxes of human skulls said to be those of Muslims killed in Bihar. The Hindus and Sikhs who had lived for centuries on the Northwest Frontier were made to abandon their homes and flee toward the Sikh and Hindu communities in the east. They had to travel on foot, in bullock carts, cram into lorries, cling to the sides and roofs of trains.

> By the summer of 1947, when the creation of the new state of Pakistan was formally announced, ten million people—Muslims and Hindus and Sikhs—were in flight. By the time the monsoon broke, almost a million of them were dead, and all of northern India was in arms, in terror, or in hiding. (10)

Mano Majra is the place of the action of the novel. In fact the novel was originally titled *Mano Majra.* It is a tiny village situated on the Indian border, half a mile away from the river Sutlej. The Sikhs, Muslims and Hindus lived in perfect harmony in this village and there was a time when no one in the village knew that the British had left the country and the country was divided into Pakistan and Hindustan. The only thing that made an impact on them was the arrival and departure of trains. But soon things began to change. Partition began to take its toll in this tiny village also.

> Partition touched Mano Majrans at both levels—at the community level and at the individual level. At the community level it effects very badly the Hindus, Muslims and Sikhs. The dark clouds of suspicion and fear arise among the Sikhs and Muslims, who have lived together for centuries. Yet feelings of brotherliness have not disappeared, and they meet for consultation in a scene that is both intensely humane and touching. (Manaver, 1998:31)

There were only about seventy families in Mano Majra, and Lala Ram Lal's was the only Hindu family. The others were Sikhs or Muslims who were about equal in number. The railway station occupied an important position and a small colony of shopkeepers and hawkers grew up around it to supply travellers with food, betel leaves, cigarettes, tea, biscuits and sweetmeats.

The routine life of Mano Majra was disturbed one evening in August 1947. The village moneylender's house was raided by dreaded dacoits:

> On the roof of his house, the moneylender was beaten with butts of guns and spear handles and kicked and punched. He sat on his haunches, crying and spitting blood. Two of his teeth were smashed.

When Ram Lal, the moneylender failed to hand over the key of his safe, one of the dacoits lunged at the crouching figure with his spear. Ram Lal collapsed on the floor uttering a loud yell with blood spurting from his belly.

The dacoity had its evil effects on Juggut Singh who was a resident of the village. The dacoits dropped bangles in his house and later he was arrested as the suspect of murder and dacoity. He was in love with Nooran which in a sense cut across religious barriers. After his release from police custody, he came to know that Nooran had visited his mother before leaving for the refugee camp carrying his child in her womb. Nooran was a Muslim weaver's daughter. Juggut Singh, meanwhile, had a dubious distinction of being 'a budmash number ten.' His father and grandfather were also dacoits and were hanged for murder. But they were reported not to have robbed their own village folk. According to Meet Singh, Juggut had disgraced his family through his acts.

Hukum Chand plays an important role in the novel. Walsh writes: "Mr. Hukum Chand, magistrate and deputy commissioner, for all his tastes for skin-lotion, perfumed talc and young girls hired from venal guardians, his administrative cunning and corrupted conscience, yet surprises us with an authentic basic human kindness—even a sort of innocence." (1990:99) Hukum Chand is perhaps one of the best drawn characters in the novel. Married to an unattractive and illiterate woman, he looked for love and sex elsewhere, but he was not exactly immoral. Cowasjee writes: "Through the portrayal of Hukum Chand, Khushwant Singh shows how the much maligned Indian bureaucracy was itself caught between the hatred of a people and the bungling of politicians." (1982:24)

Hukum Chand considered Hindu women to be unlike other women. When it was reported that the Muslim mobs had tried to molest Hindu women, they had killed their own children and jumped into wells that filled to the brim with corpses, Hukum Chand's reaction was as follows:

> Our Hindu women are like that: so pure that they would rather commit suicide than let a stranger touch them. We Hindus never raise our hands to strike women, but these Muslims have no respect for the weaker sex. (31-32)

It is interesting to hear from Hukum Chand more about how he looked at partition and its impact. He was for getting the Muslims to go out peacefully if possible. He was of the view that bloodshed would not benefit anyone. According to him bad characters would get all the loot and the government would blame people like him for the killing. For the same reason he was against killing or destruction of property. But at the same time he gave instruction to the Inspector to be careful not to allow the Muslims to take too much with them:

> Hindus from Pakistan were stripped of all their belongings

> before they were allowed to leave. Pakistani magistrates have become millionaires overnight. Some on our side have not done too badly either. Only where there was killing or burning the government suspended or transferred them. There must be no killing. Just peaceful evacuation. (32)

That there is a wide gap between what he preaches and what he practises is clear from the fact that he is revealed as a womanizer. Women were brought to him and he paid for their service generously:

> He brought the girl's face nearer his own and began kissing her on the back of her neck and on her ears. He could not hear the goods train any more. It had left the countryside in utter solitude. Hukum Chand could hear his breathing quicken. He undid the strap of the girl's bodice. (42)

He never hesitated in filling official records with half truths. Even before he received the full details of Iqbal, instruction was given to the Inspector to enter against his name that he was the son of 'Mohammed Something-or-other, or just father unknown.'

Iqbal was one who created a mild sensation in the village. He approached Bhai Meet Singh with a request for shelter and he took it for granted that he was Iqbal Singh! In fact he did not have to say what Iqbal he was "He could be a Muslim, Iqbal Mohammed. He could be a Hindu, Iqbal Chand, or a Sikh, Iqbal Singh. It was one of the few names common to the three communities." (48) He was a social worker. He had come to that village as he knew that something should be done to stop the bloodshed going on as a result of partition. His party had sent him there, since this place was a vital point for refugee movements. He had a strong feeling that trouble would be disastrous. He belonged to district Jhelum and had been in foreign countries a long time. He had his own views on morality and a host of other things.

> Morality . . . is a matter of money. Poor people cannot afford to have morals. So they have religion. Our first problem is

> to get people more food, clothing, comfort. That can only be done by stopping exploitation by the rich, and abolishing landlords. And that can only be done by changing the government. (49)
>
> For them truth, honour, financial integrity were "all right," but these were placed lower down the scale of value than being true to one's salt, to one's friend and fellow villagers. (54)

But he was well aware that criminals were not born and were made by hunger, want and justice. He always thought that if the fear of the gallows or the cell had stopped people from killing or stealing, there would be no murder or theft. Even though a man was hanged every day, ten got murdered every twenty-four hours in the particular province he was in. The population explosion also was causing great concern to Iqbal.

> The whole country was like an overcrowded room. What could you expect when the population went up by six every minute—five millions every year. It made all planning in industry or agriculture a mockery. Why not spend the same amount of effort in checking the increase in population? (58)

It might appear strange that independence meant little or nothing to the people in Mano Majra. They never realized that it was a step forward and that what they needed to do was to take the next step and turn 'the make-believe political freedom into a real economic one.' They were not quite sure why the English had left them. Iqbal tried to enlighten them as to what it all meant.

> They left because they had to. We had hundreds of thousands of young men trained to fight in war. This time they had the arms too. . . . The English were frightened. They did not shoot any of the Indians who joined the Indian National Army set up by the Japanese, because they thought the whole country would turn against them. (61-62)

But as far as the villagers were concerned, views differed. There were some among them who liked English soldiers. Meet Singh told Iqbal that his brother who was a havildar was of the view that all sepoys were happier with English officers than with Indian. Iqbal in turn asked whether he would like to continue to remain slaves all their lives. But Meet Singh had his own argument:

> Freedom must be a good thing. But what will I get out of it? Educated people like you, Babu Sahib, will get the jobs the English had. Will we get more lands or more buffaloes? (62)

Freedom was for the educated people who fought for it. He was sure that people like him were going to be slaves of the educated Indians or the Pakistanis. The lambardar was of the view that the only ones who enjoyed freedom were thieves, robbers and cut-throats.

Iqbal found himself in a predicament and was not in a position to do anything to save the situation:

> Could he stop the killing? Obviously not. Everyone—Hindu, Muslim, Sikh, Congressite, Leaguer, Akali, or Communist—was deep in it. It was famous to suggest that the bourgeois revolution could be turned into a proletarian one. (64-65)

In an unexpected move, the police arrested Iqbal. It was extremely foolish for the police to have done that and they knew that they had made a mistake, or rather, two mistakes as they had arrested Juggut Singh also.

> Arresting the social worker was a blunder and a likely source of trouble. His belligerent attitude confirmed his innocence. Some sort of case would have to be made up against him. That was always a tricky thing to do against educated people. (74)

Iqbal's pride had been injured. He was under arrest in connection with the murder of Ram Lal. Everyone knew that he had come to Mano Majra after the murder. He had taken the same train that the policemen had taken and they could be witness of his alibi. The situation was ludicrous but Punjabi policemen were not the sort who admitted making mistakes. He tried to convince Juggut Singh who was arrested along with him that he was not a villager and had come from Delhi and was sent to organize peasants.

When the truth was revealed the sub-inspector was irritated. When the fellow policemen told him that Iqbal was a stranger staying at the Sikh temple, he burst out:

> I do not suppose you have any brains of your own. I leave a little job to you and you go and make a fool of yourself. You should have seen him before arresting him. Isn't he the same man who got off the train with us yesterday? (77)

The police were doubly wrong as Jugga was out of his house on the night of the dacoity. Even Hukum Chand was angry and was surprised to see the police arresting people without finding out their names, parentage or caste. Police who were always known for their cruelty asked Iqbal to remove his dress:

> Iqbal loosened the knot in the cord. The pyjamas fell in a heap around his ankles. He was naked save for the handcuffs on his wrists. He stepped out of the pyjamas to let the policemen examine them. (80)

The Inspector thus ensured that he was a Muslim. When he said that he was sent by the Peoples' Party of India, the Inspector asked him whether he was sure it was not the Muslim League.

Mob attacks were a common phenomenon in those days and when they attacked they never waited to find out whether the persons concerned were Hindus or Muslims.

> The other day four Sikh Sardars in a jeep drove alongside a mile-long column of Muslim refugees waking on the road. Without warning they opened fire with their stenguns. Four stenguns! God alone knows how many they killed. (84-85)

A lot of women were abducted and sold cheap. Police stations were concentration camps and third degree methods were adopted to extricate 'truth' from those who were caught.

> Hands and feet pinned under legs of charpoys with half a dozen policemen sitting on them. Testicles twisted and squeezed till one became senseless with pain. Powdered red chillies thrust up the rectum by rough hands, and the sensation of having the tail on fire for several days. All this, and no food or water, or hot spicy food with a bowl of shimmering cool water put outside the cell just beyond one's reach. (91-92)

Some succumbed to hunger and others to the inconvenience of having to defecate in front of the policemen.

The arrival of the ghost train is another important 'event' in the novel which makes the reader flabbergasted. The arrival of the train in broad daylight created a commotion in Mano Majra. People stood on their roofs to see what was happening and all they could see was the black top of the train stretching from one end of the platform to the other. Later the villagers were asked to get all the wood there was in their houses and all the kerosene oil they could spare. They were asked to bring them to the motor trucks on the stationside for which they would be paid. The villagers soon 'smelt' something wrong:

> The northern horizon, which had turned a bluish grey, showed orange again. The orange turned into copper and then into a luminous russet. Red tongues of flame leaped into the black sky. A soft breeze began to blow towards the village. It brought the smell of burning kerosene, then of wood. And then—a faint acrid smell of searing flesh. (100)

There was a deathly silence in the village. The train had come from Pakistan and everybody knew what had happened. Even Hukum Chand felt feverish to see a thousand charred corpses sizzling and smoking while the train put out the fire.

> The Sikh officer said there were more than a thousand. I think he just calculated how many people could get into a bogie and multiplied it by the number of bogies. He said that another four or five hundred must have been killed on the roofs, on the footboards and between buffers. (115)

In fact fifteen hundred innocent people getting killed was only part of the story. Similar things were happening at other places also.

Muslims of some villages had started leaving for the refugee camp. Chundunnugger had been partly evacuated. Pakistan army lorries with soldiers had been picking them up whenever information had been brought. Hukum Chand believed that an individual's conscious effort should be directed to immediate ends like saving life when endangered, preserving the social structure and honouring its conventions. His immediate problem was to save Muslim lives. Meanwhile, rumours or atrocities committed by Sikhs on Muslims in Patiala, Ambala and Kapurthala began to spread.

> They had heard of gentlewomen having their veils taken off, being stripped and marched down crowded streets to be raped in the marketplace. Many had eluded their would-be ravishers by killing themselves. They had heard of mosques being desecrated by the slaughter of pigs on the premises, and of copies of the holy Koran being torn up by infidels. (141)

The Sikhs were angry and announced that Muslims would never be trusted. The last Guru had warned them that Muslims had no loyalties. All through the Muslim period of Indian history, sons had imprisoned or killed their own fathers and brothers had blinded brothers to get the throne. They had executed two of the Sikh Gurus, assassinated another and butchered his children.

> And Muslims were never ones to respect women. Sikh refugees had told of women jumping into wells and burning themselves rather than fall into the hands of Muslims. Those who did not commit suicide were paraded naked in the streets,

> raped in public, and then murdered. (142)

A trainload of Sikhs massacred by Muslims had been cremated in Mano Majra. Hindus and Sikhs were fleeing from their homes in Pakistan and having to find shelter in Mano Majra. The villagers ultimately decided to be angry with the Muslims.

Soon the Muslims began to come out of their homes, driving their cattle and their bullock carts loaded with charpoys, rolls of bedding, tin trunks, kerosene oil tins, earthen pitchers and brass utensils.

> There was no time even to say good-bye. Truck engines were started. Pathan soldiers rounded up the Muslims, drove them back to the carts for a brief minute or two, and then on to the trucks. (159)

To sum up, partition had a tremendous effect on the people of Mano Majra. It adversely affected the Hindus, Muslims and Sikhs. The communities which lived in amity for centuries became enemies overnight. There was mutual suspicion and hatred became the order of the day. However, it cannot be said that feelings of brotherhood were completely missing. When Imam Baksh, the mullah of the local mosque came to the lambardar to ask for his comments on their continuing their stay in the village, his reply was that it was as much his village as it was theirs. "If anyone speaks rudely to you, your wives or your children, it will be us first and our wives and children before a single hair of your heads is touched." (147) But he had his own problems. They were very few and the strangers coming from Pakistan were coming in thousands. Who will be responsible for what they do was the moot question as far as he was concerned. Thus they were asked to lock their houses with their belongings and move to the refugee camps. Eventually Sikhs and Muslim villagers fell into each other's arms and began to weep like children. The Muslims who were made to stay in refugee camps were later transported to Pakistan by train.

Train to Pakistan: A Thematic Analysis

S.P. SWAIN

A short story writer, novelist, historian and journalist, Khushwant Singh has established himself as a distinguished Indian writer "with an individual status in modern Indo-Anglian literature."[1] This individuality in his writings is on account of his anger and disenchantament with the "long-cherished human values in the wake of inhuman bestial horrors and insane savage killings on both sides during the partition of the subcontinent between India and Pakistan in August 1947."[2] The harrowing and spine-chilling events of 1947 had shaken the faith of the people in the innate nobility of human beings. It had driven them into a state of wonder over what man has made of man. To Khushwant Singh, this was a period of great disillusionment and crisis of values, a distressing and disintegrating period of his life. The beliefs he had cherished all his life were shattered. Giving vent to his inner struggle and agony, he says: "the division of India had been accompanied by the most savage massacres known in the history of the country. . . . I had believed that we Indians were peace-loving and non-violent, that we were more concerned with the matters of the spirit. . . . After the experience of the autumn of 1947, I could no longer subscribe to these views. I became an angry middle-aged man, who wanted to shout his disenchantment with the world. . . . I decided to try my hand at writing."[3]

The sinister and venomous impact of partition and the indignation it spawned in him has been realistically expressed in a scathing irony in *Train to Pakistan*. Originally entitled *Mano*

Majra, the novel portrays with a bold and unrelenting realism, the brutal story of political hatred and violence during the turbulent and fateful days that preceded and followed the partition of British India when the spirit of communal frenzy and a passionate zeal for self-expression were fuming and fumbling within the mass. Khushwant Singh's objective in this novel is to expose and explore the world around him and to present it in all its naturalistic setting. The socio-political theme he takes up in this novel is intrinsically a journalistic tour de force chiming in with the artistic tenets of sincerity and truth.

The novel relates the story of Mano Majra, a tiny village which becomes the microcosm of the communal strife and inhuman violence in the wake of Partition. But in the teeth of such ghastly violence we do have people who maintain a dignified stoicism, people who encounter the existential buffets of destiny with equipoise and fortitude. Jugga, the romantic deviant is one such man. "The heroic spirit of man," observes Harish Raizada, "is revealed in the novel not by men who are considered religious and respectable in the public and supposed to have innate goodness but by a man like Jugga who is treated as a confirmed ruffian."[4] A "budmash number ten,"[5] Jugga is an invincible person whom neither darkness can blind nor death scare. With his indomitable courage and unconquerable will, he becomes the symbol of self-sacrifice and goodness that humanity basically stands for. He redeems himself by saving the lives of thousands of Muslims in a thrilling climax. But all is not lost. Jugga does everything he can to assert the nobility of his self. Thus an idealistic and affirmative tone pervades the novel which imparts a silver lining to the encircling gloom in which all humanity is enmeshed. The avenger's plan to cause a gruesome accident on the train and massacre its passengers bound for Pakistan is averted by Jugga, a confirmed ruffian with a human heart. Khushwant Singh's Jugga is a character "stuffed with the so-called innate goodness of man and he is the only character which is entirely fiction."[6] The novelist thus invests a common man like Jugga with tragic grandeur in order to show "the dignity of man for all helpless littleness in the face of the universe, for all his nullity under the blotting hand of time."[7] But a deeper reading of the novel reveals that Jugga's sacrifice is an assertion of his love for an individual, not all humanity. He averts the accident because he wanted to save the life of his Muslim beloved, Nooran. Realising the danger the revenge might mean to his beloved, he manages to slash at the rope with his Kirpan: "He went at it with his knife, and then with his teeth. The engine was almost on him. There was a volley of shots. The man shivered and collapsed. The rope snapped in the centre as he fell. The train went over him, and went on to Pakistan." (158)

The train of Muslim refugees passes over to Pakistan safely but Jugga is shot by his co-religionists. His heroic death is a sacrifice, an act of self-immolation that unveils the hypocrisy and duplicity on which the so-called civilized society thrives. Khushwant Singh's genial comic irony manifests itself in his unmasking the sham pretension of the much acclaimed and glorified values of human life symbolized by the assassination of Juggut Singh. The murder of Jugga in another way symbolizes the culmination of the novelist's vision of life which is positive. This vision of life in the novelist expresses itself through love and dedication. With his intuitive understanding, he depicts things as they are and not as they ought to be. This transcription of life brings out the note of verisimilitude to life since literal transcription of life is well nigh impossible.

Khushwant Singh's is a plausible interpretation of life. R.K. Narayan and Mulk Raj Anand portray the photographic reality, a reality that is artistic but Khushwant Singh is interested in the stark and naked realism of life and thus comes closer to the French socialist realists like Balzac. Like the socialist realists, Khushwant Singh's approach is positive—not negative—inasmuch as he views the socialist order as an independent entity. Unlike a critical realist, his approach is definitely concrete, since he looks at the society from the inside, not from the outside. Like Balzac's characters, his Juggut Singh alias Jugga is a man endowed with formidable will power and individuality. The theme of the novel with all its emphasis on partition does not become a political propaganda like Raja Rao's *Kanthapura*. On the other hand, it is a tale of the fate of the individuals in Mano Majra, a small village on the river Sutlej. Sikhs and Muslims are enmeshed in a fratricidal conflict. Everywhere there is mass madness and Mano Majra too reels under the opprobrious and ghastly scene of communal frenzy. Muslims are evacuated to a refugee camp for departure to Pakistan later. As the preparation for the departure of the Muslim refugees to Pakistan is in full swing, religious fanatics are busy with vindictive activities in their underworld. They plan to blow up the bridge and the train which is to carry the Muslim refugees to Pakistan in retaliation for what Pakistani Muslims have done to Hindus on their way to India. When Jugga comes to know that his beloved Nooran is going to leave India by the train to Pakistan, he immediately rushes to the rescue of Nooran and ultimately falls a prey to the bullets of the Hindu saboteurs and is killed. With this bare outline, Khushwant Singh is able to build up a novel portraying the hard and bitter facts of life against the harrowing tale of India's partition.

In its dexterous anatomization of the real and its penetration beneath the inhuman bestialities of life to the human factor of love and sympathy, *Train to Pakistan* is a unique artistic rendering of the gruesome and vile. To Khushwant Singh, love in spite of its concomitant frustrations, "is the greatest, the most exhilarating experience of life."[8] A moving story of people in turmoil, the novel is an idyllic tale of "a village led to a moral action through its own apathy and indifference."[9]

Besides the horrors of partition and the self-sacrifice of Jugga, the novel has a deep symbolic concern. The first symbol is Mano Majra which is representative of the spirit of India herself—India, the land of Ahimsa. Here, in this idyllic village in the remote confines of the line, half a mile away from the river Sutlej, we get a picture of unity in diversity. Here the Hindus, Sikhs and Muslims lived peacefully together as they had been living since times immemorial. Though the frontier between India and Pakistan turns into a gory scene of riot and massacre, everything is calm and quiet in Mano Majra. Partition does not ruffle the normal tenor of life in Mano Majra. Mano Majrans are unaware of the political situation of the country. They even do not know that the British have left India and the India has been partitioned and is ruled now by the popular Congress ministry. Mano Majra's tranquil milieu reminds one of the famous lines of Thomas Gray's poem "Elegy Written in a Country Churchyard":

> Far from the madding crowd's ignoble strife,
> Their sober wishes never learned to stray;
> Along the cool and sequestered vale of life,
> They kept the noiseless tenor of their way.

Mano Majra is in fact a symbol of staticity, of immobility and passivity. The harmonious atmosphere and the idyllic tranquillity of this tiny village is a veritable oasis of peace. The villagers remain unruffled by the frantic acts of murder, plunder, arson, abduction and rape:

> Mano Majra is a tiny place. It has only three brick buildings, one of which is the home of the moneylender Lala Ram Lal. The other two are the Sikh temple and the mosque. . . . The rest of the village is a cluster of flat-roofed mud huts and low-walled courtyards which front on narrow lanes that radiate from the centre. . . . There are only about seventy families in Mano Majra, and Lala Ram Lal's is the only Hindu family. The others are Sikhs or Muslims, about equal in number. . . . But there is one object that all Mano Majrans—even Lala Ram Lal—venerate. This is a three-foot slab of sandstone that stands upright under a keekar tree beside the pond. It is the local deity, the deo to which all the villagers—Hindu, Sikh, Muslim or pseudo-Christian—repair secretly whenever they are in special need of blessing. (2)

Deo, the local deity, becomes the symbol of communal harmony like the goddess Kenchamma in Raja Rao's *Kanthapura*. The Kanthapurians rise to the call of Gandhiji and involve themselves in the independent movement but the Mano Majrans remain passive spectators to the whole scene of pre-independent struggle. They have heard the name of Gandhiji but remain unmoved by the call of the Mahatma to oust "the firangi from our soil." Their passivity and staticity to the violence in the wake of Partition has been very vividly described by Khushwant Singh:

> The summer before, communal riots, precipitated by reports of the proposed division of the country into a Hindu India and a Muslim Pakistan, had broken out in Calcutta, and within a few months the death toll had mounted to several thousand. . . . By the time the monsoon broke, almost a million of them were dead, and all of northern India was in arms, in terror, or in hiding. The only remaining oases of peace were a scatter of little villages lost in the remote reaches of the frontier. One of these villages was Mano Majra. (1-2)

As a contrast to the tranquil and static environs of Mano Majra, the train serves as an important symbol of mobility. It stands for all that is dynamic. Though at the outset of the story, it acts as an almanac and a regulator for the people of the hamlet, later on it acquires a sinister and formidably horrific dimension when its swift and placid tenor of life receives a shocking jolt in the wake of the bloody partition: "Trains became less punctual than ever before and many more started to run through at night. Some days it seemed as though the alarm clock had been set for the wrong hour. On others, it was as if no one had remembered to wind it." (92) The irregularity of trains symbolizes the disturbance in the smooth flow of life in Mano Majra. It presages chaos and disorder, riot and violence. The odd arrival of a train from Pakistan in the morning with heaps of mangled and mutilated corpses lets loose a reign of terror. Bestiality manifests in violence, revenge, mass rape of women in public, arson, infanticide and carnage. All this leads to the massacre of Mano Majran Muslims leaving for Pakistan by a train. The train to Pakistan reveals the humanity in Jugga, his sense of integrity in love and self-dedication. The train to Pakistan thus becomes a unique symbol in the novel. It is a symbol of motion in contrast to Mano Majra which is a static point in space. V.A. Shahane observes: "The use of the word 'train' is significant in other ways too. The train signifies groups or multitudes of people who are on the move . . . the train implies the movement of vast communities, torn from their links of nativity, from their places of birth and upbringing and areas of traditional growth in search of a new 'Jerusalem.' It indicates the harrowing process of this change, the awful and ghastly experiences of human beings involved in a historical, objective and almost dehumanised process. The train suggests the fate of the individuals, the destinies of two newly formed dominions. . . . Secondly, the train is also a symbol of the machine age. . . . Modern mechanistic, materialistic age has caused severe destruction of humanistic values."[10] Further the train is symbolic of the rhythmic pattern of the novel. It is at the heart of Mano Majra, a village which has "always been known for its railway station." (3) The villagers' activities are patterned by the to and fro movement of the train. It fills the villagers with the very pulse of life.

The arrival of a ghost train at Mano Majra stuns the villagers. They are awe-struck at the sight of the train being loaded with dead bodies giving out the acrid smell of searing flesh. The bestial scene is too terrible for the innocent villagers. It unveils the horrible and ghastly drama of communal violence—the sinking and erosion of human values. The sight of the geckos pouncing on the moth and catching it fluttering is symbolic of the genocide (since there is mass killing of Hindus and Muslims), a common feature of Partition. It points to the extermination of not only people but the annihilation of human values under the garb of religious fanaticism. Even the magistrate's fear of spending the night all alone in his room is symbolic of terror and apprehension leading to insecurity and indecision.

The summer sun going "on, day after day, from east to west, scorching relentlessly" (79) is also a very significant symbol. It suggests the "disillusioned, dejected, thirsty and sweating" (80) people of the time. The comforting and cheerful rain after the parching heat of the summer turns into a series of experiences, pertaining to death and destruction. Serpents, centipedes, scorpions and the moths fluttering around the lamps, mosquitoes and flies made life awfully irksome. The monsoon, giving a boost to the tempo of life and death, is symbolic of the inhuman acts done by the people as a result of communal violence. Life everywhere was chaotic. Man had to move on the razor's edge. Retaliation became the talk of the day and the law of retaliation the philosophers say is the law of necessary evils. Hence the Hindus and Muslims sported themselves with the lives of one another. There was no end to it. The train to Pakistan and the train from Pakistan became the symbol of man's inhumanity to man, man preying upon man. But the Mano Majrans still had some amount of sanity and wisdom, humanity and fellow-feeling. "What have we to do with Pakistan? We are born here. So were our ancestors. We have lived amongst you as brothers," (14) says one of the Muslims amidst a crowd of Sikhs. The Sikh lambardar replies forthwith: "Yes, you are our brothers. As far as we are concerned you and your children and your grandchildren can live here as long as you like. If anyone speaks rudely to you, your wives or your children, it will be us first and our wives and children before a single hair of your heads is touched." (30) The peasant folk of Mano Majra, especially the Sikhs cannot deny shelter to the terror-stricken refugees. To them "hospitality was not a pastime but a sacred duty." (9) People of Mano Majra live in amity. They are god-fearing and religious. Friendship and philanthropy was the be-all and end-all of their life. But for how long? Soon their amity and integration is going to be shattered by the train to Pakistan when they will be alienated from their near and dear ones for ever. Violence in the human world is symbolised by violence in the natural world. The flashing crash of lightning and thunder symbolize murder and looting of the people after Partition.

The swelling Sutlej presented a terrifying sight. Flood in the river suggested and foreshadowed the flood of violence. The lambardar "had never known the Sutlej to rise so high in so short a time." (121) The river's appearance in the night like a sheet of paper, symbolized the black beastly acts of violence. The new American engines, wailing "like someone being murdered" (123) also symbolized the diabolic deeds of horror and the degeneration of long-cherished socio-moral values. The cries of the jackals symbolized predatory craving. It thickened the atmosphere of awe engendered by the sight of the carcasses floating on the water and kites and vultures hovering in the sky.

Khushwant Singh does not arraign any particular party or community. He finds both the Hindus and the Muslims equally responsible for the inhuman deeds. He puts the blame squarely on both the racial factions. He feels the Mullahs actively participating in the frenzied butchery of human beings and human values. These mullahs instigate the people to mutiny and murder: "Mullahs roamed the Punjab and the Frontier Province with boxes of human skulls said to be those of Muslims in Bihar." (1) Still further, Singh's attack is on the nonchalant politicians in Delhi whiling away their time in political gossips and commitments. "Nero fiddled upon the harp, when the Roman empire was burning." This is exactly what these politicians did when the entire nation was reeling under the pangs of the two-nation theory. Partition had brought about estrangement to the lives of the people who believed in one India. They were utterly broken by the people in power sitting in Delhi making "fine speeches in the assembly" (153) in the midst of lovely foreign women. The outgoing rulers dragged the nation to utter chaos and confusion. The crazy fallacy of the two-nation theory has been fully exposed and exploited. The quest for a safe homeland had uprooted the masses of humanity. Non-violence was thrown to the winds. Religion now was found to be hollow and shorn of all moral values. Iqbal, a philosopher and social worker, says, "Ethics, which should be the kernel of a religious code, has been carefully removed." (149) But God-consciousness still haunts the minds of the people undergoing the pain of suffering and misery with their emphatic and searing realisation: "God is punishing us for our sins." (107)

Despite the note of utter despair bordering on nihilism, the novel is a message of hope and compromise. The most basic of all human instincts, i.e. man-woman love, sustains the sympathetically bitter tone of the novel. Jugga's sacrifice is an act of self-redemption, it is an identification in alienation. To William Walsh, *Train to Pakistan* "is a tense, economical novel, thoroughly true to the events and the people. It goes forward in a trim, athletic way, and its unemphatic voice makes a genuinely human comment."[11] Khushwant Singh's *Train to Pakistan* with its realistic and touching portrayal of characters, chiefly round, lays bare the grimly tragic situation of the human context in which Khushwant Singh's fictional people march towards the altar of self-immolation. To Shahane, "The concept of common man as a tragic hero is an interesting aspect of the theme and symbol in *Train to Pakistan*."[12]

The novel is a tragedy of human situation. "There is no tragedy without transcendence"[13] and true to this Jugga transcends himself. Jugga's sacrifice is the inner dynamics of tragedy since "the tragic feeling is invoked in us," observes Arthur Miller, "when we are in the presence of a character who is ready to lay down his life to secure one thing . . . his sense of personal dignity."[14] *Train to Pakistan* is a tragedy written in a mock-comic tone, criticising the celebration of freedom with mass murder and bestiality and ingeniously delineating the pity and horror of the two-nation theory. It is "a nightmare with an exciting finish, one closes the novel with a sense of relief."[15]

NOTES

1. V.A. Shahane, "Khushwant Singh: An Artist in Realism," *Critical*

Essays on Indian Writing in English, ed. Naik et al (Madras: Macmillan, 1977), p. 344.

2. Harish Raizada, "Train to Pakistan: A Study in Crisis of Values," p. 126 of this book.
3. Khushwant Singh, "Guest of Honour Talk," The Australian Broadcasting Commission's *Guest of Honour* Programme, broadcast on 5th April, 1964.
4. Raizada, p. 127.
5. Khushwant Singh, *Train to Pakistan* (London: Chatto and Windus, 1956), p. 54.
6. John Thompson, "Indian Accent," a programme of interviews with Indian Writers broadcast by the Canadian Broadcasting Commission in 1961.
7. Bonamy Dobree, "Thomas Hardy," *English Critical Essays Twentieth Century* (London: OUP, 1942), p. 328.
8. Khushwant Singh, Address to Expo 1967, Auditorium, Montreal, Canada (1967).
9. Review in *The New York Herald Tribune Book Review*, 12 April 1956.
10. Shahane, pp. 347-48.
11. William Walsh, *Commonwealth Literature* (London: OUP, 1973), p. 18.
12. Shahane, p. 350.
13. Karl Jaspers, "Basic Charcteristics of the Tragic," *Tragedy Is Not Enough* (Beacon Press, 1952), p. 41.
14. Arthur Miller, "Tragedy and the Common Man," *The New York Times*, 27 February 1949.
15. K.R. Srinivasa Iyengar, *Indian Writing in English* (Bombay: Asia, 1973), p. 501.

Train to Pakistan: A Study in Crisis of Values

HARISH RAIZADA

Khushwant Singh made his debut as a writer more by accident than by choice. But for the compulsive inner urge he felt as "an angry middle-aged man"[1] to let out his disenchantment with long-cherished human values in the wake of inhuman bestial horrors and insane savage killings on both sides during the partition of the subcontinent between India and Pakistan in August 1947, he would have perhaps continued to philander with legal profession or diplomatic assignment in the Indian Foreign Service.

Son of Sir Shobha Singh who became famous because of his association with the building plan of the city of New Delhi, Khushwant Singh was born in 1915, at Hadali in the Punjab. After his early education in Lahore and Delhi, he went to England and studied at King's College in London and took his bar-at-law from Inner Temple, one of the professional colleges of lawyers in England. On returning to India, he practised at the High Court of Lahore and taught Hindu Law and Jurisprudence at the Punjab University. The Partition of the country cut his career short as a lawyer which even otherwise was for him an inadequate and precarious source of income. The legal profession, however, extended his knowledge of human nature and made him see man and life in the raw, bereft of all its external embellishment. Like Fielding, Scott and Dickens, other fictional celebrities associated with legal profession, he got a discerning insight into complex human character. His early short stories contributed to foreign magazines, are the product of real experiences gleaned by him during his "briefless days as lawyer in Lahore."[2]

The traumatic experience of partition shook him to roots and made him restive to give vent to his indignation at the terrible holocaust which claimed innumerable innocent lives, but the pressing demands of public life in the critical early years of independence veered him to a diplomatic assignment as the Press Attache to the High Commissioner for India in London and Canada. Unable to put up with the harassing vagaries of Krishna Menon, he left his job in the Indian Foreign Service after four years and crossed the Rubicon "to launch his bark on unchartered seas of literature."[3] He took to journalism[4] to which he adheres till today, but in between contributed short stories to English, Canadian and American magazines with which he had established contacts during his stay in London and Ottawa. The collection of these stories, entitled *The Mark of Vishnu*, was brought out by Saturn Press, London, in 1950. It was followed by a historical treatise, *The Sikhs*, published by Allen and Unwin. Though both these works elicited commendable reviews in the British and Indian Press, they were not very rewarding financially.

The first major breakthrough in Khushwant Singh's literary career came with the publication of *Train to Pakistan* (1956), the book which won for him the coveted Grove Press India Fiction Prize for the year and which has been in his system for several years with the haunting memories of the unprecedented carnage witnessed by the subcontinent. The harrowing incidents of 1947 had shaken the faith of all the sensitive and thinking people of India in the intrinsic nobility of man, taught by its sages and saints including Mahatma Gandhi during various stages of its cultural evolution of thousands of years. They brought great disillusionment and crisis of values in the life of Khushwant Singh also. Describing his mental agony and distressing inner conflict of this period of disillusionment, he remarks:

> The beliefs that I had cherished all my life were shattered. I had believed in the innate goodness of the common man. But the division of India had been accompanied by the most savage massacres known in the history of the country. . . . I had believed that we Indians were peace-loving and

> non-violent, that we were more concerned with matters of the spirit, while the rest of the world was involved in the pursuit of material things. After the experience of the autumn of 1947, I could no longer subscribe to these views. I became . . . an angry middle-aged man, who wanted to shout his disenchantment with the world. . . . I decided to try my hand at writing.[5]

All the venom and indignation felt by him at the ghastly human tragedy was poured by him with scathing irony and stark realism in this memorable work of fiction depicting the sinister impact of partition on the peace-loving Hindus, Muslims and Sikhs of Mano Majra, an obscure and tiny village in the Punjab. If Kanthapura was the microcosm of the national upsurge in the country in the twenties, Mano Majra became the microcosm of vivisected India. *Train to Pakistan* is, however, a classic in the post-independence Indian English fiction not only because of the bold, brutal and unrelenting realism with which it tears asunder the mask of hypocrisy and exposes the sordidness and savagery of human life, but also because of the author's optimistic and affirmative world-view that emerges from it, his enduring faith in the values of love, loyalty and humanity and the unconquerable spirit of man in the face of the mighty forces of wickedness and savage cruelties.

This heroic spirit of man is revealed in the novel not by men who are considered religious and respectable in the public and supposed to have innate goodness but by a man like Jugga who is treated as a confirmed ruffian, "budmash number ten."[6] When powerful and potential authority of the land sulks in indifference and inactivity, religious priests cower in timidity, and the best of political and rational ideologies recoil in fright, it is Jugga, the deviant who combats the forces of darkness and sacrifices himself selflessly to save innocent lives threatened by the planned Mano Majra massacre. Like Thomas Hardy, Khushwant Singh invests the common man of the soil with tragic grandeur to show, as Bonamy Dobree remarks, "the dignity of man for all his helpless littleness in the face of the universe, for all his nullity under the blotting hand of time."[7] Describing Jugga's indubious moral stature, Khushwant Singh writes:

> I thought it was time I exploded this myth of the innate goodness in man. There is innate evil in man. And so I just wrote about it, and I did create one character whom I stuffed with the so-called innate goodness of man, and he is the only character which is entirely fiction.[8]

Though a creation of the author's imagination, Jugga is one of the most convincing and credible of the characters portrayed in the novel for in him one finds the synthesis of good and bad in the same proportion as human life presents.

II

Khushwant Singh was of forty years when he wrote *Train to Pakistan*. Everything in his life upto this point qualified him for creating just this sort of book. His childhood in the Punjab village—"My roots are in the dunghill of a tiny Indian village,"[9] he remarked once—has acquainted him with its natural surroundings and moods of changing seasons and given him an insight into its men and their morals. His British education has shorn him of his narrow parochialism and made him "a cultured humanist."[10] His involvement in legal profession and diplomatic service has given him the knowledge of the duplicity, sham and pharisaism of human character both at lower and higher levels. The bestial savagery of partition has disillusioned him about human nature and for the same reason the few in whom he found even a little of humanity, made him set an inordinate value on the virtues of loyalty and unselfishness. The hard journalistic work had given him supple precision of style.

The tone of the book was thus set by the peculiar mixture of sympathy and bitterness in the author's attitude—the strange impression that he was simultaneously inside the action as a participant and outside it as a dispassionate observer. It is therefore not surprising that *Train to Pakistan* is both a grim and pathetic tale of individuals and communities caught in the swirl of partition.

The action of the novel spans a few weeks of the fateful days of August and September in 1947 in Mano Majra, a border village, with a river fringing it and a railway bridge spanning the river. Though the frontier between India and Pakistan turns a scene of rioting and bloodshed, everything is quiet and normal in Mano Majra where Hindus, Sikhs and Muslims still live peaceably together as they have been living since times immemorial. Partition does not yet mean much to them. Many of them do not even know that the British have left and India is partitioned and is being governed by the popular Congress Ministry. One of the characters in the novel, the Sub-Inspector of Police, points out to the Deputy Commissioner: "I am sure no one in Mano Majra even knows that the British have left and the country is divided into Pakistan and Hindustan. Some of them know about Gandhi but I doubt if anyone has ever heard of Jinnah." (33)

Life in this village is regulated by the passing of trains across the Sutlej bridge nearby. The village awakes when the mail train rushes through the bridge before daybreak. The whole village then echoes with Mullah's cries of 'Allaho-Akbar' from the mosque and the Sikh priest's prayers from the Gurdwara. By the time 10.30 morning passenger train from Delhi comes in, life in Mano Majra settles down to its dull, daily routine and when the mid-day express passes people stop to rest and men and children come home for dinner and the siesta hour. As the evening passenger from Lahore steams in, everyone gets to work again and by the time the night goods train comes in, Mano Majra gets to sleep with the echoes of the prayers of the Mullah and the Sikh priest.

"Train" has been used as a significant symbol in the novel. A veritable almanac and time-guide for the people of Mano Majra in normal times, it acquires sinister dimensions when its smooth running in and out of the village is disturbed in the wake of partition: "Trains became less punctual than ever before and many more started to run through at night. Some days it seemed as though the alarm clock had been set for the wrong hour. On others, it was as if no one had remembered to wind it." (92)

The irregularity of trains presages disturbance in the smooth and quiet life of Mano Majra. A train which comes from Pakistan at an odd time in the morning with heaps of mangled dead bodies of Hindus and Sikhs, sets in motion the dark forces of violence and revenge, and leads to the attempted massacre of Mano Majran Muslims leaving for Pakistan by a train—from which the novel derives its title. It is to let this train carrying his Muslim mistress Nooran pass safely through to Pakistan that Jugga sacrifices his life. "Train" thus becomes a crucial symbol in the life of Mano Majra.

People in Mano Majra, though illiterate and superstitious, are Godfearing and religious. They live in amity with each other and have their own code of morality in which friendship counts above everything else:

> The Punjabis' code was even more baffling. For them truth, honour, financial integrity were "all right," but these were placed lower down the scale of values than being true to one's salt, to one's friends and fellow villagers. For friends, you could lie in court or cheat, and no one would blame you. On the contrary, you became a *nar admi*—a he-man—who had defied authority (magistrates and police) and religion (oath and scripture) but proved true to friendship. (54)

Very similar to this is Khushwant Singh's own credo of life: "Whatever its limitations, whatever its frustrations, love is the greatest, the most exhilarating experience of life."[11]

The quiet life of the village is suddenly disturbed when a local moneylender, Ram Lal, is murdered. Jugga, a tall, handsome, and robustly-built farmer, known as a bad character in the village is suspected and arrested for he is found absent from his house at the time of the incident and is unable to explain the cause of his absence. Along with him is also arrested Iqbal, England-educated and Communist-inspired young man who has been sent by the People's Party of India to preach Hindu-Muslim unity and stop bloodshed in the villages of the Punjab. He, being a stranger in the village, is suspected to be a Muslim Leaguer and is remanded to police custody.

Meanwhile the condition in Mano Majra deteriorates further and its time schedule starts going wrong because of the sudden irregularity of trains. People whisper about a train which comes from Pakistan at an unusual hour, carrying dead bodies of Sikhs and Hindus. Simultaneously are heard rumours about Muslims being slaughtered in Patiala, Ambala, and Amritsar, mosques being demolished, and the holy *Koran* being torn by infidels. Soon the village becomes a battlefield of conflicting loyalties. Though Mano Majrans still pledge to protect their Muslim brethren, yet afraid of the angry and aggrieved refugees from Pakistan, they shift them to the refugee camps. As the flooded Sutlej brings the dead bodies of more Hindus and Sikhs, tension rises in the village. The communal fire is fanned by the young Sikh boys who come from outside and incite Mano Majrans to take revenge upon Muslims. They succeed in getting the support of bad characters like Mali and dacoits of his gang who had earlier murdered the local moneylender and now hope to reap a profitable harvest by the annihilation of Muslims. They conspire to fire at the train taking refugees to Pakistan and tie a rope across the bridge to drag the Muslims down the roof of the running carriage.

Unable to stem the tide of violence and finding themselves helpless, police authorities release Jugga and Iqbal of whose innocence they are by now fully convinced. The authorities feel that Jugga being a friend of Mano Majran Muslims and Iqbal being a non-communal political worker, may exert some influence on the misguided people and save Muslims from being slaughtered. Iqbal, the idealist and rationalist, considers discretion to be the better part of valour and keeps himself away from the fire. But when Jugga learns of the conspiracy and comes to know that the train is carrying his beloved Nooran and other Muslims of Mano Majra, he climbs over the bridge and diverts the attention of the conspirators by cutting the rope meant for killing Muslims. The train of Muslim refugees passes over to Pakistan without any damage but Jugga dies, being shot by his co-religionists.

The heroic sacrifice of Jugga who is treated as a ruffian by the civilized society poses a challenge to it and unmasks its hypocrisy and duplicity. Khushwant Singh's irony manifests itself here with ruthless bitterness shattering the pretence of much extolled and highly glorified values of human life. Jugga, though condemned by society as a criminal and irreligious person, succeeds in achieving what the Deputy Commissioner reputed as he-man and the police authorities with all their might and power, Iqbal Singh with all his rational ideologies and convictions, Meet Singh with all his religious faith in love and brotherhood and the lambardar with all his sincere fellow-feelings fail to accomplish. Like Henry Fielding, Khushwant Singh also believes that often the most noble acts of generosity and self-sacrifice are performed by persons who are looked down upon by the people as immoral deviants. When the administrative authorities and the people of great consequence and significance in the society are either accomplices or helpless witnesses to the marauding conspiracy, the succour and safety of the hundreds of innocent Muslims come through a man who is given to swearing, stealing and other moral laxities.

III

Khushwant Singh's treatment of brutal atrocities committed on either side of the border is characterized by artistic objectivity and detachment. He exaggerates nothing, he leaves nothing. There is nothing melodramatic or ineffective about it. At the very beginning of the novel he sets the tone for his dispassionate account of the concrete details of the holocaust: "Muslims said the Hindus had planned and started the killing. According to the Hindus, the Muslims were to blame. The fact is, both sides killed. Both shot and stabbed and speared and dubbed. Both tortured. Both raped." (9)

How the emotions of people are roused by the rumours spread by both the communities about the barbaric deeds of each other, is described by the author through the mounting tension between Sikhs and Muslims who had hitherto lived in amity in Mano Majra. As the village gets divided into two halves, Muslims and Sikhs gather in separate groups and talk of inhuman savagery of each other. Muslims brood over the rumours of atrocities committed by Sikhs:

They had heard of gentlewomen having their veils taken

> off, being stripped and marched down crowded streets to be raped in the market place. Many had eluded their would-be ravishers by killing themselves. They had heard of mosques being desecrated by the slaughter of pigs on the premises, and of copies of the holy *Koran* being torn up by infidels. (141)

Sikhs on the other hand feel "Never trust a Musulman":

> Sikh refugees had told of women jumping into wells and burning themselves rather than fall into the hands of Muslims. Those who did not commit suicide were paraded naked in the streets, raped in public, and then murdered. (142)

The blood-curdling account of the bestial cruelties let loose by the partition are conveyed through the recollections of three incidents by the Deputy Commissioner, Hukum Chand. The author relates these incidents with stark realism and sardonic jibe at Prime Minister Jawaharlal Nehru, "Wasn't that a wonderful thing to say? Long ago we made a tryst with destiny and now the time comes when we shall redeem our pledge, not wholly or in full measure but very substantially. Yes, Mr. Prime Minister, you made your tryst. So did many others—on the 15th August, Independence Day." (201) Prem Singh, a colleague of Hukum Chand, made his tryst with destiny when he went back to fetch his wife's jewellery from Lahore and was killed by a dozen heads with fez caps and Pathan turbans as he emerged out of the gate of Foletti's hotel after entertaining his English friends. Sundari, the daughter of Hukum Chand's orderly, had made her tryst with destiny on the road to Gujranwala. "She had been married four days and both her arms were covered with red lacquer bangles and the henna on her palms was still a deep vermillion." She had not yet slept with her husband. She had hardly seen even his face through her veil. As she day-dreamt of her first night with her husband, her bus suddenly pulled up.

> There were large stones on the road. Then hundreds of peo-

> ple surrounded them. Everyone was ordered off the bus. Sikhs were just hacked to death. The clean-shaven were stripped. Those that were circumcised were forgiven. Those that were not, were circumcised. Not just the foreskin: the whole thing was cut off. She who had not really had a good look at Mansa Ram was shown her husband completely naked. They held him by the arms and legs and one man cut off his penis and gave it to her. The mob made love to her. She did not have to take off any one of her bangles. They were all smashed as she lay on the road, being taken by one man and another and another. (203)

Sunder Singh's case was different. Muslims did not kill his family; he killed them himself. Stranded for four days during scorching heat of summer on a wayside station in a small railway compartment stuffed with five hundred men and women, he could not bear the agony of his children whom he could not provide even urine to drink. "So he pulled out his revolver and shot them all. Shangara Singh aged six with his long brown blonde hair tied up in a topknot, Deepo aged four with curling eyelashes, and Amro, four months old, who tugged at her mother's dry breasts with her gums and puckered her face till it was full of wrinkles, crying frantically." (204)

Contrasted against these scenes of heinous crimes is the moving picture of the people who feel utterly broken as they are compelled to leave the land of their and their forefathers' birth. When Imam Baksh is asked to leave Mano Majra for Pakistan lest he be tortured by Sikh refugees, he is moved and tears trickle down his eyes:

> Imam Baksh wiped a tear from his eyes and blew his nose in the hem of his shirt.
>
> "What have we to do with Pakistan? We were born here. So were our ancestors. We have lived amongst you brothers." Imam Baksh broke down. Meet Singh clasped him in his arms and began to sob. Several of the people started crying quietly and blowing their noses. (147)

When after much deliberation, all come to the conclusion that in the interest of Muslims themselves, it will be better for them to leave the village, Imam Baksh says: "All right, if we have to go, we'd better pack up our bedding and belongings. It will take us no more than one night to clear out of homes it has taken our fathers and grandfathers hundreds of years to make." (148-49) Describing the condition of the village and its people on the eve of the departure of Muslims from there, the author writes: "Not many people slept in Mano Majra that night. They went from house to house—talking, crying, swearing love and friendship, assuring each other that this would soon be over. Life, they said, would be as it always had been." (153-54)

We learn from the novel how the common men behaved in a more balanced and sane manner than the Government officers who fanned the fire instead of finding ways to extinguish it. A Sikh officer says to Meet Singh who is sympathetic towards Muslims: "The only way people like you will understand anything is by being sent over to Pakistan: have your sisters and mothers raped in front of you, have your clothes taken off and be sent back with a kick and spit on your behind." (157-58) At another place the police inspector says to the Deputy Commissioner:

> Sometimes, sir, one cannot restrain oneself. What do the Gandhicaps in Delhi know about the Punjab? What is happening on the other side in Pakistan does not matter to them. They have not lost their homes and belongings; they haven't had their mothers, wives, sisters and daughters raped and murdered in the streets. Did your honour hear what the Muslim mobs did to Hindu and Sikh refugees in the market places at Sheikhupura and Gujranwala? Pakistan police and the army took part in the killings. Not a soul was left alive. Women killed their own children and jumped into wells that filled to the brim with corpses. (31)

IV

The crisis of values suffered by people during this period of unprecedented human tragedy is conveyed by the author through his satirical portraiture of three characters typical of their three different situations epitomizing the civilized human life. These are Hukum Chand, the high officer in the Government administration, Meet Singh, the Sikh priest, and Iqbal Singh, the rationalistic and idealistic, non-communal political worker. Jugga's moral stature stands out in strong relief against the hypocrisy, cowardice and sham of these characters.

Hukum Chand, the Magistrate and Deputy Commissioner of the district, is a worldly wise man of easy morals. He owes his rise from a foot-constable to his present high position to his sycophancy. "He always kept the Sahibs pleased and they gave him one promotion after another." (56) He is considered even by religious people like Meet Singh "a *nar admi*—and clever. He is true to his friends and always gets things done for them. He has had dozens of relatives given good jobs. He is one of a hundred. Nothing counterfeit about Hukum Chand." (56) He is, however, lascivious and carries on a liaison with a Muslim dancing girl Haseena. His fatalism has made him face the buffets of destiny with equanimity.

> He had taken the loss of his children with phlegmatic resignation. He had borne with an illiterate, unattractive wife, without complaint. It all came from his belief that the only absolute truth was death. The rest—love, ambition, pride, values of all kinds—was to be taken with a pinch of salt. He did so with a clear conscience. Although he accepted gifts and obliged friends when they got into trouble, he was not corrupt. He occasionally joined in parties, arranged for singing and dancing—and sometimes sex—but he was not immoral. (104)

He is, however, terribly shocked when he sees the heaps of dead bodies of men, women and children huddled in a train from Pakistan. A cold numbness overtakes him and all his emotions are dead. "But a trainload of dead was too much for even Hukum Chand's fatalism. He could not square a massacre with a philosophical belief in the inevitability of death. It bewildered and frightened him by its violence and its magnitude." (105) His official responsibilities, however, compel him to save the lives of people under his charge. Even by nature "he took life as it was. He did not want to recast it or rebel against it. . . . He believed that an individual's conscious effort should be directed to immediate ends like saving life when endangered, preserving the social structure and honouring its conventions. His immediate problem was to save Muslim lives." (118)

Hukum Chand's interest in saving Muslim lives is, however, not motivated by humanitarian considerations. He is only concerned about the maintenance of law and order lest his official position is compromised. The duplicity in his attitude is revealed in his conversation with the sub-inspector of police:

> We must maintain law and order. If possible, get the Muslims to go out peacefully. . . . No, Inspector Sahib, whatever our views—and God alone knows what I would have done to these Pakistanis if I were not a government servant—we must not let there be any killing or destruction of property. Let them get out, but be careful they do not take too much with them. Hindus from Pakistan were stripped of all their belongings before they were allowed to leave. (32)

Later when he feels utterly broken by the increasing incidents of arson and looting, he lapses into inactivity and wants just to maintain a pretence of having acted responsibly: "Well, Inspector Sahib, let them kill. Let everyone kill. Just ask for help from other stations and keep a record of the messages you send. We must be able to prove that we did our best to stop them." (177)

Meet Singh is a peasant who has taken to religion as an escape from work. He is not learned in the scriptures, nor has he any faculty for conversation. But he is a man of peace and goodwill and sincerely believes: "Everyone is welcome to his religion." (49) When Sikh boys try to incite Mano Majrans against Muslims, he even argues with them: "What have the Muslims here done to us for us to kill them in revenge for what Muslims in Pakistan are doing? Only people who have committed crimes should be punished." (171) But, when it comes to taking steps to avert the imminent danger to Muslims, he recoils in timidity.

When Iqbal implores him, "Bhaiji, can't you stop it? They all listen to you," he replies: "I have done all I could. My duty is to tell people what is right and what is not. If they insist on doing evil, I ask God to forgive them. I can only pray: the rest is for the police and the magistrates." (193)

Iqbal Singh is the England-educated young man of communist leanings. No other character in the novel is subjected to such an ironic and brutal exposure as he. He is very forthright, rational and logical in his criticism of social evils in the country as is evident from just one of his pointed remarks: "Where on earth except in India would man's life depend on whether or not his foreskin had been removed? It would be laughable if it were not tragic." (188) He has all the theories but lacks the courage to put them into action in time of crisis. From the very start, he is found too worried about his own safety and health. He has been sent by his People's Party of India to forge unity between Sikhs and Muslims and check them from violence, but the moment he learns of a murder in Mano Majra, he gets frightened: "Was it communal? Is it all right for me to be here? I do not suppose I can do much if the village is all excited about a murder." He winces under the sharp jibe of Meet Singh who remarks: "Why, Babu Sahib, you have come to stop killing and you are upset by one murder? I thought you had come to stop such things, Babu Sahib." (51) As the communal tension mounts in the village, he wishes "they had sent someone else to Mano Majra. He would be so much more useful directing police and clearing the cobwebs from their minds." (65)

Iqbal Singh's moral inadequacy comes under the bantering ridicule by the author when he shows him funking at the time of threatened attack on Mano Majran Muslims. Replying to Meet Singh's ironical remark, "When you came you were going to speak to them about something? Why don't you tell them now?" he says, "Bhaiji, when people go about with guns and spears you can only talk back with guns and spears. If you cannot do that, then it is best to keep out of their way." (193) Instead of resorting to bold steps to avert the tragedy, he drowns himself in pegs after pegs of whisky and muses over the futility of any action in the present situation:

> If there were people to see the act of self-immolation, as on a cinema screen, the sacrifice might be worthwhile: a moral lesson might be conveyed. If all that was likely to happen was that next morning your corpse would be found among thousands of others, looking just like them—cropped hair, shaven chin . . . even circumcised—who would know that you were not a Muslim victim of a massacre? (194)

Lacking the courage to act to his convictions, Iqbal remains only too self-conscious about his image.

Contrasted against these moral decrepits respected by the civilized society, is Jugga, a robust and tall Sikh who is feared and condemned as a bad character. He has no pretensions about himself and candidly confesses before Iqbal, "I am a *budmash.* All governments put me in jail." When Iqbal asks him, "But what makes you *budmash*? The Government," he interrupts him in the middle and replies, "No, Babu Sahib, it is our fate. It is written on our foreheads and on the lines of our hands. I am always wanting to do something. When there is ploughing to be done or the harvest to be gathered, then I am busy. When there is no work, my hands still itch to do something. So I do something, and it is always wrong." (76) Jugga is in reality a typical Punjabi peasant in his strength and weakness, in his courage, fearlessness, loyalty, unsophistication, roughness and bluntness. He is self-sacrificing and humane. He shows his mettle on several occasions. His silence about the cause of his absence from his house on the night of Sahukar's murder, reminds us of the Italian novelist Ignazio Silone's *The Secret of Luke.* Like the peasant Luke, he also courts imprisonment to protect the honour of the girl he loves. Later he gives a thrashing to Mali for disturbing the peace of the village by murdering the village Sahukar. It is, however, his heroic self-sacrifice to save the lives of the innocent Muslims of his village, that makes him put to shame all those time-servers who notwithstanding their resources, power, learning and prestige falter and vacillate to take a decision. There is a rare grandeur and singular nobility of character about his heroic resolution to save Mano Majran Muslims from death-trap. He goes to Gurdwara and asks Meet Singh, avoiding all unnecessary talk, to read "the Guru's words" from the *Granth Sahib*, "Will you just read me a few lines quickly? . . . It does not matter what you read. Just read it." (198) As the Bhaiji comes to the end of his recitation and tells him, "It is just the Guru's word. If you are going to do something good, the Guru will help you; if you are going to do something bad, the Guru will stand in your way. If you persist in doing it, he will punish you till you repent, and then forgive you," (199) he gets up and goes away uttering "Sat Sri Akal." A little later we see him twining round a rope tied across the bridge for killing Muslims:

> Somebody fired another shot. The man's body slid off the rope, but he clung to it with his hands and chin. He pulled himself up, caught the rope under his left armpit, and again started hacking with his right hand. The rope had been cut in shreds. Only a thin tough strand remained. He went at it with the knife, and then with his teeth. The engine was almost on him. There was a volley of shots. The man shivered and collapsed. The rope snapped in the centre as he fell. The train went over him, and went on to Pakistan.

V

The horror accompanying the transfer of population as a sequel to the independence and partition of India, has been the major theme with Indian English writers. Mulk Raj Anand and Khwaja Ahmad Abbas have treated it in their moving stories of rare power and many other writers like B. Rajan, Balwant Singh Gargi, Attia Hosain, Manohar Malgonkar, Raj Gill and Chaman Nahal, in their full-length novels of artistic excellence, *The Dark Dancer, Cruel Interlude, Sunlight on a Broken Column, A Bend in the Ganges, The Rape* and *Azadi* respectively. But none of these works approach Khushwant Singh's *Train to Pakistan* in extraordinary power and unrelenting realism. It still remains the most forceful and exquisite of the creative works born out of the agonized torments and travails of body and spirit endured by the sacred soil of the five rivers.

NOTES

1. From the transcript of a talk for the Australian Broadcasting Commission's *Guest of Honour* programme, broadcast on 5 April 1964.
2. Khushwant Singh, "Compulsions to Write," R.K. Dhawan, ed., *Explorations in Modern Indo-English Fiction* (New Delhi: Bahri, 1982), p. 185.
3. *Ibid.*
4. Khushwant Singh has edited *Yojna*, *The Illustrated Weekly of India*, *National Herald* and *The Hindustan Times*.
5. The *Guest of Honour* talk.
6. Khushwant Singh, *Train to Pakistan* (London: Chatto and Windus, 1956), p. 54.
7. Bonamy Dobree, "Thomas Hardy," *English Critical Essays: Twentieth Century* (London: Oxford University Press, 1942), p. 328.
8. From the transcript of "Indian Accent" by John Thompson, a programme of interviews with Indian writers broadcast by the Canadian Broadcasting Commission in 1961.
9. Khushwant Singh's Address to Expo 1967 Auditorium, Montreal, Canada.
10. V.A. Shahane, "Khushwant Singh: An Artist in Realism," M.K. Naik et al, ed., *Critical Essays on Indian Writing in English* (Delhi: Macmillan, 1977), p. 346.
11. Address to Expo 1967 Auditorium.

Train to Pakistan: Some Reflections

D. PREMPATI

Like the War fiction of the West the Partition fiction of India made a first-class use of the worn-out formula of a simple, dramatic narrative with a gaudy and spicy plot interspersed with lots of violent action. Often the insensate violence shocks the reader into a stony silence. He does not have the heart to re-read it, let alone partake of the human suffering at any level. The least episodic of the Partition writers was the celebrated Urdu writer Saadat Hasan Manto who is universally recognized to have succeeded in objectifying the disaster into a universal suffering.

Unlike several Partition novelists, Khushwant Singh's *Train to Pakistan* has a gripping narrative which by itself is no mean achievement by any standards. Partition novels like the War novels of the West must needs have a reportorial quality, which makes them documentaries of the social milieu of a certain representational type. *Train to Pakistan* is a rich and colourful documentary having achieved not a little from Khushwant Singh's long association with creative journalism.

Generally Indian English critics being a generation raised on the "international fictional achievements" of a Henry James or a James Joyce are averse to social realism in fiction and other genres. Whether they would tend to accept or not, increasing attacks on social realism are now part of the deepening cold war attitudes in the divided world today. Even for his toothless and innocent humanism which often fails to distinguish the good from the bad, Mulk Raj Anand had to pay rather dearly for a social realism of some sort. Khushwant Singh's case is slightly different. For what all we know he has never been on the wrong side in the cold war theatre. And yet his general acceptability got slightly vitiated when his fiction refused to transcend the social realistic form. This was bound to make him the paradox he grew into in the Indian English literary establishment.

Refreshingly *Train to Pakistan* is free from any pretentious and murky dabbling in symbolism, psychology, philosophy and anthropology with the Partition providing only a dramatic background. To dig out from this charming and straight-forward novel all kinds of estoeric symbols will be a wasteful effort, for Khushwant Singh is not made of such stuff. Whether the train in the novel represents "modernity" or "mobility," and to argue that the novel as a whole represents a well-regulated architectural pattern will take us probably nowhere. The sort of criticism which a Robert Barthes invites will be bland and irrelevant to a writer of Khushwant Singh's orientation. Indeed it is amazing to see that votaries of pluralism have been so deadeningly monistic in the art and technique of literary criticism. The contradictions which have come to exist between rooted literature and modernistic literature of international standards are suggestive of a plurality of literary assessments and that there isn't a single set of standards whether national or international. The Indian English critics have lost their freedom to see the rich diversity of different fictional strains, which explains why their critical output has remained irrelevant to creative problems of the larger Indian literature.

How do we approach *Train to Pakistan*? A look back to the social milieu reveals that Sikhs, Hindus and Muslims made the traditional structures of the Punjabi society in the pre-Partition India. Culture, language and customs contributed to the larger Punjabi identity though at a certain level religion divided them into communal groupings—almost separate identities. Another identity—a tense emotional belongingness to the village—also operated at the immediate level which subsumed even the separate religious identities. It was something like the old school tie, but in no case the class concept which it was in the British hierarchical society. Except for the varying percentage of religious groupings the village Mano Majra, the focal point of *Train to Pakistan*, was by and large typical of the rural Punjabi life. In terms of economic sluggishness and cultural backwardness, the village was like any other village of the entire subcontinent.

The Punjabi rural people were not at all prepared for the big holocaust which the Partition proved to be. It came as a big destabilizing factor in the smug and contented "self-sufficiency" of the Indian rural life. The people were caught in a disaster beyond their understanding. The national leaders had proclaimed that India would be partitioned only after their bodies had been cut into two pieces. This had got into the Punjabi folklore. *Train to Pakistan* chronicles the frightened reactions of a people suddenly thrown over to an uncertain destiny.

The very character of the national liberation struggle contributed in no small measure to the unpreparedness of the Punjabi rural life. Lahore, the capital of the undivided Punjab, emerged as the epicentre of all kinds of revolutionary and reformist movements in northern India. It was also the largest concentration of the emerging Punjabi ruling class. While the Government College located in Lahore provided the British a good chunk of obsequious bureaucrats, the non-government colleges of the city turned out a very impressive number of revolutionaries and reformists who made an all-India impact in course of time. The Punjabi rural life, however, remained unaffected by these middle-class movements. The feudal consciousness that "Government" was God remained ingrained in the rural consciousness as a whole. Perhaps nothing as much contributed to this as the British policy of recruitment to the armed forces and the proven failure of the national liberation movement to secure for itself the grassroot support all over the country.

Hostility to the British presence in India found a trenchant expression in the rising middle class and also in such sections of the rural masses as could be involved in the national liberation struggles. Mano Majra had none of these opportunities and so it had no other option than to submit passively to the forces let loose by the Partition. It didn't have to think for itself.

The lecherous ruling class which the British gifted to India was symbolised in the flabbiness of Magistrate Hukum Chand who camped at Mano Majra during the partition ordeal. A pastmaster in the art of lying, cheating, inventing alibis, he cared a fig for the butchery of thousands of innocents. The police administration he reared was comparable to the feudal system under the Nawabs and the Rajas. With the whole of the Punjab drowned in flames, Hukum Chand must have almost every night a sweet sixteen to respond to his impotence. The extra flesh hanging loose on his decaying body was pointer to the whole system gone plump and fluffy. We do not know how posterity will find *Train to Pakistan*, but we are quite certain it will prize the book for the way the writer recaptured the police savagery with corresponding savagery of expression. The police system which continues to this day in yet worse forms was the worst fedual gift the so-called British liberals chose to make for the modernisation of India.

Train to Pakistan was not conceived in terms of either Carlyle's heroes or the subsequent little heroes of little or no significance. The Australian critic H.M. Williams discovers in the novel what he calls "doomed heroes," perhaps Hukum Chand, Jugga and Iqbal are the "heroes," of this category "being a mystic archetype totally out of touch with the modern age's scepticism and banalities, an age for whom the natural heroes are not kings but pop-singers and footballers." As far as Khushwant Singh is concerned, no "mystic archetypes" will do. While a criticism of this sort would make a plain and simple novel unnecessarily ponderous and heavy, the text as well as the genre, I would argue, does not warrant such extraneous findings. The social milieu of the novel was at the receiving end. Precisely for this reason the novel remains a significant documentary. Jugga being peripheral to the main theme was maverick, perhaps no better than an adolescent hardly bothering about the need to interact with the holocaust which overtook his society.

The weakest link in the structure of *Train to Pakistan* is Iqbal. Khushwant Singh contrived this character as one with no flesh and no blood. A repuslive abstraction he seems to have been projected, rather satirically, from caricatures of such persons often referred to by Indian careerists studying in the British universities. Iqbal defends the political freedom of 1947. Conversely the Communist Party with which Iqbal was associated denounced the freedom as false and deceptive. It was only after some years that the CPI recanted its earlier assessment and resolved to dismiss it as a Stalinist error. Both Dange and Ranadive were equally responsible for their earlier error and subsequent revision. Besides, he was assigned no significant role in the novel. Like Jugga, he, too, appears to be a maverick, a political adolescent rather than a functionary deputed by a political party. Iqbal represents Khushwant Singh's extra-literary dimension, and to the extent he remained adventitious to the text he was no better than a dispensable commodity, an interpolation dictated by non-textual considerations.

What sort of social realism does one find in *Train to Pakistan*? The formula which got this novel its well-deserved popularity was: a sincere belief in traditional moral and social standards of Indian society (agrarian in this particular case) and a charming narrative skill. An occasional dose of sexual sensationalism is also contrived to punctuate the text here and there. It is, therefore, obvious that *Train to Pakistan* is a documentary novel with no claims whatsoever to the artistic techniques and extra-artistic philosophies of social realism and naturalism.

Khushwant Singh is a sensitive observant and accomplished craftsman in the world of Indian English fiction. A popular novelist, he does not have any pretence to fictional greatness. His was a simple formula which made the novel episodic in more than one sense. It was, again, this formula which made him turn his skill to sentimental glorification of adolescent behaviour (as in the case of Jugga) and also to a celebration of false and feudal values of the static agrarian society. No wonder the novel does not disturb us to any deeper awareness. The villains are dull and promiscuous. The criminality which the writer found overtaking Mano Majra's agrarian world does not give us a sharp awareness of the tormented psyche. The people's sufferings are not of the spirit, just of the flesh, and so their misfortunes are just pitiful, and not universally significant.

Though a very fascinating novel, *Train to Pakistan* does not carry the achieved significance of the modern Indian fiction at a higher level. It certainly is Khushwant Singh's masterpiece and its abiding popularity has stood the test of time.

The Conflict between Imperialism and Nationalism in *I Shall Not Hear the Nightingale*

BASAVARAJ NAIKAR

The conflict between the colonizer and the colonized happens to be a major thematic concern in many Indian English novels like R.K. Narayan's *Waiting for the Mahatma*, Raja Rao's *Kanthapura*, Malgaonkar's *A Bend in the Ganges*, Chaman Nahal's *Azadi* and Khushwant Singh's *I Shall Not Hear the Nightingale*. In these novels different aspects of colonial encounter between Indians and Britishers like protest, submission, love-hate relationship and compromise are highlighted and are, therefore, comparable to similar novels by Commonwealth writers like Chinua Achebe, Ngugi and Patrick White.

In *I Shall Not Hear the Nightingale*,[1] Khushwant Singh presents the colonial encounter between Indians and the British Government against the background of the Punjab. Punjab, the land of five rivers is known for its own distinctive geographical features, its military history and Sikh religion which easily set it off from the other ethnic cultures of India, although it belongs to India politically. Khushwant Singh has tried to give a very microscopic picture of the Punjabi life in the novel even when he concentrates his attention on the political theme.

The novel deals with the India of 1940s, when the colonial encounter between the Indians and the British was moving towards a climax on account of the emergence of nationalistic consciousness among the Indians. There had always been a mixed reaction among Indians towards the British Raj. Khushwant Singh presents a microscopic picture of the strange mixture of attitudes to the alien rule through the depiction of life in Amritsar district. The situation presented here is easily comparable to those in other colonized countries like Africa and West Indies.

The characters in *I Shall Not Hear the Nightingale* can be broadly classified into two groups: one, Sardar Buta Singh, Wazir Chand, John Taylor and Lambardar are pro-British in their attitude; two, Sher Singh, Madan and other student leaders are anti-British in their attitude.

The central irony in the novel is evident in the fact that both the pro-British and the anti-British ideologies are cherished by different members of the same family. (This situation provides a very good contrast to the one depicted in Chinua Achebe's *Things Fall Apart.*) Buta Singh, for example, happens to be a District Magistrate who has a great admiration for the British rule in India: "loyalty to the Raj had been as much an article of faith with him as it had been with his father and grandfather who had served in the army. He, like them, had mentioned the English king or queen in his evening prayer, 'O, Guru, bless our Sovereign and bless us their subjects so that we remain contented and happy.'" (23) Buta Singh tells his son that the Indians should help the British in their war against the Germans and other European powers: "I do believe that in this war our interests and that of the English are identical. If they lose, we lose. If we help them to win, they will certainly give us something more than we have now. We should know who are our friends and who are our enemies. The English have ruled us for over a hundred years, and I don't care what you say. I believe they have treated us better than our own kings did in the past; or the Germans, Italians, or Japanese will do if they win and take our India. We must stand by the English in their hour of trouble." (23)

Buta Singh knows that his sympathy for the British rule in India may earn him the scorn of his own countrymen. But he does not mind being unpopular with his countrymen as long as he has the patronage of the British rulers like, for example, the District Commissioner, Mr. John Taylor. Buta Singh's attitude to life is opportunistic in that he wants to accept the contingencies of political life and turn them to his own best possible advantage so that he can lead a life of security and ensure happiness for his family.

Buta Singh's son Sher Singh believes in a diametrically opposite philosophy of life. A young and energetic student in the local college, he heads the Student Union as its President. He is not very serious about his studies, but he is fired by the patriotic zeal and nationalistic philosophy popularized by Mahatma Gandhi, Nehru and other leaders. He questions the very rationale of the British rule in India and pleads for self-government for the motherland. He is not influenced by his father's loyalty to the British. He, therefore, reacts very strongly to his father, "We are far too concerned with other people. Our Communist friends are only worried about what will happen to Russians; others think only of what will happen to Britain. Very few of us are bothered with our own future." (23) Sher Singh is, thus, deeply concerned with the Indian life. He becomes an embodiment of the nationalistic ideal. He enjoys the support of a large mass of students and consequently conducts several secret meetings of students thereby planning to carry out terroristic activities in the city of Amritsar.

He has the cooperation of other leaders like Madan, son of Wazir Chand. Thus the conflict between the pro-British attitude and the anti-British comes into operation in one and the same family which may be said to be a microscopic symbol of the macroscopic phenomenon of the Indian political life.

The women folk of Buta Singh's family or of Wazir Chand's family are not bothered about the political life of the country. They are mainly concerned with the security of family life and comfortable living. Sabhrai, wife of Buta Singh, for example, happens to be a very religious lady who believes in the sanctity of *Granth Sahib* and supremacy of Guru Govind Singh. She believes that what her husband does is right and that her son Sher Singh should not be cross with his father. Likewise, Sher Singh's young wife Champak is also not bothered about his public life and nationalistic and terroristic activities. She is very keen on the enjoyment of regular matrimonial sex and even commits adultery with Madan secretly. The sisters of Sher Singh and Madan are concerned only with their studies. But all of them tacitly agree with their parental sympathy for the British rule in India.

Buta Singh's sympathy for the British rule is supported by his knowledge of the internal contradictions and conflicts of Indian life. He knows that there is no homogeneous society in India and that it is a mosaic of many castes and cultures, like the Sikh, the Hindu and the Muslim among others. He knows that the ethnic conflicts are sparked off in the country at the slightest provocation and result in violence and chaos. He, therefore, believes that the British rule can keep these violent and conflicting forces under check and offer a political unity to India.

The conflict between the pro-British and the anti-British continues all through the novel. Sher Singh expresses his nationalistic ideology in the fiery speech he delivers at the gathering of patriotic students, "Comrades, we meet at a crucial time. The enemy is at our gates. . . . Comrades, we not only have the enemy at our door step, we have enemies within our own house. . . . Those who sacrifice the interests of the motherland for foreign countries are our enemy No. 1. They have been rightly named as the *Kaum nashts*—destroyers of the race. . . . There are also people who want to cut off the limbs of Mother India and make another state of Pakistan. The two are our enemies. . . . But we are Sikhs who do not fear any enemies. We shall destroy all those who stand in our way." (9) His patriotic speech whips up the nationalistic zeal in the audience and elicits a great applause from them.

Buta Singh does not encourage his son to indulge in anti-British activities. Though he knows the general trend of his son's thinking, he does not know any details of his secret activities. He enjoys the confidence of the D.C. John Taylor and offers his suggestions to the latter in solving some of the local problems. When, for example, John Taylor issues an order banning the Hindu procession in the city, the Hindus feel insulted and irritated because the Muslim and Sikh processions were not banned earlier. Wazir Chand who is a Hindu wants to meet the D.C. and get permission for the Hindu procession by explaining the situation. But he is not permitted by the District Commissioner. He, therefore, seeks the help of Buta Singh and requests him to explain the sensitiveness of the communal issue to John Taylor and get at least a relaxation of the ban order. Buta Singh who enjoys the confidence of John Taylor meets the latter at his residence, explains the possibility of communal explosion in the city and finally but gently persuades him to relax the ban order against the Hindu procession at least for a few hours. Wazir Chand and his friends thank Buta Singh for helping them.

The ideological conflict between father and son continues all through the novel. When Buta Singh habitually admires the British people and their impartiality, and suggests that "We Indians have a lot to learn from them," Sher Singh boldly crosses his father and argues that the British "too have something to learn from us . . . like hospitality . . . tolerance." (77) Buta Singh pinpoints the mutual intolerance among Hindus, Sikhs and Muslims and highlights the so-called impartiality and tolerance of the British people. Sher Singh does not hesitate to show the racial discrimination practised by the British elsewhere, "You can find examples like that everywhere. Most white people are anti-Semitic. It's not only Hitler who has been putting Jews in gas chambers, the Russians have killed many. Everywhere in Europe and America there is prejudice against them and only because they have better brains and talent than others. We do not have any racial discrimination." (77) Sher Singh's mother Sabhrai does not like his being cross with his father and asks him, "Tell me, son, what will you get if the English leave this country?" (78) Then Sher Singh replies that the country will be free. He waxes lyrical and hopes that "Spring will come to our barren land once more . . . once more the nightingales will sing." (79) The song of nightingales thus becomes a symbol of freedom and joy for Sher Singh.

Meanwhile, the members of Buta Singh's family grow closer to those of Wazir Chand's family. Buta Singh's daughter Beena and daughter-in-law Champak join Wazir Chand's son Madan Lal and daughter Sita and all go to Simla to spend sometime in summer. The ideological similarity between Sher Singh and Madan Lal has, obviously, brought the two families closer. Madan Lal, in spite of being a nationalist, is an unfailing seducer of women. On account of his physical handsomeness, sophisticated manners and abundant chivalry, he succeeds in tempting and finally seducing Champak, thereby creating a sexual jealousy between Beena and Champak. Even when Sabhrai joins them in Simla to prevent the possible damage to Beena's virginity or Champak's chastity, she is very cleverly fooled by Madan Lal who shows her extraordinary respect and courtesy and silences her suspicion about the violation of the family's sexual morals.

Meanwhile, Sher Singh associates himself with the terrorists of Amritsar and begins to indulge in the terroristic activities in the city. He is so much preoccupied with the nationalistic-cum-terroristic activities that he remains blissfully ignorant about the loss of his wife's chastity. In spite of his knowledge about Madan Lal's being a notorious womanizer, he fails to know that he has been cuckolded by the latter. Though Sher Singh hates the British rule and the British officers, he is persuaded by his father to meet the District Commissioner Mr. John Taylor to develop some familiarity with him and consequently to change his attitude towards him. Buta Singh expresses his pure admiration for the British people, "As I was saying, these Englishmen take a lot of interest in other people, and it is not just curiosity, it is a genuine concern with their problems. Now Taylor knows all of you by name, what you are doing, how you have fared in your examinations—everything. He has an excellent memory." (94) Far from being impressed by his father's Anglophilia, Sher Singh offers his severe comment on the Englishmen, "They have learnt from Americans. . . . They have reduced human relationships to a set of rules. They say you must know the name of the person you are talking to and use it as often as possible. You must know his or her interest and talk about them and never of your own. They write down whatever they have discussed with anyone in their diaries and refresh their memories before the next meeting. It does not mean much because their real desire is to create a good impression about themselves. They are not one bit concerned with the affairs of the person they happen to be talking to." (94) In spite of Sher Singh's strong dislike for the Englishmen, he yields to parental persuasion and wifely order and meets John Taylor by way of courtesy.

But when he meets John Taylor much against his willingness, he feels angry with himself. Although Taylor treats him with courtesy and advises him to relax in the summer holidays at Simla and even offers him permission to own a rifle, Sher Singh feels confused between the contradictory feelings in himself like respecting the authority of the District Commissioner on the one hand and his hatred for the British rule on the other. Similarly he feels confused between his fear of the empty cartridges fingered by John Taylor and his eagerness to drive out the British from India. He feels a sense of humiliation at having agreed to meet John Taylor and a sense of anger at his parents and wife for having pressurized him to meet the officer. He, therefore, returns home with a decision never to repeat such a compromising act.

Sher Singh dreams of harmonizing the contradictory philosophies of his family somehow or the other, without realizing the impossibility of such a happening in real life, i.e., in 1942 in India. "Britain had to get out of India herself or be kicked out, and Sher Singh would say that to Taylor's face. Could he? What about his father's views? his cousin in service and his hope of finding his name in the next Honours list? And the unique honour he was getting in the way of an armed police guard outside his house—the sentry who sprang to attention and smacked the butt of his rifle even when Sher Singh passed by with his college friends? Couldn't it somehow happen that these opposite factors could be combined into one harmonious whole? He visualized scenes when his Nationalist and terrorist colleagues honoured him as their beloved leader, where Taylor read an address of welcome and his father proudly looked on. Such were the dreams with which Sher Singh tried to dope himself. They were based on the non-discovery of one party by the other." (118) Thus Sher Singh dreams of achieving his ideal and hopes to concretise his plans by resolving the confusion in his mind.

As his will power grows stronger with the passing of time, he decides to resort to terroristic action. He, therefore, calls a secret meeting of his student friends near the canal bridge outside the city. He hides the arms in his garage to escape the notice of the Government police. He also knows that some of his fellow conspirators might be informers against him and therefore remains quite alert.

One day the village headman Lambardarji meets Sher Singh at his home and pretends to be very friendly with him. Sher Singh treats him with buttermilk. The village headman cleverly tries to elicit some information about the Hindu boys who participated in the shooting party a few days ago. Then Sher Singh begins to suspect that the village headman may not be really as innocent as he appears, in spite of his courteous behaviour and fine manners. Suspecting him to be an informant to John Taylor, Sher Singh offers him some money as a gift, though inwardly he knows he has given it to him as 'black money.' He also knows that he may have to give more money to the village headman to keep his secrets concealed by the Government.

By this time, the nationalist activities begin rigorously in north India under the influence of Mahatma Gandhi. The Gandhi-cap covered patriots begin to attack the shops and public offices. The British soldiers try to beat the patriots violently. Thus the nationalistic struggle gathers force and occupies the mind of Indians who tend to forget or neglect their personal problems. Shops are looted, roads are blocked and trains are stopped by the nationalist agitators. Sher Singh reads the newspapers full of news about the nation-wide agitation. He also receives a cyclostyled letter with a caption, 'A Manifesto of the Hindustan Socialist Republican Army.' "It drew attention to the arrests of the leaders and asked the youth of India to arise and rid themselves of foreign rule. It did not mince its words, 'Shoot English officials and the Indian toadies who serve them. Destroy roads and bridges; cut telegraph and telephone wires; create chaos and paralyse the administration. This is your sacred duty. Long live the revolution!'" (151)

After learning about the spread of nationalistic movement all over the country, Sher Singh's rebellious impulse grows more and more intense. Finally he overcomes his confusion and oscillation and decides to indulge in terroristic action. He, therefore, calls a secret meeting of his fellow rebels and takes the oath of liberating the country from the foreign rule. They take the oath of secrecy before indulging in terroristic action. They are inspired by Mahatma Gandhi in general and by Bhagat Singh in particular. They define their terroristic targets clearly. As Sher

Singh makes it clear, "The call is to destroy means of communication. A few bridges blown up, a few roads barricaded and the British Army will be stuck where it is." (153) Accordingly they take six hand grenades and initially blow the central bridge and think that nobody knows about themselves.

Since the nationalistic activities spread all over the country, the British officers, especially John Taylor, become very alert and try to control the situation as far as they can. John Taylor, therefore, sends for Buta Singh to track down the agitators unofficially. He also suggests to Buta Singh that he knows about Sher Singh's nationalistic activities. He explains to him clearly that they would leave India as soon as the war is over: "Your son could do a good service to his friends and his country. You know we are anxious to get out of India and hand over the reins of power to you people as soon as the war is won. But we will not leave the country to the Japanese or the Germans. And these acts are calculated to do just that—hand over India on a silver platter to the Fascist powers." (159) An ardent admirer of British rule, Buta Singh decides to advise his son at his leisure.

Meanwhile, the village headman Lambardar meets Sher Singh at home and asks for compensation of Rs. 300/- for the medical treatment of his bullock which has broken its leg in the holes created by the grenades in the canal. Sher Singh treats him nicely by giving him buttered toast and asks him to see him at the canal bridge in the evening. Sher Singh inwardly suspects that Lambardar, being an informer to the British Government, was trying to exploit the situation. When Lambardar sees Sher Singh and his friends including Madan Lal near the canal bridge, there is an exchange of hot words between them. Lambardar's behaviour changes from the modest to the arrogant. Sher Singh and his friends like Madan grow certain about his being an informer to the Government and therefore, Sher Singh shoots him to death. Lambardar sags to the earth cursing them, "I'll sleep with your mothers. . . . I'll sleep with your sisters. . . . I'll . . " (168) Immediately they bury the dead body and disperse from there.

After the death of Lambardar, his son Jimma Singh is appointed as the village headman and is given a revolver to defend himself. Jimma Singh has three wives and yet he has no single progeny. One day he disappears from the village for three days without telling anyone of his wives. The disappearance of Jimma Singh is attributed to his murder by one of his relatives. The same is reported to the Police Commissioner who sends the file to the Deputy Commissioner to have the case closed as 'untraced.' But the Deputy Commissioner sends a warrant to search the house of Sardar Buta Singh, the seniormost Indian Magistrate of the district and another one to arrest Sher Singh. John Taylor wants to treat Buta Singh gently and therefore sends for him. When Buta Singh meets John Taylor at home, his house is searched by the Police Commissioner. The police constables beat Sher Singh, Mundoo and the dog called Dyer. They arrest Sher Singh and take him to prison. Champak is simply flabbergasted by the sight of what has happened to her husband and family. Buta Singh does not know what is happening in his house in his absence. He narrates the history of the loyalty of his family to the British Crown right from the days of Sikh rule: "Sir, we can almost go back to the days of Sikh rule. In the annexation of the Punjab and the disbanding of Sikh force my great grandfather, who was a subedar and had fought against the British in the Anglo-Sikh wars, joined the British army. He served under John Lawrence. He also fought under Nicholson in the Mutiny of 1857 and was awarded a medal for the capture of Delhi; we still have it in the family. My grandfather was also in the British army. He rose from the ranks and retired as a Jamedar—in those days to be a Jamedar was a big thing for an Indian. My father did not join the army, but he recruited many soldiers in the 1914-18 war and our family was given lands in the Canal Colonies. I have kept up the tradition of loyalty to the British Crown and will do so till the day I die." (180)

Although Buta Singh expresses his loyalty to the British Crown, John Taylor knows that the British are going to leave India in the near future. He, therefore, says to Buta Singh, "I appreciate your sentiments of loyalty, Buta Singh, but I do not agree with you about the future of Indians and I am British. I feel we should pull out of this country as soon after the war as we can—and let you Indians manage your own affairs. I, for one, have no intention of continuing in the Indian Civil Service a day after the ceasefire. In fact I am not on the side of Mr. Churchill but on that of Mr. Gandhi and Mr. Nehru—except, and this is important, I do think the war has to be won first. Otherwise the Nazis and the Fascists will put the clock back for you and for us. I may be wrong, but that is my belief." (180) Then John Taylor gently asks Buta Singh about his son's nationalistic and terroristic activities and his possible connection with the murder of the village headman Jimma Singh. Buta Singh is simply shocked out of his wits and begins to cry for shame. He covers his face with his palms and blurts out, "My nose has been cut. I can no longer show my face to the world." (182) John Taylor tells him further that his son Sher Singh has been put into jail and gives him fifteen days's leave and allows him to see and advise his son as often as he can.

On receiving a telegram from Buta Singh, Sabhrai and Beena return from Simla by train and are unexpectedly received at the Railway Station by Mrs. Joyce Taylor and dropped at her home. Buta Singh explains to his wife how their son has been sent to jail for his being connected with terroristic activities and murder of the village headman. Champak also feels crestfallen. Sabhrai is totally confounded by her son's behaviour. Although she does not fully understand the implications of her son's activities, she wants to have her piece of the moon back at home. Her emotional attachment for her husband as well as her son makes her not to bother too much about political ideologies. A lady of deep religious bent of mind, she believes in the spiritual powers of Guru Govind Singh and the holy *Granth*.

Buta Singh with his pro-British attitude is so much angered and insulted by his son's arrest that he refuses to go to the prison to talk to Sher Singh. Likewise, Sher Singh also knows that his father will not spare him in case he visits him in the prison. When Sher Singh's parents-in-law hear about his imprisonment, they take away their daughter Champak back to their place.

Meanwhile, Sher Singh is interrogated by the Sahibs. But Sher Singh wants to consult his father or a lawyer before that. Finally he is allowed to consult his father. But since Buta Singh flatly refuses to see him in prison, his wife Sabhrai wants to see him after four days.

Buta Singh fears that his son's anti-British activities may cost him his own job, pension and other amenities of life which he owes to the British sympathy. Feeling terribly insecure in life, he grows unusually religious and reads the holy *Granth*. Sabhrai spends a whole night in the golden temple bathing in the cold water and meditating and praying all through the night. She waits for the spiritual guidance from the Guru in the present crisis. The next day she visits her son in the prison, gives him the holy dust from the temple and advises him not to name the other culprits. She knows that Sher Singh has done wrong but she invokes the Guru to guide him.

After returning from the prison, Mrs. Sabhrai sends a letter thanking Mrs. Taylor for all the kindness shown to her. The letter is full of filial tenderness and touches the heart of the addressee. "Dear Taylor Memsahib, I am an uneducated Punjabi woman who cannot write nice words of thanks in English. Ask one of your clerks to read this to you. God bless you for what you have done. You wanted to share the grief of a mother whose child has been stricken. There is no greater act of kindness in this world. May the Guru's blessings be on you, your Sahib and on your children. May you have many sons. May God ever keep your household full of plenty and keep sorrow and suffering away from your door." (211) Sabhrai sends the letter with the chauffeur to Joyce Taylor. Then she is down with fever and pneumonia.

Buta Singh thinks that only the Englishman i.e. John Taylor can help him out of the crisis. He wants to please the Englishman with some Christmas gifts. He, therefore, arranges to send some fine oranges to John Taylor and his wife and a finely composed letter in the name of his wife which shows their admiration for the British authorities. It reads as follows:

> Respected Mrs. Taylor,
>
> Pray accept this humble gift of oranges for Christmas Day. They are the first pick of the year from our garden. I hope you will like them. To you and to your noble husband

> and children our most respected Deputy Commissioner, my husband and children owe their all. Madam will do us an honour by receiving this very little gift on the auspicious occasion of the birthday of the World Saviour, Lord Jesus Christ.
>
> Your humble servant
> Sabhrai
> (Sardarini Buta Singh)
> Wife of Sardar Buta Singh,
> B.A. (Hons.) Magistrate, First Class (214)

The Christmas gift of oranges is luckily received by Joyce Taylor who shows the humanitarian courtesy by visiting Sabhrai. Joyce Taylor, who was trained as a nurse before marrying John Taylor, examines the health of Sabhrai. Sabhrai is in delirium and cannot speak but she shows her gratitude to Joyce Taylor by the quivering movement of her lips. Joyce Taylor tries to enhearten Sabhrai and her husband and daughter. She knows that Sabhrai is suffering from pneumonia. She is so much touched by the plight of a religious mother i.e. Sabhrai that she persuades her husband John Taylor to give a real Christmas gift to Buta Singh's family in the form of release of Sher Singh on the Christmas Day itself. John Taylor knows that he has ordered the arrest of Sher Singh on mere suspicion without having any solid proof about the murder of the village headman. His knowledge about Buta Singh's firm loyalty to the British, Sabhrai's religious bent of mind and physical suffering and his wife's pressure finally compel him to order for the release of Sher Singh on the Christmas Day. Sher Singh is ecstatic about his release when he is taken out of the prison into the city in a procession by his friends and nationalist zealots. Thus Sher Singh becomes a hero in the eyes of his fellow rebels and nationalists. He is garlanded, photographed and cheered by the enthusiastic audience. He thumps his chest and declares, "Comrades . . . I will cherish the honour you have done me today for the rest of my life. I've proved that I was called upon to do a small duty to my country and I did it. . . . You all know how well the King Emperor—may peace be upon him—looks after his guests. . . . But they could not break the spirit of the son of India and God willing they never will." (224-25) Obviously, Sher Singh's father, mother, sister and wife are very happy about his release. Sabhrai recovers her health temporarily and spends some happy moments with the members of her family. The doctors opine that she should not be allowed to be excited. The release of Sher Singh is followed by another happy event i.e. the declaration of O.B.E. title for Buta Singh in the New Year's Honour's list. Buta Singh initially refuses to believe it, but when the newspaper correspondents, colleagues and friends come to garland and congratulate him, he accepts it as real. Everybody in the family is very happy.

But alas, the happiness does not continue for long because Sabhrai, after four days's cheerfulness, begins to sink suddenly. She knows that she is going to die and says, "My time has come." (231) She sends for all the members of her family and makes them read the holy *Granth*. Then she dies while uttering the prayer. Her funeral is conducted with due honour and dignity. The Taylors and many officials send wreaths as a mark of their respect for the late Sabhrai.

Buta Singh's loyalty to the British Crown has earned him the right kind of reward. He, therefore, wants to thank Mr. John Taylor for the O.B.E. title and for his releasing his son so quickly and unexpectedly and Mrs. Joyce Taylor for her kindness shown to his family. He also wants to seek the help of John Taylor in fixing a job for his son. He wants to build a memorial for his late wife Sabhrai in consultation with the Taylors. He buys a new tie and wears it before meeting them and thanks them profusely and consults them about his son's job and a memorial for his late wife. The Taylors treat him with great courtesy and friendliness so much so that Buta Singh feels that he is one of their family friends. Thus the novel *I Shall Not Hear the Nightingale* delineates the paradoxical picture of the colonial encounter between the Indians and the British including both the positive and the negative aspects, the submission as well as rebellion simultaneously involved in it. The novel can be easily contrasted with Chinua Achebe's *Things Fall Apart* where the same theme is depicted in a reverse fashion. Whereas in *I Shall*

Not Hear the Nightingale, the son rebels against the British rule and the father submits to it, in *Things Fall Apart*, the father rebels against the British rule and the son submits to it in the form of being converted to Christianity.

Apart from the colonial conflict depicted in *I Shall Not Hear the Nightingale*, there are other details in the novel which are very realistic and interesting. Khushwant Singh is known for his stark realism and evocation of the Indian, especially the Sikh culture, in the novel. He is not a puritanical writer who sugar-coats the truth of life. On the contrary, he is a realist and modernist in the sense that he has the courage to look into the face of harsh reality and describe it precisely and objectively without any sentimentalism or exaggeration. For example, apart from the depiction of Buta Singh's admiration for the British rule, Sher Singh's antipathy for the same and Sabhrai's religious nature, Khushwant Singh offers a very realistic picture of Champak's sexuality, like her shaving of pubic hair, Mundoo's juvenile curiosity about feminine nakedness, Shunno's anal bleeding and her sexual surrender to the Peer Sahib, Madan's shameless womanization etc., without any hypocritical slurring over them. In this sense, Khushwant Singh can be easily compared to Mulk Raj Anand, Chinua Achebe, Ngugi wa Thiong'o and other Commonwealth novelists.

NOTE

1. Khushwant Singh, *I Shall Not Hear The Nightingale* (1959; Bombay: IBH, 1973).

I Shall Not Hear the Nightingale: A Re-evaluation

SUBHASH CHANDRA

Khushwant Singh's creative oeuvre consists of *Mark of Vishnu and Other Stories, Train to Pakistan, I Shall Not Hear the Nightingale, The Voice of God and Other Stories, Black Jasmine and Other Stories, A Bride for the Sahib and Other Stories* and his latest historico-fictional work *Delhi*. It is surprising that of the two novels, *I Shall Not Hear the Nightingale* (1959) has not received as much critical attention and acclaim as *Train to Pakistan* (1956) did. The latter, in fact, earned for Singh a place in the galaxy of Indian English fiction writers of the fifties. So much eulogy and scholarship have been devoted to *Train to Pakistan* that *I Shall Not Hear the Nightingale* came to be overshadowed by the former's sprawling popularity and got relegated to the secondary position in the hierarchy of the two novels. There were certain factors, contributing to the resounding success of *Train to Pakistan*: the intensity of the traumatic event of partition, the topicality of the theme, and above all the dramatization of the transforming and ennobling power of love which is a life-sustaining and life-furthering force. The triumph of the ideal appeals to the noble instincts of the reader, makes him believe in his own innate goodness and gives him hope in a world darkened by bestiality, violence and evil. But the fictional process by which the triumph of the ideal is achieved is not altogether flawless (to which I shall revert later). The intention of the present paper is to suggest that *I Shall Not Hear the Nightingale* is an equally great work of art in its own right and is a better crafted novel than *Train to Pakistan*.

II

The story of *I Shall Not Hear the Nightingale* revolves round a Sikh senior magistrate, Buta Singh, in the Punjab in the pre-partition days, and his family, and their relationships with the white Deputy Commissioner, Mr. Taylor and his wife, Joyce Taylor, another Hindu magistrate, Wazir Chand, his cricketer, rakish son, Madan, and shy, but academically bright daughter, Sita. Buta Singh's family comprises his intensely religious, illiterate wife Sabhrai, his sexually inadequate, but politically ambitious son, Sher Singh, Sher Singh's buxom, beautiful, sex-hungry and sexually loose infidel wife Champak, Buta Singh's daughter, Beena, maid-servant, Shunno, boy servant, Mundoo and an Alsatian dog, Dyer (he is treated as a member of the family in terms of affection he receives and the services he renders).

Not that *I Shall Not Hear the Nightingale* is entirely free from novelistic blemishes, which tend to detract from its merit. First of all, it begins with the indications of developing into a political novel, with a focus on the pre-partition activities of the revolutionaries and the terrorists. But it does not. Politics remains the background for putting into relief other statements. The reason for this perhaps could be the sub-conscious predilections of the *artist* in Singh which made him expand the thematic horizon and turn the novel into a more encompassing study. The loosening control of the artist over his materials and parametres is a well-known phenomenon of which E.M. Forster and D.H. Lawrence talk in different contexts. Something akin probably happened in the case of *I Shall Not Hear the Nightingale* during the course of its composition and Singh found himself dealing with a much larger theme than he had originally envisaged—the realization of the political ambition of Sher Singh, coupled with the complications arising for him and his family from the peculiar mould of his character and his sexual inadequacy.

The second flaw in the novel is the incorporation of or rather super-imposition of overdoze of sex, which is not surprising, coming as it does from Singh. This is a journalistic stance he has adopted—sex sells—and he cannot help introducing a lot of sex, whenever he can. The latest novel, *Delhi,* is a confirmatory example, and Singh does not mince words when he says, "I am a dirty old man, I will remain a dirty old man and I will write as a dirty old man."[1] It appears Singh delights in baring as many female bodies and buttocks as possible, and getting as many females laid as he can during the course of the novel. Champak, Sher Singh's wife, is constantly in quest of quenching her excessive sex desire. Besides getting her buttocks massaged (actually caressed) by Mundoo (the boy servant) who goes into convulsions because of the rising sex in his body (he is fourteen), has lots of sex with Madan, Sher Singh's friend. Madan, a married man, seduces Beena, Sher Singh's sister, who gets a "feverish longing in her body" for the tall, handsome Madan whom she imagines "stripping her and taking her as a man should take a woman." Beena is prevented from copulating with Madan (she does get up from her bed at night with that desire) because he at that moment was ravishing Champak. Though it would have been equally probable, if the author had sent Beena into Madan's room, who discovered Champak there and both, promising to keep each other's secret, had taken turns in the bed. Shunno, the almost old maid-servant is made to experience sex once again after a lapse of thirty years and the young holy mullah, leading a celibate life, guarding the tomb of a sacred soul and praying a dozen times a day, justifies his mating with Shunno.

But these flaws notwithstanding, the novel's artistic stature remains unassailed. At the deeper level, the book turns into a clash between and evaluation of two sets of values, two ways of life: conventional, non-violent, staunch faith in religion and God and pure, ascetic, unostentatious but dignified and moral life on the one hand and the modern, sexually promiscuous, morally loose, hypocritical, opportunistic and violent ways on the other. This juxtaposition of the two modes of life—the old and the modern—is comparable with Aldous Huxley's *The Brave New World* in which the author pours fun on the ultra-modern values through the Savage.

III

Singh exposes the innate smallness of most of the people who camouflage their petty desires under righteous idealistic facades. They manage to convince themselves about the genuineness of the purity of their pursuits and the ennobling image it would create for them among their relatives, friends and masses. Sher Singh is a pertinent example of this type, who professes patriotism, practises terrorism with a view to bringing about an armed revolution to throw out the British, but gets exposed as a coward, who cringes shamelessly at the first blow that is struck on him. He weeps and sheds tears when he is kicked by a white sergeant in his groins. He feels helpless, loses self-esteem, because "Even his dog had shown more fight." Sher Singh "did not realize that strength was not a natural development of his own personality but nurtured behind the protection provided by his father's position as a senior magistrate and a respected citizen. He was like a hot-house plant blossoming in a greenhouse."[2] When he is questioned by the village headman, Jhimma Singh, about the licence of his shooting gun, he gets pathalogically frightened. His conduct during his incarceration, especially during his questioning is ignominous, and presents him shorn of all that is worthy in man. He "knew that if they used any violence, he would tell all he knew without considering the rights and wrongs of making a confession." (197) A significant feature of the modern literature, beginning with James Joyce's *Ulysses* is the anti-heroic hero it portrays, and Sher Singh fits the bill, though I would like to suggest that *I Shall Not Hear the Nightingale* is not hero but a heroine-oriented novel and that Sabhrai, the true heroine is in the classical mould of the hero. Sher Singh's moral corruption and his political rise (glorying in the mantle of leadership which falls on him by default) become symptomatic of the malaise afflicting the modern society (in India or elsewhere). Madan, Beena, Champak epitomize the unbridled lust which has replaced the classical concept of love, reducing the relationships to mere body contact, devoid of deeper emotional fulfilment. This is reminiscent of T.S. Eliot's depiction of the joyless sex in *The Waste Land.* Buta Singh is a double-faced sycophant who professes his loyalty to the British, when he is in the presence of his superior, Mr. Taylor, the Deputy Commissioner, but changes colour when he is in the company of his son or the natives.

Against this bunch of moral midgets, who represent one way

of life, is posited the heroic figure of Sabhrai whose mode of life is totally different.. She is a repository of towering moral strength and emotional warmth. She valorizes religiosity, integrity, quiet dignity and unpretentious steadfastness to the principles of selflessness, love, loyalty to the family, nation and even humanity. Acting as a cohesive, harmonious force in the family, she displays indomitable courage, integrity of character and sacrificing spirit. Having prayed all night at the Golden Temple for the Guru's guidance in the matter of advising her son whether or not to disclose his accomplices' names and get pardoned by turning into Crown's witness, she tells her son that she would not set eyes on him ever again if he got his friends implicated. She loved her son dearly; she fondly recalled the joys of motherhood, when Sher Singh was an infant and a boy. But she does not flinch from the right course, once she has seen the light by the grace of the Guru. Sitting through the cold night on the bare floor and facing the chilly winds while praying at the temple, she catches pneumonia and dies. Her courage, her sacrificing spirit, her suffering and her death make her a heroine of tragic stature. Love, not the narrow familial love, but the love for humanity and faith triumph. K.R. Srinivasa Iyengar's words about Sabhrai are significant, in this context: "Sabhrai wholly redeems the dimness and murkiness of the general atmosphere. The fever of sensuality is easier to describe than the radiance of Faith and this is the reason why Sabhrai 'steals' the novel."[3]

Now let us compare the victory of nobility of love in *Train to Pakistan,* which results in saving the lives of a whole trainload of Muslims, leaving for Pakistan. First, Juggut Singh's love is confined to his beloved, Nooran, whom he wants to save from death. Sabhrai's compassion is all-enveloping and it disregards the safety of her beloved son. Hence, in *I Shall Not Hear the Nightingale* the moral vision is broader in its horizon. Secondly, the final act of compassion in the case of Sabhrai springs from her religiosity, selflessness, and kindliness which are fundamental aspects of her personality. There is no discordance between what she does eventually and what she has been. But Juggut Singh (Jugga) has been a *budmash*, a man devoid of finer feelings. The change in him, is too sudden and, therefore, largely incredible. It follows the pattern of the popular Bombay cinema, where the protagonists, immersed in degenerate ways, abruptly metamorphose into noble characters. Thirdly, Juggut Singh is more in the nature of wish-fulfilment of the novelist than a probable hero. This is borne out by Khushwant Singh's own words: "The beliefs that I had cherished all my life were shattered. I had believed in the innate goodness of the common man. But the division of India had been accompanied by the most savage massacres known in the history of the country,"[4] and "I thought it was time one exploded this myth of the innate goodness in man. There is innate evil in man. And I just wrote about it, *and I did create one character whom I stuffed with the so-called innate goodness of man and he is the only character which is entirely fiction.*"[5] (emphasis added)

IV

A lingering sadness envelops the end of *I Shall Not Hear the Nightingale* which is not merely the result of the death of the good woman, Sabhrai. It is the novelist's strident awareness of a world passing, a set of values getting eroded and a "brave new world" (with a new connotation of 'brave') emerging in which people like Sabhrai and all that they uphold in the midst of trying and unnerving situations will become either strangers, out of place or extinct. Her death is marked by as much dignity as was her life; and her life was the embodiment of life-sustaining virtues. The title of the novel clearly suggests the brooding, sombre vision of the author and can be interpreted in two ways: i) as Sabhrai's lament that she will not be able to witness the Independence of the country, and ii) as the death of beauty and goodness of the nightingale—symbolized by Sabhrai.

Thus, the deceptively structured surface of the book contains underneath a message, or a lament far more profound and shocking that can be discerned by a rapid, superficial reading of the novel. *I Shall Not Hear the Nightingale*, excelling in artistic qualities and thematic expansiveness needs to be placed alongside, if not higher than its counterpart, *Train to Pakistan.*

NOTES

1. Interview with Ashok Chopra, *The Hindustan Times* (Sunday Supplement), 14 January 1990, p. 2.
2. Khushwant Singh, *I Shall Not Hear the Nightingale* (London: John Calder, 1959), p. 192.
3. K.R. Srinivasa Iyengar, *Indian Writing in English* (Bombay: Asia, 1973), p. 504.
4. From the transcript of a talk for the Australian Broadcasting Commission's *Guest of Honour Programme* broadcast on 15 April 1964.
5. From the transcript of 'Indian Accent' by John Thompson, a programme of interviews with Indian Writers broadcast by the Australian Broadcasting Commission in late 1961.

Fact and/or Fiction?: A Study of *Delhi*

CH. A. RAJENDRA PRASAD

What is so proud of any Nation
The whole history of mankind is a saga of mutual oppression.[1]

Khushwant Singh in his characteristic down-to-earth attitude reconstructs the history of Delhi, and in a way of whole India as the fate of the former has always affected and moulded the destiny of the entire country. This is not a historical novel in the ordinary sense. In his *Delhi*,[2] the novelist lets the history of Delhi 'relive' and 'speak' for itself. This "reliving" of past at times borders upon 'fact and fiction combine' as the novelist does not mean to maintain fidelity to "facts" only. The aspect of romanticization of past is admitted by the novelist himself: "History provided me with the skeleton. I covered it with flesh and blood and a lot of seminal fluid into it."[3]

In *Delhi*, the novelist is not merely interested in reenacting the past of Delhi. While reconstructing the history of Delhi, he intends to throw light on the higher reality—the cyclic phenomenon of birth-growth-decay—that governs the lives of City and Man. Further, the novel in a way endorses the fatalistic aspect that lies behind the man-inflicted havoc against another man, there is a greater and omnipotent Force, i.e., Time.

In his foreword to the paperback edition of the novel, Khushwant Singh states: "All I wanted to do was tell my readers what I learnt about the city . . . my aim was to get them to know Delhi and love it as much as I do." This is certainly understating the magnitude and significance of the novel which actually chronicles the sagacious study of city and man. While narrating the saga of Delhi, and its people and rulers, Khushwant Singh in his typical realistic style unveils all the gory incidents that have made up the story of Delhi. Perhaps there is so much horror and agony in the life of Delhi, and for that point the situation may be the same in the case of any city, the novelist does not hesitate to speak of 'reality' in all its details uninhibitedly: "The essence of Khushwant Singh's art of fiction is his innate capacity to capture reality in all its magnificence and horror."[4]

Like in *Train to Pakistan,* herein also Khushwant Singh, in spite of his acknowledging the near-all-pervasive inhumanity of the humanity, does not fail to notice the brighter side of the humanity. He rightly highlights the contribution of gracious people in strengthening and vitalizing the life of Delhi.

While unfolding the saga of Delhi, the novelist tries to view every historical situation and the personages in a detached manner. The historical figures turn into three-dimensional and speak for themselves. The novelist tries to grasp the innate feelings and the essential strengths and weaknesses of the rulers who have moulded the destiny of Delhi, and of India.

Despite the high seriousness of the theme of the novel, he deals it in his typical comic and ironic vein. In fact, the Bhagmati episode which is present in every alternating chapter puzzles the reader. Perhaps the novelist attempts to tone down the seriousness of the theme by creating highly hilarious situations involving the narrator and Bhagmati, a hermaphrodite.

However, Bhagmati episode is in accordance with the novelist's established narrative mode—the comic. In Khushwant Singh's fictional world "the comic inextricably linked with social and moral criticism and also with the free play of mind in a spirit of detachment."[5] Further, in his fictional world comedy "is connected with laughter, which is also a corrective and arises from fragments of action and utterance."[6]

While unravelling the saga of Delhi and its people, Khushwant Singh makes his best attempt to remain as a detached observer. This stance is possible for Khushwant Singh as he sees himself essentially as agnostic: "Being an agnostic without any prejudices, I may have become the loudest voice against religious fundamentalism and stupid beliefs in miracles, astrology, and that of hocus-focus."[7]

The novelist begins the "reliving" of the past of Delhi with the times of Ghiasuddin Balban and of sufi saint, Nizamuddin Aulia. It is essentially a time of great transition, and society is in a state of flux. The novelist hints at that society, of Delhi or of any city and place, is never static and hence constantly evolves. Perhaps it is a time of bigotry, and also a time of reconciliation and reintegration, made possible, through the self-sacrificing efforts of sufi saints like Nizamuddin. Through a fictious character, Musaddi Lal, a new Hindu kayastha convert to Islam, the transitional times of Delhi are poignantly viewed at.

The life of the new convert to Islam along with his wife stand as testimony to the then-fast-changing society of Delhi. This kayastha's best efforts to get assimilated into the just-emerging new society, and his half-successful attempts to this end speak volumes of trying times. But for the ironic and comic vein adopted by the novelist, the reader would have been swept by the winds of prejudices. The comic and ironic mode of the novelist help him and readers rise above prejudices, and lighten the weight of the subject. The predicament of Musaddi Lal, presented in a comic manner, speaks of him and also of many: "I was disowned by the Hindus and shunned by my wife. I was exploited by the Muslims who disdained my company. Indeed I was like a *hijda* who was neither one thing nor another but could be misused by every one." (55)

The times are not devoid of saviours. The one to save Musaddi Lal and the like has appeared in the shape of Nizamuddin: "Nizamuddin was our umbrella against the burning sun of Muslim bigotry and the downpour of Hindu contempt." (62)

By making clear his view of religion, Nizamuddin stands as a pillar of sanity amidst the prevailing frenzy of bigotry: "I believe that the best way to serve god is through love of his creatures. . . . God is an experience." (56) Further, he could stand aloof from the royal patronage, and pronounce: "Kings come and kings go. The will of Allah is eternal." (82)

The Oxford History of India records the saintly greatness of Nizamuddin and the like who have won the hearts of masses among Hindus and help spread Islam in India in a faster and easier manner: "sufi saints or pairs were present in the Punjab in the eleventh century . . . some like Khwaja Moin-ud-din Chisti of Ajmer and Khwaja Nizamuddin Aulia of Delhi settled near cities where their tombs become centres of devotion. They appealed direct to the people and were the evangelists as well as spiritual preceptors of Islam. The sufis rather than kings, warriors, or adventurers, were responsible for the bulk of the Muslim in the subcontinent."[8]

The novelist's attempts to step into the shoes of Taimur result in an 'almost convincing' argument for the invasion of Taimur against India. It is aptly suggested that behind the facade of holy wars, there lies the question of personal ambitions and interests who take precedence always. It is also made clear that most of the rulers and the people, irrespective of their religious affiliations, are simply men of their times only. Hence, one does not wonder at the expression of smugness by Taimur.

It is no wonder a book of history which views Taimur from another perspective and enlists the devastation caused by him during the invasion: "The city was thoroughly plundered for the days . . . all the accumulated wealth of generations being carried off to Samarkand along with a multitude of women and other captives."[9]

In the episode of Banda bairagi, one can discern the spreading of Sikh religion among the lower classes of society of Delhi, and in what manner this bairagi has helped the lower classes develop self-esteem. But in the eyes of history, Banda bairagi remains an "imposter"[10] only.

Likewise the novelist aptly captures the highly complex and multi-faceted personality of Aurangzeb Alamgir who remained to a large extent shrouded in mystery and misunderstanding, in the annals of history of Delhi and India. The novelist ably visualizes the penitent and god-fearing Aurangzeb. Aurangzeb is in his death-bed and is sour and sad, not because of the fast approaching death, but with the augurs of impending dismantling of his closely-guarded empire, and with the sense of unfulfilment: "I came alone and I go as a stranger. I do not know who I am, nor what I have been doing. The instant which passed in power left only sorrow behind it. . . . Life, so valuable, has been squandered in vain. . . . I fear for my salvation, I fear my punishment. I believe in god's bounty, but I am afraid because of what I have done." (162)

The fall of mighty personality like Aurangzeb pushes Delhi into the hands of weak rulers. Presently it faces the invasion of Nadir Shah and has to suffer his plundering it. It is aptly suggested that the wheels of juggernaut of oppression and victimization have rolled further and Delhi as a whole has suffered.

Come the year of 1857, the year of "First War of Independence" along with all its "intrigues," Delhi finds itself in a new situation. For a change, the roles of victims and perpetrators of oppression have been taken up by a new set of people. In the episodes of "Alice Aldwell," "Bahadur Shah Jafar" and "Nihal Singh," it is clearly proved that what is ultimately significant is the manifested "inherent evil" in man. During this period all sections of the people including Europeans have suffered. Perhaps in certain cases victims have turned into perpetrators of oppression and vice versa.

The novel also marginally takes into consideration the havoc that was wreaked upon Delhi and a part of India during the partition and during the post-partition period. In the caricature of Mahatma Gandhi and in the fictionalization of his assassination, the novelist points out the corrupting influence of evil of bigotry and violence on the young minds as seen in the person of Mahatma's assassin, Nathuram and also the ultimate and undying victory of Mahatma over violence, and the sustenance of the voice of sanity. The novel also takes into consideration the recent incidents that have taken place in Delhi which stand as examples of further perpetration of evil and oppression.

It is not out of place here to establish the thematic affinity of the novels *Delhi* and *Twilight in Delhi.* Khushwant Singh's *Delhi* compares and contrasts with Ahmed Ali's *Twilight in Delhi.* Both the novelists are ardent lovers of Delhi and its past. The plot of *Twilight in Delhi*, mostly viewed through the eyes of the protagonist, Mir Nihal, unravels the saga of Delhi from the watershed year of 1857 to 1911, the year of Coronation Durbar held by King George V and to the Home Rule movement. The novel progresses along the climb-down of Mir Nihal and the city, Delhi. Khushwant Singh's *Delhi,* though the span of time taken into consideration is long, is not thematically alien to Ahmed Ali's novel. In a way both the novels testify to the existence of the higher reality—the cyclic process of birth-growth-decay—that governs the lives of City and Man.

NOTES

1. These lines are a free translation of two lines of late Srirangam Srinivasa Rao's (popularly known in the field of Telugu literature as Sri Sri) magnum opus, *Mahaprasthanam,* an anthology of poems written in Telugu.
2. Khushwant Singh, *Delhi* (New Delhi: Penguin, 1990).
3. "A Note from the Author," *Ibid.*
4. V.A. Shahane, "Khushwant Singh: An Artist in Realism," M.K.Naik, ed., *Critical Essays on Indian Writing in English* (Madras: Macmillan, 1977), p. 354.
5. *Ibid.,* pp. 344-45.
6. *Loc. cit.*
7. Atma Ram, "Interview with Khushwant Singh," *The Quest,* Vol. 7, Nos. 1 & 2 (Oct. 1993), p. 2.
8. Vincent A. Smith, *The Oxford History of India* (London: Oxford, 1961), p. 801.
9. *Ibid.,* pp. 260-61.
10. *Ibid.,* p. 432.

A Note on Bhagmati in *Delhi*

SUBHASH CHANDRA

Talking about the central character, Bhagmati, Khushwant Singh writes, "Those who do not know her find her unattractive. She is dark and has pock-marks on her face. She is short and squat; her teeth are uneven and yellowed as a result of chewing tobacco and smoking beedis. Her clothes are loud, her voice louder; her speech bawdy and her manners worse."[1] That Bhagmati symbolizes Delhi and that the narrator is in love with her is made clear in the very first sentence by the writer: "I return to Delhi as I return to my mistress Bhagmati when I have had my fill of whoring in foreign lands." (1) Bhagmati is a eunuch (hermaphrodite). *Delhi* has been extensively reviewed along the predictable lines of its being fictionalized history of Delhi; the veracity of the major historical personae and events and the extent of infusion of the novelist's imaginings (wild at times) into the narrative structure (larded heavily with sex and violence) have also been discussed. But why does the writer make Bhagmati, a character who plays a central role and functions as a fictional parallel to the subject of the book, a eunuch? This aspect of the novel has remained unexplored. Therefore, in the present paper I attempt to suggest certain factors which made the author choose Bhagmati, a eunuch, as the central character. Simultaneously, I shall try to explain certain ambiguities that creep into the narrative when Bhagmati and Delhi are equated in absolute terms, as the novelist appears to do.

Khushwant Singh gives the reason in an interview for making a *hijra* (eunuch) the symbol for Delhi, for "The *hijra* stands for a symbol of sterility. It can never conceive and I thought this was a wonderful symbol for a city in which so much has happened like a sexual intercourse that repeats itself. With Delhi all that has happened to it in the way of violence, in the way of change of dynasties, it has still not produced anything as great as one would have expected of it."[2] This is rather an ambiguous thesis. It is incomprehensible how violence committed on a city and the change of dynasties it witnesses should make it produce something great. Secondly, a problem arises when Delhi is identified with Bhagmati in toto. While Delhi, as Singh states, was raped repeatedly, Bhagmati, on the other hand, seeks pleasure with or without money. Her stormy sexual escapades with the narrator indicate the satisfying sexual orgasms she derives from cohabiting with the narrator. Not only that, she develops an intimate and lasting emotional, sexual relationship with the narrator. These differences become stumbling blocks while considering the structural unity of the novel. However, these differences are explainable, when locked upon from a different perspective. And this plank is that of androgyny. The hermaphrodite fuses in himself/herself the elements of the male and the female or to use the Jungian terminology, Anima and Animus. An idea of what androgyny is may be got from Virginia Woolf's musings who wondered "whether there are two sexes in the mind corresponding to the two sexes in the body. . . . And in the man's brain, the man predominates over the woman, and in the woman's brain, the woman predominates over the man. The normal and comfortable state of being is that when the two live in harmony together, spiritually cooperating. If one is a man, still the woman part of the brain must have effect; and a woman also must have intercourse with the man in her."[3] According to Heilbrun, androgyny is an ancient Greek word which is covered from *andro* (male) and *gyn* (female) and it "defines a condition under which the characteristics of the sexes, and the human impulses expressed by men and women, are not rigidly assigned. Androgyny seeks to liberate the individual from the confines of the appropriate."[4] Bhagmati conforms to this concept of androgyny.

Androgyny at one level underlines the absence of sexual conflict, which the malignant feminists of today are forever feverishly and frantically stressing between the genders. On the other, and at an extended level, androgyny embodies complete harmony in every sphere of human existence, generally riven with conflicts and bickerings. She, the androgynous being (the narrator chooses to call Bhagmati "she" as she like women menstruates, even though she has several male attributes), speaks Hindustani, larded with Urdu words, the *lingua franca* of India and thus stands for linguistic harmony. More importantly, even though her name is Hindu, she has equal respect for all the religions and exhibits the essential secularity of her thinking.

I now come to another difference between Delhi and Bhagmati which needs to be explained. Delhi does not remain tolerant and understanding as Bhagmati is. Following the assassination of Mrs. Gandhi, Delhi becomes bloody and violent—mass murders and mayhem becoming widespread. The city is soaked with the blood of humans and the narrator and Bhagmati witness traumatic happenings in shocked anguish. Bhagmati here represents the narrator's wishfulfilment: in Bhagmati he envisions Delhi of his dreams, free from violence, cruelty and full of compassion. Bhagmati acquires a larger stature than she commanded during the early parts of the novel, when she appeared to be no more than a fucking-machine for the narrator, which he used to his satiation and delight. Bhagmati, through her person, points to a state and time when conflictual situations would be ironed out and the society would live in an androgynous harmony. Androgyny itself acquires a larger connotation of a happy state in which there is no room for hostile turbulence.

It is this androgynous being, Bhagmati, who thinks of and feels concerned about the narrator, when there is danger to his life during the fierce riots raging in the city of Delhi in 1984. No male or female around the narrator comes to his rescue, but a male-female member of society is anxious to save his life. Bhagmati comes to the narrator's house and insists on taking him along to a safe haven, Lal Kuan, the *hijra* headquarter. Seen in this light androgyny becomes a universally tranquil (and therefore safe) environ which has no place for dissension, contrariness and conflict. And herein lies the wider relevance and meaning of the character of the petty *hijra*, who is introduced in the novel as a mean-looking pathetic figure, lying on the road in a fit of epilepsy. Every writer cherishes a vision of an ideal world, a utopian ambience in which there is no antipathy, marring human relationships. In *Delhi* this vision is embodied in Bhagmati.

Yet another dimension to the character of Bhagmati is her resemblance to Tiresias, the blind priest in Sophocles's *Oedipus, the King*, with the only difference that Tiresias is blind. Both Tiresias and Bhagmati are hermaphrodites and both of them are represented as repositories of wisdom, which inheres in the visionary power to perceive things and penetrate men's minds and events. The blind priest Tiresias's revelations play a crucial role in the context of the play; Bhagmati's sagacious pieces of advice to the narrator, delivered albeit in an affectionately chiding manner, bear close resemblance to Tiresias's wisdom. But why did Sophocles and Khushwant Singh choose to invest this type of unfaltering wisdom in bisexual being? A possible clue again seems to lie in the phenomenon of androgyny. Wisdom is neither nationality (which has often led mankind into blind and disastrous alleys, involving world wars and mass tortures and murders) nor purely instinct which uncoupled with rationality may remain an inadequate guide. It is the combination of the two which becomes wisdom. Both the blind priest Tiresias and Bhagmati possess this wisdom by virtue of their being male (rationality) and female (instinct) at the same time.

Bhagmati, as the chief persona, acts as the counterbalancing force to the all-pervasive violence that marks the history of Delhi. The fictional cosmos of the book permeates with the descriptions of violent acts and violent situations/events. To wit some of them: Mahmud of Gazni who invaded Hindustan seventeen times "used to chop off the fingers of the Hindu rajas he defeated in battle; his treasury was full of Hindu fingers." (54) Referring to Ghiasuddin Balban, the writer says he "was known to execute anyone who as much as raised his eyes to look at him. He kept two huge Negroes beside him to hack off the head of people he sentenced to death." (55) There are several other depictions of ambitious intrigues and lust for power (throne) leading to gory and terrible violence, the most monstrous being the bloodshed and treachery involving the capture of throne of Hindustan by Aurangzeb. Bhagmati's character epitomises reconciliation: reconciliation between the antithetical elements, reconciliation to one's situation—physiological, social or economic—she is not greedy for money (though she is extremely poor), she is not power-hungry, she is no egoist. In a sense through her, Khushwant Singh sketches out the paradigmatic example of a perfect human being, a model individual, interested in the business of living and trying to get as much out of the inevitably troubled and sombre human existence as possible, without causing hurt or harassment to any other person. She represents what Virginia Woolf calls "the unity of being."[5] Even though she is presented as a vulgar and crude person, she is witty, sharp and intelligent. She has the requisite resilience to survive the crises and yet not lose the desire for life. Nothing can deter or depress her into leading a vegetable existence: she has verve and vivacity, vigour and *joi de vivre*. She takes life as it comes; she is never down or out.

Khushwant Singh's other two celebrated novels, *I Shall Not Hear the Nightingale* and *Train to Pakistan*, I would like to suggest, also posit counterbalancing forces to the urge for violence which overtakes people every now and then. Sabhrai, the prototypical mother-figure in *I Shall Not Hear the Nightingale*, who plays a pivotal role in the novel, becomes the condensed symbol of love and compassion, while the lout, Jugga in *Train to Pakistan* is made to perform the noblest act of self-sacrifice for the sake of love. Khushwant Singh prizes humaneness, tolerance, compassion and fellow-feeling, and is against bigotry of all types, and more so against the violence that follows in the wake of bigotry. All these values are invested in the persona of Bhagmati in the novel *Delhi*. In a fictional cosmos marked by disharmony, discord, violence and mayhem, the writer, through Bhagmati, communicates the message of harmony, peace, and love of life and humanity.

NOTES

1. Khushwant Singh, *Delhi* (New Delhi: Viking, 1989), p. 1.
2. Ashok Chopra, Interview with Khushwant Singh, *The Hindustan*

Times, January 14, 1990, p. 2.

3. Herbert Marder, *Feminism & Art: A Study of Virginia Woolf* (Chicago: The University of Chicago Press, 1968), p. 108.
4. Carolyn G. Heilbrun, *Toward A Recognition of Androgyny* (New York: W.W. Norton, 1964), p. x.
5. Herbert Marder, p. 198.

'Time and Tide': History in Khushwant Singh's *Delhi* and Ivo Andric's *The Bridge on the Drina*

G.R. TANEJA

Delhi: A Novel[1] has, much like *The Satanic Verses,* had the unfortunate distinction of receiving a great deal of public notice. But the attention that has been focused upon it has no relevance to the book at all, with the result that the genuine strength of one of the major works of fiction published in the eighties has not been adequately appreciated. Behind the narrator's endless adventures with American *missi babas,* German stenographers, British dowagers, and lonely army wives; behind a long and complex interaction with a hermaphrodite that Singh dwells upon with an insistent attention to detail—behind, briefly, the quintessential dirty joke that *Delhi: A Novel* is expected to embody—lies a point of view which illuminates some of the larger issues of life and living.

Singh told a journalist soon after the publication of *Delhi:*

> Gone is the culture of Delhi . . . it breaks my heart. I no longer want to see Hauz Khas or go to Suraj Kund which was a good four mile walk or visit Tughlakabad that was almost another city. Today they are in the middle of slums with construction all around. I came here when there was no New Delhi. I saw the whole city being built. At that time all these ruins were accessible to us. You could see them for miles. There were no roads. One walked to them. Now they are smothered in the name of development, art or what have you. . . . Delhi has not produced anything that will last. Apart from Ghalib.[2]

Singh tells us that he was inspired to write Delhi by Ivo Andric's *The Bridge on the Drina* (1945).[3] The Yugoslav Nobel Laureate's celebrated trilogy (*Bosnian Chronicle* and *The Women from Sarajeo* are the other two novels) which was written during World War II, presents a tableau of Bosnian history from 1916 to World War II. One of the two major contemporary Yugoslav authors, Andric in his work combines the twin traditions of realism and modernism. Born in Dolac in 1892 (he died in 1975), the Serbo-Croatian author was awarded the Nobel Prize for literature in 1961. While his early reputation was established with *Ex Ponto* (1918), a ruminative lyrical prose work written during his internment for nationalist political activities during World War I, his world-wide fame rests on the trilogy referred to above. His novels reveal epic force, and a deterministic philosophy. He has a great sense of compassion. He expresses himself with objectivity and sobriety in a language of "great beauty and purity."

The Bridge embodies and exploits many of Andric's preoccupations since his early days of writing in the twenties. Here Andric depicts the life of the people of Visegrad through the events of centuries, and the description of countless characters and their reactions, though not necessarily inter-actions, take the place of plot. The Drina is the river which marks the boundary between Bosnia, Andric's native village, and Serbia. Spanning it at Visegrad, the Turks built a bridge in the sixteenth century, and the novel describes life as it moves around and over the bridge during the course of three and one-half centuries, upto the time of World War I.

As an historical symbol the bridge united Serbia to the east and Bosnia to the west. The bridge also has a suprahuman existence. It endures and unites all the inhabitants of Visegrad through time. In the sixteenth century mothers screamed when their sons were taken to Stambul as a blood tribute to the Vezir, and almost four centuries later they shout and plead again when their sons are forcibly recruited for the Austrian army. Viewed in Biblical terms the bridge serves as a Calvary, for in the course of the novel a peasant, a religious pilgrim, a young mill attendant, and a parish priest—all innocent of any real crime— are impaled on the *kapia*, the wide terraces on either side of the middle of the bridge.

Yet if the bridge claims human sacrifice, it is also the place of spiritual purification. Also, a strand of Moslem thought present in the novel suggests that the bridge stands for man's creativity which achieves something lasting and good. In this world anything can happen, except that we must cherish wise and great men who build bridges for the love of God and the beauty of the world. The absence of such men who nourish human creativity would mean that God no longer existed.

But through the centuries the bridge appears overshadowed by conflicts rather than harmony. Thus, for Andric, the bridge becomes an idealistic symbol of what could be. Andric's sympathy for idealism is evident. He values man's endeavour and finds in his failures tragic waste. Obviously Andric does not share the existentialistic view of human existence.

As in Andric's *The Bridge*, or in Ruttmann's *Berlin, Symphony of a City* (1927), the protagonist of Singh's novel is the city itself. What *Delhi* most certainly is not is a book of history, its scrupulous adherence to the facts of history notwithstanding. Apparently the city lays itself bare chronologically—from 1008 AD to the 1984 Massacre. But when one looks back after reading the book, one is not conscious of a sequential narrative but of numerous voices that the city speaks to us through, voices that rise in tumultuous multitude, mingle and become a symphonic concerto: voices of kings and noblemen and their hirelings; rebels and turn-coats; lowly *kayasthas*, and half-caste anglo-Indians; sepoys, Gurus and *aulias;* perfidious women and treacherous friends; *Khwajasaras*, Hindus, Muslims, the untouchables and Christians; whores and hermaphrodites. Singh's triumph is to present a city which disregards the logic of time. He transforms it into an organic whole by according the time past and time present of the historical, 'time-bound' Delhi a simultaneous presence.

The unmistakable voice of the persona that Delhi dons to speak to us is that of the author himself The vehicle that Singh employs to communicate to his readers is the metaphor of the hermaphrodite:

> I return to Delhi as I return to my mistress Bhagmati when I have had my fill of whoring in foreign lands. Delhi and Bhagmati have a lot in common. Having been long misused by rough people they have learnt to conceal their seductive charms under a mask of repulsive ugliness. It is only to their lovers that they reveal their true selves. . . . What you have to do for things to appear different is to cultivate a sense of belonging. (1)
>
> To the stranger Delhi may appear like a gangrenous accretion of noisy bazaars and mean looking hovels growing around a few tumbled down forts and mosques along a dead river. (1)

But love can transform ugliness into beauty: "Then the skies over Delhi's marbled palaces turn an aquamarine blue; its domed mosques and pencil-like minarets are spanned by rainbows." (1) Singh points out that hermaphrodite "stands for a symbol of sterility. It can never conceive and I thought this was a wonderful symbol for a city in which so much has happened like a sexual intercourse that repeats itself."[4]

Delhi is not a ready reckoner for the prurient. Khushwant Singh's use of the bawdy is deliberate and seriously handled. It is the chief weapon and metaphor through which he expresses his disgust. Bawdiness by definition draws upon the witty and the comic, the absurd and the ingenious, even the gross, and seeks to startle and shock. Wit needs subtlety, and a degree of indirectness; metaphors and allusions rather than four-letter words. Bawdy has in fact been equated with caricature. In Erica Jong's *Fanny* (1980) bawdiness is used to create the eighteenth-century ethos. More recently Upamanyu Chatterjee employed it to startle and delight as well as to establish the lingering traces of adolescence in the youthful protagonist of *English August: An Indian Story* (1988). Singh's use of the bawdy is funny and comic. As often he is gross. He employs it discriminatingly to condition the reader's response to his subject matter.

Responding to the charge of deliberate obscenity, Singh told a journalist: "I have been deliberately misunderstood by many people who have not bothered to read the book. . . . I have used four-letter words. Perhaps the text is racy, bawdy and has a lot of sex. That is me. And that is also a lot of people."[5] To the charge levelled against him in a Pakistani newspaper, *Jung*, that Singh's novel makes him a Sikh Salman Rushdie because he has described Muslim emperors drinking or indulging in an orgy, Singh says: "Nowhere in the novel have I said a word against Islam or the Prophet or the Koran. I have described the lives of Monarchs who happened to be Muslims. It is all taken from their diaries. . . . Why should Islam be linked with the decadence of [a] monarch." As Anees Jung has remarked, Singh "has not attacked the faith of the man but the man himself who has betrayed that faith."[6]

In the ultimate authorial judgement the city in *Delhi: A Novel* emerges as "sterile" (30) and "a dying city." (380) The Hindus live on "a stale diet of past glory," (54) are "fawning flatterers," (100) "ungrateful and cowardly," (182) their manners "unlikeable," (192) and their ethics "questionable." (336) The 'Delhiwalla' is portrayed, to borrow the words of the master of anger himself, as "the most pernicious race of little odious vermin that nature ever suffered to crawl upon the surface of the earth." The anger is Swiftian; the accusatory finger, with its relentless logic, reminds one of Nirad Chaudhuri; and the pain of a harrowing realization is familiar from Saadi, Mir and Ghalib.[7]

The city as a phenomenon has always fascinated the creative eye. While Ruttmann's *Berlin, Symphony of a City* (1927) is too depersonalized, and Strand and Sheeler's *Manhatta* (sic) (1921) too abstract, *Delhi* is a human document. Anger veils admiration, disgust, love, and gross sexual nausea suggests the protagonists', and the author's, intense fascination. Singh's hatred of the object of his desire gives him remarkable insight into the heart and soul of the city and its inhabitants. *Delhi* is the story of a grand failure, the failure of a city and its inhabitants, its past and its present. It is the story of a people who have failed to exploit their potential; a society which has failed to appropriate for itself values that make a people discover and realize themselves; a civilization that has crumbled before attaining its true destiny. Traces of the glory that could have been, serve to heighten one's sense of the magnitude of that failure.

Delhi is not without its faults. The novel is the form through which the present century has expressed its insights into the human predicament. This is the age that has given us North American metafiction, Latin American magic realism, the French New (sic) Novel, concrete prose, and science fiction. Singh's craftsmanship reveals no awareness of the myriad approaches to literary ontology, or post-modernist fiction's ability to construct, or deconstruct, the world through its strategies of form and language.

Despite its utterly conventional idiom, its failure to create three-dimensional characters, fuse thought and action (which makes his earlier novels read like dramatized essays), and the unchanging, often monotonous, tone of the speaking voice that pervades Singh's entire narrative, it remains a major work. *Delhi: A Novel* is not a dirge sung over lost empires. It is a celebration of the unique power of a culture and civilization: the power to generate some of the finer values of life; the power to ensure the survival of these values in the face of a nation's collective debasement; and above all, the power to ensure that when all is lost an awareness of that loss remains. What makes the novel an enduring work of art, and lifts it above the deep despair that pervades the whole narrative, is the testimony that it provides to a haunting sense of that loss.

NOTES

1. (New Delhi: Viking, 1989).
2. Anees Jung, "Man—Not the Faith," *The Times of India Sunday Review*, 18 March 1990, p. 7.
3. Khushwant Singh, "I am a dirty old man. . ." [Interview], *The Hindustan Times Sunday Magazine*, January 14, 1990, p. 1.
4. *Loc. cit.*
5. Anees Jung, p. 7.
6. *Loc. cit.*
7. "It is a saga of greed, violence, oppression and injustice. . . . There is little to counter the gloom with which the book ends.

. . Yet one cannot help but going back to the transforming and healing power of those who oppose such divisive forces of hatred, those holy men from Nizamuddin Aulia to Guru Arjun Singh to Mahatma Gandhi . . . who are the real *badshahs* of Delhi." Makrand Paranjape, "The City is the Hero," *The Times of India Sunday Review*, 28 January 1990, p. 3.

Amrinder's *Lajo* and Khushwant Singh's *Delhi*: Sikhs in a Crisis of Identity

O. P. MATHUR

The strategies of contemporary fiction have been struggling to escape the grips of external reality. But, as Alison Lee notes, "Realism still has control over the way in which literature is read, taught and evaluated."[1] In developing countries, in particular, the presence of socio-political problems are too strong to allow the novelists in general to transcend the immediacy of the treatment of visible approaches. Irving Howe, feeling the vibrant pulse of the political novel, comments, "Abstraction, then, is confronted with the flow of experience, the monolith of programme with the richness and diversity of motive, the purity of ideal with the contaminations of action."[2]

In India the hard political realities, ranging from foreign subjugation and struggle for freedom to the varied but nonetheless disturbing post-independence political scenario, impinged upon the consciousness of writers for whom the subjects were in God's plenty. One of the most provocative of these themes was that of the relation between the followers of different religions, many of whom forgot the quintessential teachings of their faiths and indulged in violence of all kinds to which even the Partition provided no permanent solution. The Sikhs, in partition provided no permanent solution. The Sikhs, in particular, were always one with the Hindus—with common names and families, numerous inter-communal marriages and their venerations for each other's scriptures and places of worship—and had acted as the advance guard of the Hindu community. They had fought and suffered together in the communal riots and the holocaust that preceded and followed the Partition. This long-standing feeling of oneness which had received a jolt at the hands of our politicians in search of vote banks and of the terrorist fires lit and fanned from without, is now fast returning. Though many in the Sikh community underwent a transient crisis of identity, the heart of the community remained by and large in the right place. Any temporary feeling of alienation which might have been there was superficial, for it hardly permeated through literature and the arts, which continued to act as the vehicles of the message of universal love and brotherhood. The intellectuals on both sides too were never ranged against each other. A significant pointer is the fact that while works of literature dealing with the divide between the Hindus and the Muslims are many, there are an extremely small number of such works dealing with the temporary alienation of some of the members of the Sikh community. In fact, there seem to be only two in English, both by Sikh writers. Amrinder's *Lajo* has this as the main theme, while Khushwant Singh's *Delhi* ends its panoramic, though fragmentary, survey with a section on the Operation Blue Star, the assassination of Indira Gandhi and the anti-Sikh riots of 1984, not to mention a Sikh soldier whose monologue points at another moment of crisis faced by the Sikhs at the time of the Indians' first struggle for freedom in 1857.

Amrinder's *Lajo* primarily focusses on a small number of characters, both Hindus and Sikhs, and the changing flux of their emotional relationships wrought by external events. It has much of the paraphernalia of a popular thriller—love, explosive passion, mass killings, revenge leading to the 'murder' of the same person twice by two different persons, both closely related to him, secret love, elopement, near-insanity—once or twice relieved by the idyllic charm of rural life. The characters also are varied and they face unpredictable situations and undergo sudden transformations. As the title indicates, the chief character is Lajo, a sturdy young woman from Punjab, who, during her childless existence in Delhi with her meek and passionless husband Mohinder, finds that her tempestuous passion is awakened by a young Hindu neighbour Vikram resulting in the birth of a boy

Sharan. The burning to death of her husband, with the connivance of her lover, as she believes, during the anti-Sikh riots of 1984, she decides to take a double revenge—murder of Vikram and bringing up of Sharan as a devout Sikh, potentially a terrorist to take revenge for the killings of 1984. The warp and woof of the novel consists of the consequences of the failure of both her missions and of the ultimate regaining of their mental equilibrium and the realization of their true identity.

In her commendatory note on *Lajo*, Amrita Pritam comments that it is "full of raw, rough and blind passions for identity." The remark applies most to Lajo whose crisis of conscience and of identity are spread over the whole novel—her illicit passionate responses to a Hindu lover followed a little later by her resolve to make her son a true Sikh.

> No one could extinguish a race like this. The young would grow into sturdy, strapping youths and produce further progeny and the Sikhs would flourish and prosper. Only one thing was that they were caught unawares by people who they thought were their own. They had never considered themselves separate from the Hindus and had celebrated Holi and Diwali with equal enthusiasm and gusto as the birth anniversaries of Guru Nanak Devji and Guru Gobind Singhji.[3]

Her Sikh identity surfaces and she is full of contempt for all those Sikhs who, to save their lives, wanted to pass off as Hindus by shaving off their beards and hair. She begs them to die as Sikhs "with dignity and pride." (52) She wants to hate and despise herself for having loved a Hindu. (56) She even sows the seeds of hatred among the children by repeating before them the incidents of 1st November 1984 on which the Hindus deprived them of their homes. To Sharan in particular she says, "you have a greater responsibility on your shoulders because you are a man. God has spared you for the express purpose of taking revenge for the unjustifiable evil done to us." (57)

Lajo's Sikh identity, forced upon her by her tragedy, is rudely shaken when she meets Vikram again, alive, arousing her old passion and revealing to her that he had no hand in her husband's brutal murder. She realizes: "I was just swept along with this tidal wave of destructive humanity." (75)

> She was appalled at the way she had brought up her child. Such religious fanaticism in a child barely eleven years old was like a cancer poisoning his blood. She must stop it if it was not already too late. She realized with horror how wrong she had been. (78)

Now she again becomes "a warm, affectionate lively woman," (81) helping Vikram and his family in their times of need, and even taking Sharan's crime of murder upon herself to save him from prison. The Lajo who dies in prison is hardly the same Lajo who had responded to Vikram's love, for the vicissitudes of life have matured her and made her less impulsive and more thoughtful and self-sacrificing. Her life is a long and tortuous journey from ignorance, wild passion and animal love to knowledge, serenity and consideration for others.

If Lajo's journey through changing identities is longer, her son Sharan's is shorter but more painful. Ignorant of his Hindu paternity and brought up on the poisonous diet of hatred and revenge, the double shock he receives on his being told of his paternity just when he has stabbed to death his real father replaces his long cherished Sikh identity with that of a Hindu murderer of his father. He remains in his "private hell," (126) bitterly hating his mother, and consoled only by his sweetheart Channo:

> He was suffering from an identity crisis and till now was unable to accept, leave alone face, the reality of the situation. . . . The tall trees of his confusion with their enmeshed, intermingling branches would not let sunlight of reason to enter and in the chaos that prevailed he searched for his lost identity. (132)

When he asks her, "What am I who am I? All my life I was a devout Sikh and now suddenly I don't know," she assures him that he is "a wonderful human being," "one of the lucky few who belong to two religions," and "humanity is the best of all religions." (133) Gradually "the glacier of his mind thawed to a certain level of reception" (132) and pendulous between Sikhism and Hinduism, finds that "there were good and bad Hindus just as there were good and bad Sikhs" (138) that religions are but different routes to the same goal. Now he feels "as enlightened as the Buddha in a Hindu temple." (138)

The core of the novel seems to consist in the impalation of his false identities. With the "cobwebs of confusion swept away by a giant broom," (138) he is irradiated by the true identity of a human being, and driven by the subconscious while moving about in the city on his motor-cycle he reaches his father's house and brings home his handicapped real sister. This puts a final stamp of peace on the 'development' worked out in the novel. Sharanjit Singh has finally become Sharan Kumar, with an identity in which all identities find their refuge and merge. This religion of humanity is "the ultimate religion" which the novelist deliberately projects chronologically into the future.

This is also the impression that the novelist wishes to create through the portrayal of other characters—Mohinder Singh, gentle like a lamb, quite unlike the then popular image of a Sikh; Vikram, a Hindu who tries to save the lives of a Sikh family, and later a true lover of a Sikh woman for whom he does everything possible; Channo, a Hindu girl in love with a Sikh boy, later revealed to be a Hindu, but without any difference to her love; or, above all, the most helpful and gentle orphan Guddi whose sole identity is that of a human being.

The final assertion of the human identity is marked only by the novelist's repeated sermonizing, either in her own person or through her characters' words or thoughts which are too well argued and expressed too clearly and repeatedly, considering their class and intellectual level. They all become the author's spokesmen.

In this respect it would perhaps be fruitful to mention two other novels by writers who have powerful links with this subcontinent and whose messages are similar. Taslima Nasrin's *Lajja* brings out the miseries undergone by the Hindu minority in Bangladesh, but in this novel too the author's repeated interventions obfuscate the aesthetic impression much more than is done in *Lajo*. The characters of *Lajja* produce statistical data like a computer, an exercise that would not be easy even for a specialist. The novelist's purpose or message should not be poured upon the reader but should arise from the work like fragrance from a flower. This is rightly the case with Rushdie's *Midnight's Children*, where through the medium of irony, parody, humour and satire and through exaggerated, even laughable, characters, the novelist conveys a similar message of peace, love, tolerance and brotherhood in a highly sophisticated manner. The 'message' in a work of art is best communicated if it is not too obtrusive, otherwise it becomes a pamphlet.

The question of Sikh identity and the crises it faced has been treated in some detail by Khushwant Singh in his novel *Delhi*. The novelist's object seems to be to catch the historical dynamics of the spirit of Delhi through the last few centuries and to emphasize its sterility, which can also be put as hermaphroditism, i.e. a combination of diversities, which has characterized its culture, the symbol of which in the novel is Bhagmati. Only the concluding chapter of the novel in an ambivalent manner attempts to illustrate the message of love and communal harmony, which has perhaps been communicated much more effectively in the earlier historical episodes. The narrator of the novel bears a marked resemblance to the author, though a complete identification is belied by chronology. Khushwant Singh, born in 1915, could not have witnessed the coming up of New Delhi or the Delhi Durbar. The narrator tries to have an overview of the movement of certain fragments of historical time, returning to the present and to his beloved Bhagmati, a *hijra*, after every such foray. In the last two sections dealing with the twentieth century, he has selected only the building up of the city and the anti-Sikh riots of 1984 which may be an indirect portrayal of his progenitors and an oblique statement of his own reactions, but neither of the two is treated so as to highlight the secular theme which he is so fond of. One can understand his avoidance of the theme of Partition which he had already treated so powerfully in *Train to Pakistan*. But perhaps a monologue given to any political leader, worker or freedom-fighter, known or unknown, would have been an appropriate celebration of the capital of free India and of the contemporary strivings after secularism. Moreover, he has not a word about the Emergency, perhaps because of his closeness to the Nehru family. Even the anti-Sikh riots he has treated could have provided him an opportunity to reassert his non-communal stance. But it is an opportunity which he has largely missed, consciously or sub- consciously. The events have been largely portrayed objectively and no Hindu or Sikh has been given a monologue. Even a monologue given to a terrorist or to a victim of the riots or even to one of the rioters could have been so handled as to reaffirm the author's values. Instead, there is so much of the portrayal of the riots but so little of the terrorists and their 'irreligious' acts, to say the least. No doubt, Bhindrawale has been mentioned, but that is only once, and that too in a way as to appear as a lawyer's defence in a murder case: "one demented monk and his gang of armed goons."[4] There is no mention of the large-scale killings in the Punjab and elsewhere and of the raising of the banner of secession under the garb of religiosity. And the timely Operation Bluestar, which perhaps saved the nation's unity and integrity is called "a stupid thing." (383) Bhindrawale and Indira Gandhi are, surprisingly enough, equated. The narrator does dislike the Sikhs' celebration of Indira Gandhi's assassination, but it is on the human plane only and not as a catastrophic event for the whole nation perpetrated by traitorous religious fanatics. Could the act have been condemned if, instead of a "frail, little woman" (386) the victim were a big burly man? Even in her case the narrator almost seems to suggest a rational justification of the assassination as one crime following another. (386)

There are two Sikh characters in the novel. In the section entitled '1857' there is a Sikh soldier Nihal Singh (who perhaps derives his name from the Sikh battle-cry "Sat Sri Akal, Bole so Nihal"). Nihal does speak up and that in the defence of the Sikhs' role in India's first struggle against foreign rule. As a man, Nihal is a brave fighter and occasionally a deeply sympathetic man who once quietly lets off a pious Muslim woman whom he has orders to shoot. But there is much on the other side of the scale. He is loyal to his British masters and is not repulsed by their acts of massacre, loot and rape of Hindus and Muslims alike. He seems to be a bundle of contradictions, who can partially be understood only with reference to his creator, a historian of the Sikhs, for, like his co-religionists, he has a reason to support the British, for Aurangzeb had cut off the head of their Guru, and the leader of the Indian fighters for freedom was "the grandson of the same Auranga," (273) a Muslim Emperor Bhadur Shah Zafar. Nihal Singh seems never to have heard of the Hindu leaders of the revolt who far outnumbered the Muslims. And the narrator too has not a word to say about it! Everywhere the narrator seems to shy away from an outright condemnation of the Sikhs.

There is another Sikh character, Budh Singh, who is presented as a butt of mockery, the author's favourite pastime with regard to 'Sardars' in particular. Lacking in intelligence and even in common sense, he is something of a Shakespearean character, generally an object of both sympathy and laughter, who evokes nothing but our pity in his gruesome end.

It appears that the sturdy secularist that the novelist is, he is silently gnawed at the heart by his own Sikh identity when he tries to portray a crisis in the Sikh psyche. Such delineations therefore seem to be marked by ambivalences and self-contradictions. From the point of view of narrative technique, *Delhi* is much more sophisticated than *Lajo*. The author attempts to erase himself out of the monologues given to different characters representing the selected moments of Indian history, though, as has been suggested by the present writer elsewhere,[5] his political beliefs cast an unmistakable shadow on the novel. *Lajo*, a much shorter work, like Taslima Nasrin's *Lajja*, is characterized by a forceful expression of the author's feelings and convictions which sometimes burst the seams of fictional technique. Khushwant Singh refers with approval to Shaw's famous remark about there being a hundred versions of religion.[6] This lesson shines forth perhaps with greater luminosity in *Lajja, Lajo, Midnight's Children* and many other such works than in *Delhi*. In fact, what he writes about himself in his "Introduction" to *I Believe* seems to be nearer the mark: "But I am a Sikh and want to continue to have a sense of belonging to the religious community in which I was born and reared."[7] However liberal and tolerant he may be, he cannot walk but in his own shadow. While *Lajo* ends with "The Eternal Religion," the last page of *Delhi* is smeared with petrol and is full of the stench of the burning body of Budh Singh. While in *Lajo*, it is the characters who undergo crises of identity, in *Delhi* it is the narrator who seems to do so through the patina of the events of the novel.

Amrinder's *Lajo* has more artistic integrity than Nasrin's *Lajja* and a strength of affirmation and a total absence of ambivalence, when placed beside Khushwant Singh's *Delhi*. *Lajo* may not be a great work of art, but it has a plot that is well-constructed, in spite of the intrusions of chance and accident, characters who are not always types but often affect us as living individuals and a highly significant message relevant to our times which may have been rubbed a little too much but not unjustifiably so, for the patient perhaps needs that much of pressure. And the characters, especially Lajo and Sharan, "work a development" rather than simply "propose a change."[8] It is undoubtedly a thriller, but it thrills us into thought.

The work aptly illustrates a recent remark by another Sikh writer emphasizing the importance of the social relevance of the artist's purpose in the contemporary Indian scenario: "God has seemingly given us up. The writer is the only hope left. He must play his role to awaken both the government and the people to put the house in order."[9]

NOTES

1. Alison Lee, *Realism and Power: Postmodern British Fiction* (London: Routledge, 1990), p. xiii.
2. Irving Howe, *Politics and the Novel* (New York: Fawcett, 1967), p. 25.
3. Amrinder, *Lajo* (New Delhi: Sharma, 1990), p. 37.
4. Khushwant Singh, *Delhi* (New Delhi: Viking, 1989, rep. 1990), p. 386.
5. *Modern Indian English Fiction* (New Delhi: Abhinav, 1993), pp. 184-91.

6. Khushwant Singh, *Need for a New Religion in India and Other Essays*, ed. Rohini Singh (New Delhi: UBS, 1991), p. 1.
7. Khushwant Singh, ed., *I Believe* (New Delhi: Orient Paperbacks, n.d.), pp. 9-10.
8. Derwent May, "The Novelist as Moralist and the Moralist as Critic," in Shiv K. Kumar and Keith Mckean, *Critical Approaches to Fiction* (New York: McGraw-Hill, 1986), p. 178.
9. K.S. Duggal, "The Writer is the last hope," *The Hindustan Times*, October 9, 1994, p. 13.

Inscription of the Repressed: A Study of *Delhi*

ANITA SINGH

Khushwant Singh claims in his foreword: "History provided me with skeletons, and I covered it with flesh and injected blood and a lot of seminal fluid into it." My reading of *Delhi* finds there are indeed the skeletons in the cupboard that are exorcised, conjured and animated with flesh, blood and glandular secretions. I see this work as a corollary to Singh's earlier history novels: *Train to Pakistan* and *I Shall Not Hear the Nightingale.* Singh uses historical events and documentary evidence for his framework to excavate the sub-text—the hidden portions of history. In his attempt to conjure his history he has assimilated other stories—other than history; concocted, fantastic, voyeuristic, even private lurid tales which put the official records in question. One may see *Delhi* as Singh's revision of history that subverts the officious view and offers a critique of the conventional historiography that is often authoritarian, monologic and prescriptive. The text resists from linear referentiality and releases multiple referentiality producing the effect of a carnivalesque.

It records the major historical events that have endowed Delhi with a glorious past, a mystic and an aura in the annals of history over a period of 600 years. From the Muslim invasion—the year 1265, the beginning of the reign of Sultan Ghiasuddin Balban—to the assassination of Indira Gandhi, followed by the massacre of the Sikhs. Malcolm Bradbury's definition of historical novels in the Preface to "The History Man" as the narration "Whose approximation of history is delusory as history itself" could be examined in relation to this novel.

Any discourse of *Delhi* must involve the narrative mode that builds up the assumptions, cultural moorings sexual taboos and fetishes. The novel embraces a large number of autonomous, dissonant voices unintruded by the anonymous narrator, a sikh. Travelling in time, space and history he discovers his beloved city Delhi: her invasions and possessions are revealed through the network of intricate metaphors.

Mirza Ghalib's couplet stated in the epigram:

> I asked my Soul: What is Delhi?
> She replied: The world is the body and Delhi its life.[1]

sets the tone of the novel. Delhi is a site/text/persona that assumes multiple identities. The eunuch whore Bhagmati could also be seen as a metaphor for Delhi and for history simultaneously. In the very opening lines of the novel, the narrator confesses: "I return to Delhi as I return to my mistress Bhagmati. Delhi and Bhagmati have a lot in common." (i)

Delhi, trampled, destroyed, dismantled and divested of all her precious possessions, is equated with Bhagmati having met with the same fate: "Long been misused by rough people they have learnt to conceal their seductive charms under a mask of repulsive ugliness. It is only to their lovers among whom I count myself, that they reveal their true selves." (1)

The ugliness of Delhi/Bhagmati is highlighted; "To a stranger Delhi may appear like a gangrenous accretion of noisy bazaars and mean looking hovels growing round a few tumble down forts and mosques along a dead river. It is the same with Bhagmati. Those who do not know her find her unattractive." (1) He affirms his liaison with Bhagmati/Delhi when he writes: "What you have to do for things to appear different is to cultivate a sense of belonging to Delhi and an attachment to someone like Bhagmati." (1)

The narrator's oedipal relationship with Delhi/Bhagmati could be gauged in the lines: "I detest living in Delhi and I am ashamed of my liaison with Bhagmati, I cannot keep away from either for too long." (2) The psychological ambivalence explodes into a confession that marks the end of the novel: "I am beginning to tire of Bhagmati as I am of Delhi. One of these days when I have enough money, I will buy myself a one way ticket to London . . . and slip out of Delhi without telling Bhagmati." (315) But later concedes: "I no longer want to buy myself an air ticket . . . get away from Bhagmati and Delhi. I told you once you are in their clutches there is no escape." (315)

The narrative is imploded with tales recounted in the first person of Emperors, untouchables, poets, saints, sahebs and a myriad of people who have participated in and have been witness to the major historical forces that have shaped Delhi. I find Singh sharing stance of history with Rushdie who questions; "Is history to be considered the property of the participants only."[2]

Both show concern with the plight of the common man. What it meant for a plebeian to "be" in a historical epoch. The "nonhistorical" or the fictional characters are constantly lurking in the foreground, countering the "memory" of the history. The historical characters set the stage, on which the imaginary characters move about. In the gradual unwinding of the novel we watch the drama of love and passion, laughter and tears of a set of puny figures whom history has not cared to remember. As the first flashback takes us to the scribe Masaddial who recalls his ancestors who had been scribes and had served Raja Anangal, Prithvi Raj and Sultan Qutubuddin Aibak. These historical facts are assimilated with incidents regarding his own life. He writes of Balban, when the Emperor's eldest son died: "The mighty Sultan who had ruled Hindustan for twenty two years with an iron hand wept like a woman." (63)

Masaddilal paints the perversities of King Qutubuddin Mubarak Shah and Khusro Khan and portrays them as degenerate transvestite. Thus showing how one sodomite catamite followed another to the throne.

The next flight into the past takes us to the memoirs of Taimurid coming alive. History describes him: "The wealth of India naturally excited the temptation to invade this land, for which the disintegration of the Delhi Kingdom afforded him a suitable opportunity. He used his championship of faith as a pretext to win support of the nobles and warriors, who were not in favour of his mediated invasion of this distant land."[3] Taimur writes: "Our object in undertaking the invasion of Hindustan was to bring infidels to the path of true religion and to purify the country from the filth of polytheism and idolatry." (96)

One may identify the tongue-in-cheek attitude of the narrator reporting the event. The hegemony has always sanctified and justified its surreptitious and devious designs. It is one of the "sensational designs"[4] for which the class in power politics has to indulge in order to exercise control over their subjects. The truth gets displaced in the form of a subterfuge.

Delhi casts a garish and glaring light on the historic/histrionic performances of the Badshahs like Jahangir and Shah Jahan. One feels amused at the autobiographical version of an untouchable: "The badshah [Jahangir] could drink twenty cups of arrack and eat tolas of opium every day and yet poke his queen and the other women of harem every night." (124)

The emperors are divested of their traditional aura and dignity. The exposé of *harem* life trivializes them, erodes their facade of nobility, they appear licentious, debauch, dedicated to the surfeit of their libido. Interestingly, Aurangzeb is presented asserting his authority over history: "Misguided historians have written many falsehoods about the way we came to acquire sovereignty over Hindustan while our father Emperor Shah Jahan was still alive. They have maligned our name as a scheming self seeker and a plotter." (151) Yet his intrusion in history can be seen as a foil to history, both keen on serving personal goals never disinterested.

The illustrations of the interweaving of personal reflection, historical information and anecdotal format conjures the carnivalesque in history. The loot and plunder of Nadir Shah is succinctly stated in his own words: "Those who remonstrated were brought before us, we had them flogged in front of their kinsmen . . . their women stripped naked. Many, unable to face themselves after the chastisement they had received, ended their miserable existence with their own hands. Gold and silver and precious stones flowed into our treasury as the waters of oxus flows into the sea." (187)

The crass profligacy, sexual excess juxtaposed with religious fanaticism of the Muslim emperors described in *Delhi*, calls for finding a parallel in Singh's *A Train to Pakistan:* "All through the Muslim period of Indian history, sons had imprisoned or killed their own fathers and brothers had blinded brothers to get the throne. And what had they done to the Sikhs? Executed two of their Gurus, assassinated another and butchered his infant children; hundred of thousands had been put to the sword for no other offense than refusing to accept Islam."[5]

History is made piquant and pungent, not the dust dreary reconstruction of a pedant but warm beatings excitingly alive. We have Meer Taqi Meer recounting his life as a poet and a lover of Begum Sahiba, who had spun a web of intrigue to ensnare him. The narratives of Alice Aldwell, Bahadur Shah Zafar, Nihal Singh and Rama Rakha from 1857 provide a panorama of the time by synthesizing the great entities with non-entities. For the Mirza and his eunuch it is a feather in their cap, a fetishism long harboured and enacted with brutality: "It's been my heart's greatest desire to make love to a white woman . . . Mirza Sahib. I have to thank you for fulfilling my ambition."

The account of a white woman's molestation is not found in history and Alice's revelation could be seen as the suppressed, tabooed issues in history: "Confusion and shame together describe what I passed through that afternoon. I narrate what happened to me so that the world knows how rotten, villainous, treacherous, degraded and lecherous these Indians are." (256)

Bahadur Shah bemoans the insults suffered at the hands of the British who ask him, "Budha man where are all your young wives?" (311) The trauma of dispossession wounded his sensitive soul and Singh's novel finely transcribes his rendering in verse the unrelieved melancholy:

> My beloved tormented me so much
> We were forced to leave our native land;
> As drops wax from the burning taper
> So we quit the circle of life
> Fell tears from our eyes
> The gardener forbade us sporting in his garden
> With laughter we came,
> With wailing we parted. (313)

Nihal Singh's version subverts the popularly revered notions of the freedom struggle: "They talked of Satyagrah and ahimsa but gloated over bombing and political murder" (342) further derogatively refers them as: "Freedom Fighters, my foot; . . . hired yellers of slogans who spent more comfortable time in jails than in their own hovels. And now want to be compensated with life pensions." (345)

Delhi's history is presented through a rich pageantry of variegated colours. The time is shortened, tampered, broken and finally disjointed, but with immaculate balance and proportion. The protagonists are misplaced and replaced, comprising a "backstairs" view of Gandhi's role as a politician. He is variously described by Ram Rakha: "Gandhi is our enemy number one," "Gandhi is a double fraud," "Gandhi did not like military tamasha, he has his own special kind of Tamasha," "When the old man comes out for his afternoon meeting he seems very happy, and why not he has one arm resting on one girl, the other on another." One may view Ram Rakha's opinion as the narrator's design. The intellectuals of Singh's generation and 'Style' have made their political stance by stirring controversy around the deified historic figures. The novel reaches its climax with the chaos and carnage triggered by the assassination of Indira Gandhi.

Singh's involvement with truth telling takes outrageous forms in his blunt depiction of the voyeuristic fantasies of the Emperors. I am however inclined to see this penchant as obsession—an excess that undermines the serious intent of the work. The slickly drawn vivid descriptions appear to be competing and defeating Salman Rushdie.

To articulate the past historically, does not mean to recognize the way it really was. The repressed portion of history is relocated. The text seems to be liberating itself from the high seriousness of history—the protocol of historical convention. History is parodied, transvestied and travestied. The novel could be hailed as Singh's significant contribution to Indian English fiction for its erudite content and insightful recreation. In comparison to many other novelists of the late eighties and early nineties, Delhi displays intellectual content. The author's sensitive grip on history, its ramification make an impression upon the reader.

NOTES

1. Khushwant Singh, *Delhi* (New Delhi: Penguin, 1990).
2. Salman Rushdie, *Shame* (Calcutta: Rupa, 1983), p. 28.
3. Majumdar, Ray Chaudhari and Dutta, *An Advanced History of India* (Madras: Macmillan, 1976), p. 328.
4. Jane Tompkins, Preface to *The Sensational Design: The Cultural Work of American Fiction* (New York: O.U.P., 1985).
5. Khushwant Singh, *A Train to Pakistan* (Bombay: Pearl, 1967), p. 106.

Trapped in Sexuality: An Analysis of *The Company of Women*

P.S. KASTURE

Khushwant Singh is one of the most significant contemporary Indian English novelists. A lawyer by vocation, he took to writing as a profession after Partition. Though Khushwant Singh has always been a prolific writer, he claims to write under compulsion, "The decision to write comes at the same time as when one has found something compelling to write about. I can best illustrate this theme from my own career as a writer."[1] He has to his credit a few famous novels like *Train to Pakistan*, ample journalistic writing with remarkable and highly popular column 'With Malice towards One and All,' a lot of translation work and an excellent history of the Sikhs. He is noted for his sharp writing as his equally sharp wit. He minces few words, spares no one and believes he is the best. He is always in the news if not for his writing then for his social comments. Presently with his latest novel *The Company of Women* (1999) he has once again evoked an extremely controversial response.

He is immensely popular, but controversy is something he revels in, the more the better. In "Provoking people has become part of my character," Pavan Varma unpeels the mask and gets to real Khushwant Singh: "his new book, *The Company of Women*, has just exploded on India's fairly moribund literary horizon. I recall having told him the book was capable of giving a hard-on to any healthy man. He laughed and said it could be a good substitute for Viagra."[2]

It has been pointed out by Purabi Panwar that his *Train to Pakistan* has a depth of feeling unsurpassed in his later works, his next famous novel *Delhi* also contextualises the city in an original and interesting manner, but *The Company of Women* does not compare with either of them,

> He agreed and said that every period in one's life has an obsession. "I was obsessed with Partition when I wrote *Train to Pakistan*. The novel *Delhi* was born out of an obsession with the city. Similarly *The Company of Women* was also born of an obsession." Khushwant Singh gave me the example of a novel by Muriel Spark called *Memento Mori* which was about fantasies of old people who lived in a home for the aged.
>
> But why does Mohan Kumar, the main character die of AIDS at the end of the novel? The end is so very abrupt and dissatisfying and hardly in keeping with the general mood of enjoyment in the book. Khushwant grinned broadly and answered with his usual candor. "I did not know how to kill him. This seemed a fitting end to reckless philandering."
>
> I point out that any group working towards prevention of AIDS would find it useful. "It could be made compulsory in such a case and that would add to my royalty," he says with a grin.[3]

To Makarand Paranjape this sizzling new novel of Khushwant Singh is easy to read and just as easy to forget. It is neither erotic nor funny but only sad. He comes down heavily upon Khushwant Singh for the unconvincing end.

> Kumar's lovers usually entreat him, "For God's sake, don't stop." Readers, of course, might wish for just the opposite. Sensing this, Singh brings the novel to a rather abrupt and unconvincing end. Kumar gets AIDS, all in a matter of just six months, from one unprotected encounter in Mumbai, and soon dies. I find this a clumsy finale. It is also a trifle dishonest: condemning lasciviousness at the end after revelling in it throughout.[4]

Hasan Suroor has no doubt about the saleability of the book but he regards it as a stigma on Khushwant Singh.

> At 85, Khushwant Singh has written a novel that should go down as this millennium's last great Indian, lascivious novel. *The Company of Women* from the first lustful glance to the last grunt, not to mention the atmospherics in between. . . .
>
> There is no doubt that cash registers are going to ring until the last copy is sold, but is that all Khushwant Singh's last (?) novel should be remembered for? Here is hoping he will write something to redeem his "Company of Women."[5]

Dubbed as the original 'Dirty Old Man,' Khushwant Singh is actually far from so, says V. Sudershan in "Old yes, but 'dirty' no."[6] In an interview with Suchitra Behal, Khushwant Singh claims the *Company* is entire fantasy. He heard of that sort of a person who indulged in various liaisons after a broken marriage. The outline was there, the rest is dictated by an evolving character. But G. Rajaraman is shocked with Khushwant Singh's fantasies. The book is indeed, as the flap jacket advertises, uninhibited and erotic, but not an entertaining celebration of love. Far from it. It is what Khushwant Singh claims it is: the sexploits of Mohan Kumar are the result of senile fantasies. Khushwant Singh feels if a writer does not write, his pen is rusted by disuse. "A writer's work is never done till he dies. . . If he stops writing, he feels frustrated and often finds his pen has rusted."[7] To Rajaraman *Company* is an evidence of rust in Khushwant Singh and he desires to be spared of Khushwant Singh's fantasies.

> Khushwant Singh is true to his word, drawing out his colourful fantasies from the grey cells in black and white and attempting quite successfully to change his image of a gifted story teller. . . . One isn't overly concerned by his penchant for the libidinous, but there is clear evidence of rust. . . .

> After *The Company of Women*, it is hard not to ask: why does Khushwant Singh not put his pen away in the remotest corner of his cupboard? . . . Indeed, Khushwant Singh has astonished us with his choice. In the twilight of his career as a writer, he would well have done without making his fantasies public.[8]

II

Khushwant Singh presents man not as a figment of spirit, but as a being with a body who lives with all his elemental passions. Naturally sex-lust-sex has always been present in his fictional world.

Jugga in *Train to Pakistan* (1956) is a man of flesh and blood. His love for his sweet-heart Nooran is not only spiritual but equally physical.

> His hand strayed from the girl's face to her breasts and her waist . . . slipped his hand inside her shirt and felt the contours of her unguarded breasts. They became taut. The nipples became hard and leathery. His rough hands gently moved up and down from her breasts to her navel.[9]

R.K. Dhawan perceptively talks about Khushwant Singh's provoking tendency as a revolt against the established norms. "Khushwant Singh wants to shock and provoke existing norms of Victorian morality, which he must have been discomforted by in his younger days."[10]

Khushwant Singh's second novel *I Shall Not Hear the Nightingale* (1959) based on the war years (1942-43), once again, has sexual theme intertwined with the political one. Sher Singh's wife—the tempestuous, sex-hungry Champak strikes a contrast with the traditional morality embodied in Sabhrai, her mother-in-law. Here, too, Khushwant Singh does not lag behind in providing all possible details of her sex-hungry indulgence. "She wore a close fitting Punjabi dress which accentuated the largeness of her bosom and narrowness of her waist."[11] She shaves her private parts and revels in observing her nude body standing before the dressing-table mirror. Champak seeks sexual satisfaction in her amorous flirtation with Madan Lal.

> He undid the top button of her shirt and let his hands slip on to her warm, rounded breasts. She turned her face up to him; their mouths met with hungry passion. (113)

Peer Sahib is a pseudo holy man who combines spiritual ministrations with medicine. He seduces simple women like Shunno, a domestic servant in the household of Buta Singh. "The holy man turned and saw a fat middle-aged woman lying bare from the navel to her ankles . . . the infidel woman has perfumed her privates. . . . He explored the depths with his fingers." (140-41) As a sociologist, Khushwant Singh locates this perversion of mind in India rooted in inhibited and repressed sex. "Unfulfilled sexual impulses result in an obsession with sex."[12]

Sex is the principal driving force in the life of Mohan Kumar in Khushwant Singh's *The Company of Women* (1999). The book traces Mohan Kumar's amorous adventures in full detail. Not only the title of the book, but even the chapter names (Dhanno, Sarojini, Jessica Browne, Yasmeen . . .) indicate that the book is an account of Mohan Kumar's relationship with various women.

Mohan Kumar's sex life does not begin with Dhanno. He has been initiated long back at Princeton by Jessica Browne. When Mohan Kumar admires Jessica's figure, she questions, "Want to see what I'm really like?" and strips herself off. She takes him to her bed, pulls him over her. Mohan Kumar vividly recalls how he lost his virginity at twenty.

> This was first time and I spent myself, moaning helplessly, almost as I entered her. I had never imagined sex could be so thrilling. But I wished it had lasted longer.[13]

He thinks his friendship with Jessica will hold as long as he is in the States, but it does not last long beyond spring. When he sees her go out with another boy, he feels "a stab of jealousy in my heart" (95) and then begins an unending sex game.

> Many were eager to date me. So I wrote Jessica off my list of dates and went on a rampage like a stud bull in a herd of cows on heat. I lost count of the girls I bedded. (95)

He only remembers "a most bizarre experience" with Yasmeen.

After thirteen years of troublesome marriage, Mohan Kumar gets separated from his wife. He has everything except a happy home and satisfying sex. To celebrate his newly won freedom, he decides to reinvent his life. Convinced that 'lust is the true foundation of love,' he embarks upon an audacious plan to advertise for paid lady companions to share his bed and his life on temporary basis. Thus begins his journey of easy, unbridled sexuality in the company of some remarkable women, says the front cover flap.

> There is Sarojini Bhardwaj, the demure professor from small town Haryana who surprises Mohan with her ardour and sexual energy. Molly Gomes, the free spirited masseuse from Goa, mistress of the sensual impulse; and Susanthika Goonatilleke, the diminutive seductress from Sri Lanka. After each affair ends and before the next begins, Mohan Kumar finds solace in the practised charms of his obliging maid, Dhanno, and in the memories of his first loves: the American Jessica Browne to whom he lost his virginity and the Pakistani Yasmeen Wanchoo, who brought him the heady passion of an older woman.

Mohan Kumar never tires in re-living, as it were, every physical detail of each encounter.

> Each time Mohan made love to a new body, it was like exploring a new landscape. Women were much the same in their essentials but enchantingly different in detail. Dhanno's body had a musky odour unlike his wife's which always smelt of French cologne. (23)

With Sarojini, once again, the same round of 'Let's have a dekho,' beginning with slipping gown, round breasts, ending in 'the ecstasy of a multiple orgasm' (48) or 'Oh God, this is heaven heaven heaven' (222) with Molly Gomes or, 'By God, that was the greatest fuck I've had in my life' (271) for Susanthika.

III

Khushwant Singh's basic concern as a novelist has been the need to find the meaning of human existence in man's struggle against various negative forces. In spite of the loss of values in traumatic situations, Khushwant Singh is able to shore the essential human element, often surging from an unexpected corner.

He was distressed and disillusioned due to the crisis of values in Partition. The myth of the innate goodness in man was exploded. His belief that Indians are more spiritual and hence more peace-loving and non-violent was shattered. As a result he became "an angry middle-aged man, who wanted to shout his disenchantment with the world. . . . I decided to try my hand at writing."[14] *Train to Pakistan*, with scathing irony and stark realism, exposes sordidness, wickedness and savage cruelties in human life. It also sounds a note of affirmation through the values of love, loyalty and humanism. The most ruffian 'badmash' Jugga, though a creation of the author's imagination ("the only character which is entirely fiction"[15]), is presented saving the situation even at the cost of his own life.

Khushwant Singh's *I Shall Not Hear the Nightingale* deals with various polarities in the family of a Sikh magistrate, Buta Singh. Buta Singh is a moderate nationalist, a strong supporter of the British Raj but his son Sher Singh is a staunch nationalist. The family pragmatically inherits this split in loyalty. Another polar pair is Sher Singh's amorous wife Champak and his pious mother Sabhrai.

Sher Singh looks to his political career as a way to impress Champak and cover his failure to satisfy her strong urge for sex. Sher Singh's terrorist activities land him in criminality. Taylor, an Englishman, assures full help to Buta Singh, if Sher Singh confesses his crime and gives the names of his accomplices. Though torture and humiliation in police custody demoralize Sher

Singh, his uneducated mother's moral strength saves him from committing another great wrong of treason.

> My son had done wrong. But if he named the people who were with him he would be doing a great wrong. He was no longer to be regarded as a Sikh and I was not to see his face again. (208-9)

Though sex appears, in both the novels, as an elemental force that shapes human drives, Khushwant Singh locates the source of human essence in love—a sense of relatedness in *Train to Pakistan* and moral strength of character in *I Shall Not Hear the Nightingale.* Now, it remains to be seen if Khushwant Singh in *The Company of Women* is able to give anything beyond physical passion.

From the memoirs of Mohan Kumar emerges a human figure who is cursed with lust but also has some good qualities of head and heart. He is a clever student with special aptitude for arithmetic. He is gifted with a good memory. He wins a state scholarship to DAV college. He tops the university in the degree examinations and wins a scholarship to Princeton. He does well in his studies. He finishes his final year at Princeton and stays another year to do an advanced course in finance.

> As a sophomore I was the only one in my class to be admitted to Phi Beta Kappa, and in my final exam I was the only Princetonian to earn a summa cum laude, the highest academic distinction anyone could earn in any American university. (114)

He is much attached to his father. From Princeton he writes to his father almost every week and sends him money every month. In spite of a bright opening in America he comes back for his father. "I would not abandon him in his old age." (116) After coming to Delhi, Mohan Kumar goes along with whatever his father wants him to do. Though he does not like the social system, for his father's insistence he remains "a mute spectator, eyeing one girl after another." (126) For his father's satisfaction he visits Haridwar to have a dip in the holy Ganga as an act of penance. With Sonu's resentment his father shifts to Haridwar Though Mohan Kumar cannot stop his father, he sticks to his resolve of being in Haridwar on full moon nights with his father. He makes Sonu accept his father's stay for four/five days of the month with them. Because of his father's sudden death, Mohan Kumar cannot attend him. His sorrow over losing his father turns into sour resentment against Sonu who has treated him so shabbily. He has no forgiveness left in him and resolves to lead his life as he pleases.

Though he comes from a middle-class family, he does not depend upon his rich father-in-law. On his own he becomes a successful businessman—a young millionaire. He is a good master, caring for his employees and appreciating their work and loyalty, not only in his active life, but also provides for them in his will.

> The first charge on his estate was Rs. 50,000 in cash to be given to the people who had served him faithfully—his cook, the bearer, the driver Jiwan Ram and Vimla Sharma. . . . His car was left to Jiwan Ram who had served him longer than the other servants. (293)

He is a loving father. The day his son is born, he names his new house after him—'Ranjit Villa.' He and his son are deeply attached to each other.

> He looked forward to my coming home in the evenings and clung to me till it was time for him to have supper and be put to bed. He insisted on my telling him stories till sleep overtook him. (194)

His daughter Mohini is born six years after Ranjit. He loves his children deeply and for their sake tries to keep the marriage going. Ultimately he is exasperated and gives up. Sonu goes to her father's house with the children. Later when he wants to see them often, they are not receptive to his advances.

> Sonu had thoroughly brainwashed them. I was a bad man who had done the dirty on their mother . . . they did not enjoy their visits and wanted to get back as soon as I let them. I gave them expensive gifts; they accepted them without enthusiasm. . . . Mohini showed a little more affection for me but was scared of her bother sneaking to her mother. (275-76)

In his will he left his property to his two children equally.

Though his response to other human relationships is normal and natural, Mohan Kumar is not successful in his domestic life. His married life is most unhappy. His wife, Sonu, is sadist and revengeful. In spite of his sex adventures at Princeton, he tries to begin his married life anew with no hankering back, but Sonu has no desire either to develop or continue that relationship. She always finds fault with him, never responds to any of his efforts to be happy. Instead of welcoming the happy surprise of their new house 'Ranjit Villa' and all the arrangement done by Mohan Kumar, Sonu is most dissatisfied and overtly critical. As a result, Mohan Kumar is also extremely dejected.

> 'All I have to do is to eat what is offered to me, sleep with you when I'm expected to and be the wet-nurse for my own child.'
>
> I was exasperated. 'Is there anything I do which pleases you? I've done all this to make you happy. All the thanks I get is a barrage of criticism.' (174)

She makes his life impossible. He cannot even enjoy his evening drinks and TV. He slowly drifts away from her. Sonu's keeping him away for months before and after delivery, tries Mohan Kumar's patience. "Sonu would not let me come near her. . . . I had not had proper sex for over six months. Another six months of abstinence would be hard on a lustful man like me." (176) One night he falls for Mary Joseph and then there is no end to it.

It is true that Mohan Kumar has an exceptionally strong urge for sex. His personal life seems to be entirely governed by his sex instincts. For example, sex decides his choice of Sonu.

> Ultimately, it was fantasizing about deflowering Sonu, the haughty little memsahib, and having her in bed whenever I wanted to that made me decide in favour of accepting the offer. (139)

Still he truly assures Sarojini: "I'm not a sex maniac." (47) Only at Princeton he is made aware by the boys about the singularity of his sex organ. His initial reactions indicate normal Indian attitude to sex.

> I was shocked to see them strip naked and exchange obscenities about the sizes of their penises. . . . Very reluctantly I took off my shorts, . . . Very gingerly I undid my towel. . . . I knew what he meant but refused to answer what seemed to me a very vulgar question. (90-91)

But the reaction of the boys to the size of his sex organ, perhaps, makes him self and sex conscious.

> 'Holy Moses!' cried the boy. 'Look at this one. A real Hindu lingam.'
>
> I became the centre of attention. (90)

The surprised reception of his organ by every mate, as if, enthuses him further.

> 'Goodness gracious me!' she chortled. 'Where on earth did you buy that one? Black boys have bigger dicks than the whites but yours is bigger than any I've seen. (93)

This new awareness may have given him a sense of superiority. As penis is the thing that differentiates a man from a woman, it is regarded as a sign of his manhood. When the ancients wished to represent the life-giving power of the Sun and the action of this power on all living creatures, they adopted the emblem of masculinity, called by the Greeks 'phallus.' It is this source of energy, stored more conspicuously in the male than in the female throughout nature, that induces man with a sense of living God in him, having realized his Self. Naturally Mohan Kumar unconsciously starts identifying his manhood with his sex-adventures. Because of this misconception, he is not able to accept the decline of sex desire as a natural sign of adult life. Normally a man with advancing age outgrows the hungers of youth, but Mohan Kumar is, as if, trapped in sexuality.

> The most difficult thing Mohan Kumar had to deal with in his adult life was the loss of his sex drive. . . . He tried the wildest of fantasies. . . . There was no response. He did not like this. Sex was the most important thing in his life: with the sex urge gone, there was little left for him to look forward to. . . . But he could not accept impotence as natural in a man not yet fifty who had lived such a full sexual life. (279)

When he is able to enjoy sex in Bombay, he is happy that he has not gone 'kaput.' Once again he recovers his zest for life. Though sex has lost its urgency, he is content that he can rise to the occasion. When he comes back to Delhi, he starts enjoying evenings with his friends. When the wife of one of his friends asks him the reason—lottery, another million, new sweetheart?

> 'All those and more,' he replied and added cryptically, 'I have rediscovered my manhood.' (283)

Ultimately it is this obsession with sex that leads him to his doom. He recklessly exposes himself to an unsafe sexual contact and becomes HIV positive. When he has AIDS, he ends his life with sleeping pills.

IV

Like his other novels, Khushwant Singh deals with elemental human passions in his *The Company of Women* too. So here too the seed is equally promising. In *Company* the main theme is sex. Khushwant Singh is not the first author in the history of man to write about sex. There are authors like D.H. Lawrence who deal with more controversial aspects of the experience. But they are not trapped in sexuality as Khushwant Singh is in *Company*. They explore psyche through sex. They deal not only with human body but with man As Chaman Nahal says:

> 'Phallic consciousness' has a sort of symbolic meaning with Lawrence which need not necessarily refer to the sexual moments alone of our life and which covers the whole span of our existence, organic and inorganic. Applied to sex, it would mean an implicit acceptance of the power and the glory of the body and a sense of love for this power and glory. Virility is one of its aspects, but that it passes beyond virility and is with Lawrence more a projection of the beauty of the union is obvious from the tenderness, from the softness of his theme of marriage.[16]

Khushwant Singh successfully deals with sex in his earlier novels like *Train* and *Nightingale*. There is no contention to forbid Khushwant Singh to write about sex as he is an old man now. It must, however, be remembered that *Company* is projected not as a journalistic report of Mohan Kumar's sex adventures, but as a work of art—'his first novel in ten years.'

In *Company* Khushwant Singh seems to stick only to the surface level, giving a factual account of each encounter with all possible details. It seems that he revels in the very act of description. An artist's ability to recreate essential reality that lies beyond the solid seeming wall of reality endows his work with multiple meanings. But Khushwant Singh seems, in *Company*, to be lured by the banal description.

There is no compulsion for Khushwant Singh to treat sex only in a particular standardized way. He surely has a full claim to the artist's freedom of creation. But he must also be quite clear about the nature of his creation—a work of art or otherwise and the consequent responsibilities. Not only Mohan Kumar is obsessed with sexuality, but Khushwant Singh is also obsessed with overt exposure. The repetition of the same details does not achieve any additional effect.

Though sex is a physical action, it is also related to human psyche, and personality as a whole. It is not the companionship that Mohan Kumar seeks; only the company, not of a human being of opposite sex, but of female body just for mating. As a result, this long line of paramours points to no development or awareness in Mohan Kumar. It only confirms his belief that lust rather than love shapes human life. "Love cannot last very long without lust. Lust has no time limit and is the true foundation of love and affection." But Mohan Kumar consciously lives only on the level of lust, guarding himself from any attachment. "As soon as I sensed a girl was getting emotionally involved in me, I dropped her." Mohan Kumar's approach to sex and his identification of manhood with sex drive tragically ends his life.

Such allegations as Khushwant Singh kills Mohan Kumar abruptly, that the end is unconvincing or that he is unable to do anything else with Mohan Kumar, so he kills him are answered by the natural result of an erroneous value-scale. At the same time to say that *Company* is a documentary highlighting the evil effects of licentious sex is too simplistic. Mohan Kumar's dual awareness is a significant pointer to Khushwant Singh's attitude. When Dr. Malhotra tells Mohan Kumar that he is HIV positive; a pall of gloom envelopes Mohan Kumar. He rebukes his 'baby python' with a stream of expletives, but "He was reminded of all the pleasure he had known in life, and knew that he only had this little snake to thank for all of it. He felt stupid." (291)

'Author's Note' for *Company* declares, "No characters in this expose are real: they are figments of my senile fantasies." Perhaps, with his sharp wit, Khushwant Singh senses a possible attack. Whatever may be his aim or his justification or explanation, a work of art stands on its own. It is a self-existing and self-sufficing world to be understood and judged by its own norms. *The Company of Women* may prove to be the most provocative and sensational of Khushwant Singh's creations.

NOTES

1. Khushwant Singh, "Compulsions to Write," *Explorations in Modern Indian-English Fiction*, ed. R.K. Dhawan (New Delhi: Bahri, 1982), p. 184.
2. Pavan K. Varma, "Writers' Dialogue," *The Hidustan Times*, Oct. 3, 1999.
3. Purabi Panwar, "Confessions of an Old Teenager," *Pioneer*, Saturday, Sep. 25, 1999.
4. Makarand Paranjape, "Khushwant Singh's One-Night Stand," *The Express Magazine*, Sep. 19, 1999.
5. Hasan Suroor, "Khushwant Singh's Great Fling," *Hindu*.
6. V. Sudarshan, "Close-up," *Hindu*, Sep. 19, 1999.
7. Khushwant Singh, "Compulsions to Write," p. 186
8. G. Rajaraman, "Khushwant, Spare Us Your Fantasies," *The Hindustan Times*, Oct. 3, 1999.
9. Khushwant Singh, *Train to Pakistan* (Bombay: India Book House, 1976), p. 12.
10. R.K. Dhawan, "The Artist as Historian: Some New Writers," in *Commonwealth Fiction*, ed. R.K. Dhawan (New Delhi: Classical, 1988), Vol. 3. p. 253.
11. Khushwant Singh, *I Shall Not Hear the Nightingale* (Bombay: IBH, 1983), p. 162.
12. *Commonwealth Fiction*, Vol. 3, p. 258.
13. Khushwant Singh, *The Company of Women* (New Delhi: Viking Penguin India, 1999), p. 93.
14. Khushwant Singh, The transcript of a talk for the Australian Broadcasting Commission's *Guest of Honour* Programme, broadcast on 5th April, 1964. *Commonwealth Fiction*, Vol. 1, p. 162.
15. *Commonwealth Fiction*, vol. 1, p. 163.
16. Chaman Nahal, *D.H. Lawrence: An Eastern View* (Delhi: Atma Ram, 1971), p. 123.

The Fantasy-Erotica Paradox in *The Company of Women*

NOVY KAPADIA

Is the novel *The Company of Women* (1999) autobiographical or is it a work of fantasy and adultery? Is the book an uninhibited, erotic and endlessly entertaining celebration of love, sex and passion or is it a parody of the hedonistic upper middle class urban society of Delhi? Can this book be compared to the celebrated novels of Shobha De because of the frank and candid expressions of love and lust and uninhibited employment of salacious detail? Is it sheer pornography, a mediocre novel or a swan song gone wrong? These are some of the various questions raised by the fourth novel of the "Ancient Mariner" of Indian writing in English. Viewed in the context of public and critical reactions and acclaim, Khushwant Singh's novel is a grand success. It has aroused extreme reactions, contrasting critical viewpoints, high visibility and subsequently successful sales. The novel got orders for over 10,000 copies before the first book appeared in print. For several weeks it topped the list of most read and most sold fiction in India, as is evident from the TOP 10 Fiction list published by *The Hindustan Times*. As a novel it is difficult to categorise. The immediate reaction is to label it as "Khushwant Singh's great fling." (*The Hindu*, Sunday, October 3, 1999) In the review, erudite critic Hasan Suroor says, "At 85 Khushwant Singh has written a novel that should go down as this millenium's last great Indian lascivious novel." (X) From the first lustful glance to the last grunt, this novel has elements of fantasy, erotica and seduction. The narrative is racy, though the prose admittedly lacks the fluency and subtlety of his earlier novels *Train to Pakistan*

(1956) and *Delhi* (1989). It also lacks the seriousness of tone and theme of his earlier novels and his scholarly work on the history of the Sikhs. But maybe this is what Khushwant Singh wants to achieve. At one level the novel lives up to Khushwant Singh's deliberately cultivated image of a man obsessed with sex and scotch. The novel is an apt outpouring of the public persona of India's most successful syndicated columnist. Dubbed as the 'Original Dirty Old Man,' Khushwant Singh is often a victim of his public image. In an interview with Suchitra Behal, Khushwant Singh has admitted that such labels have stuck to him because of his journalistic writings. He says, "Since I laughed loudly, praised good looking women and the wine I drunk, people chose to call me that—It hurts." (xiv) Talking to Samita Bhatia, Khushwant Singh has admitted that he is multi-dimensional, "certainly not one-track."

The reality is quite different. Khushwant Singh is a restless, prolific and disciplined writer still active and creative at an age when most people either indulge in maudlin nostalgia or get extremely religious or complain endlessly of aching limbs and muscles. He has written several scholarly works such as the *History of the Sikhs,* a biography of Maharaja Ranjit Singh, translations from Urdu classics, poetry and excellent prose articles on nature and politics. He has been a successful journalist. As editor of *Illustrated Weekly* magazine for a decade since 1969 and later as editor of *The Hindustan Times* in the 1980s, Khushwant Singh became a legend in Indian journalism for the gamut of subjects that he wrote about. Yet the pubic image of a rollicking Sardar who loves his Scotch and women prevails. Khushwant Singh himself is surprised at the prevailing public image and the fact that the maximum royalty he gets is from his several joke books. Now in the twilight of his career, Khushwant Singh tries to rationalise about the difference between his public image and his private self. Typically Khushwant Singh is not hesitant to ruffle a few feathers in offering his analysis to Samita Bhatia. He says flatly, "Being an iconoclast I write very openly about things. And Indians being constipated with humbug pick up with what suits them. They enjoy running people down more than praising them. It is not entertaining enough to call a person a serious scholar. But to call him a drunkard and debauch is far more interesting." (Bhatia, 7) Similar sentiments are expressed in an interview with Pavan K. Verma in the series, "Writers in Dialogue." Khushwant Singh admits, "this is a country which has so many sanctimonious humbugs that if you write or speak openly about drinks or about women, they think you are a drunkard or a womaniser." (6) Later in the same interview, Khushwant Singh explains his outlook on life: "They must know that a man of my age with so much output in writing doesn't have time. He can't afford to get drunk. He can't afford to waste time on women. I work from 4.30 in the morning till 7 p.m." (6) In the introduction to this interview, Pavan Verma upholds a similar view that there is a lot of difference between the public image of Khushwant Singh and the actual man himself. Pavan Verma writes, "For all his cultivated image of a debauch, I know with long association that I am meeting a disciplined workaholic. For a book I am editing on New Delhi, his 4000 word chapter came in first and dot on the deadline. He's a stickler for time and amazingly prolific as a writer even at the age of 85." (6)

Throughout his career Khushwant Singh has been an iconoclast. He minces no words and spares no one. He has come to accept the contradiction between his public image and his actual lifestyle and attitudes to life. By writing a novel of sexploits and the voyeuristic view of male and female anatomy and titillating accounts of the innumerable sexual encounters, Khushwant Singh is parodying all the religious and moral taboos and codes of social respectability imposed on individuals in contemporary Indian society. By cleverly presenting and highlighting masculine fantasies about seductive women, the crafty old man of Indian English fiction could thus be having a last laugh at the pomposity and sanctimonious morality of middle class India. His works have always provoked extreme reaction. The novel, *The Company of Women* is in keeping with that trend. Khushwant Singh's agenda for this novel could thus be an exposure of middle class morality and moral hypocrisy that in his interview with Pavan Verma he has termed as "middle class Victorianism." (6) Shiela Reddy in her review of the book has appropriately called it. "The Truth about a Dirty Old Society." (7)

In the brief Author's Note, a sort of preface, the 'Grand Old Man' of Indian English fiction says,

> I started writing this novel when I was eighty-three. I finished it at eighty-five. An equally apt title for it would be: 'The Fantasies of an Octogenarian.' No characters in this expose are real; they are figments of my senile Fantasies. (1)

Khushwant Singh's novel, like his celebrated syndicated columns, has aroused controversy and numerous comments and reactions. In the interview with Suchitra Behal, Khushwant Singh categorically denies that this novel is autobiographical: "Oh no, it is far from it. It is entire fantasy." (xiv) The Author's Note is a kind of a disclaimer. The author stresses that the fantasies are only an attempt to catch up with lost time. He admits, "as man gets older, his sex instincts travel from his middle to his head." So the life of his protagonist Mohan Kumar fulfills the wishful fantasies of many young men who are often unable to indulge in such passionate, amorous adventures because of nervousness, lack of response or opportunity. Thus Khushwant Singh's novel is a parody of the social taboos of society which restrict the natural yearnings of youth and consider a natural desire like sex as something vulgar and obscene. What Khushwant Singh implies is that many men have the same desires as his protagonist Mohan Kumar but are unable to fulfill them. He also suggests that the veneer of morality is only skin deep. Due to social restrictions, many young Indian men and women curb their passions and they give it a cloak of respectability by masking it with taboos of religion and tradition. So it is a novel of exposure. The novel also parodies middle class aspirations, the concept of arranged marriages in India which are often akin to business bargains and the desire for scandalous gossip of the urban elite. Through the introspection of his protagonist Mohan Kumar, the author cleverly parodies the concept of arranged marriage. As his marriage is collapsing Mohan Kumar starts ruminating about the institution of marriage as the "sacrosanct bonding for life" (26) attitude and holy status that it is given in India. He comes to the following conclusion:

> Marriages, he concluded, are not made in heaven. They are made on earth by earthlings for earthy reasons. The first priority is money: it may be property, a profitable business or a well-paid job. The couple concerned fell into line without bothering to find out whether or not the person they are committing themselves to will make a good life-long companion. (17)

Mohan Kumar concludes that even modern young children agree to arranged marriages because "their sex urges are of explosive dimensions, and they are eagerly looking forward to exploring other's bodies." (17)

In a candid exposure of arranged marriages and middle class morality, Mohan Kumar says that sexual fantasies are inevitable in arranged marriages. "The possibility of a pleasant diversion in an adulterous relationship is never far from their minds. When an opportunity guaranteeing secrecy presents itself, they succumb to it." (8)

With characteristic candour, Khushwant Singh's protagonist Mohan Kumar provides a solution which is that of an iconoclast. He says that occasional adultery did not destroy a marriage but "proved to be a cementing factor." (8) Such outrageous suggestions are used as shock therapy by Khushwant Singh to expose sanctimonious attitudes towards sex, arranged marriage and adultery in modern urban India. Thus it can be seen that the novel is not just the libidinous exploits of the main character Mohan Kumar, as is claimed by several critics. The candid exposure, used by the author, makes this novel similar to the works of Shobha De in several respects.

Celebrated critic R.S. Pathak in his learned essay, "Feminist Concerns in Shobha De's Works: A Study in Attitudes" says: "Shobha De tears to pieces all notions of respectability associated with marriage. Her women discuss and practise sex with unusual candour. All sexual taboos are broken by them with gusto. The novelist makes them put forth candidly what they always feel but are afraid and inhibited to show." (42) Pathak explains that Shobha De's unique success is not just due to her sublime skills in the art of story telling, the use of language and popularising "Hinglish" but above all in her candour about the desire for sex. "According to Shobha De, all people need sex. It is something special, something beautiful, something shared. . . . In fact sex is the bedrock of all relationships." (41) Khushwant Singh is attempting something similar in *The Company of Women*. He is exposing cant, hypocrisy, double speak, double standards and pomposity in the attitudes to sex in predominantly patriarchal urban India.

So *The Company of Women* also belongs to the tradition of the critique of society novels. Now what type of Indian society is Khushwant Singh exposing. The focus is on the urban, modernised, westernised men and women. R.S. Pathak in his essay on Shobha De says that her novels explore the world of the urban woman in India. Similarly it can be said that Khushwant Singh's *The Company of Women* explores the world of the urban Indian man in a hedonistic society which fluctuates between a life of tradition and an Americanised attitude to the body with an unIndian amorality. The type of society which Khushwant Singh depicts is aptly presented by Dipanker Gupta, a professor of Jawaharlal Nehru University, New Delhi in his article "Nor'westerly winds." Writing about Punjabi culture's present dominance in India and the route to Westernisation, Dipanker Gupta shows that demonstrative and ostentatious consumption is one aspect of this new culture. He writes, "New money is ideologically self-confident in its material possessions and is not in the least overawed by manners and customs of yore. The indicators of success have to be tangible for respect to follow." (12) Khushwant Singh's protagonist Mohan Kumar inhabits such a society. The stepping stones to success are membership of the Millionaire's Club (a group of young, prosperous and successful businessmen) and the lifestyle of five star hotels, posh clubs and material desires. "He had enough going for him in life; his company brought him over twenty lakhs every month; he had the looks and the sophistication to charm women; he was a member of three elite clubs—the Delhi Golf Club, the Gymkhana Club and the Indian International Centre." (10) Smoking imported Havana cigars, drinking

Scotch whisky and fondness for foreign cuisine are other symbols of success. Mohan Kumar belongs to the generation of Indians with changing tastebuds, who have forsaken the traditional Indian 'mithai' for tempting chocolate brownies and chocolate cherry cakes. Mohan's preference for Western cuisine is also an expression of his cosmopolitanism and departure from traditional moorings. The food and wine that he prefers also reflects the changing lifestyle of the urban elite. He fantasises about "avocado pears with chilled Pouille Fusse; wild rice with creamed mushroom sauce and juicy steaks with rich Barolo or Burgundy; trifle followed by sips of Drambuie, Cointreau, orange Curacao, Grand Marniere or Cognac." (195)

Despite all the trappings of success, Mohan Kumar remains uncertain and dissatisfied. It is the anxieties and confusions of the protagonist of such a society, like Mohan Kumar, that Khushwant Singh depicts. So the novel is not just the senile fantasies of an octogenarian but a critique of the aspirations of the Indian yuppie who remains a cultural hybrid torn between tradition and a hedonistic lifestyle. In the case of Mohan Kumar, tradition is represented by his religious father, a superintendent at Northern Railway in Delhi, dips in the holy Ganges at Hardwar and an arranged marriage with the affluent Sonu.

The storyline is simple. It is the search for the complex existential dilemma, an individual's quest for the truth of existence within society. Mohan Kumar is an Indian yuppie, the only child of a government clerk whose aspiration for a better life is hastened by a stint at Princeton University. He returns home to all the trappings of middle class success and comfort, a thriving export company, a house at Maharani Bagh, one of South Delhi's posh colonies, a wife from a wealthy family and two children. But his desire to live life to the full remains unsuccessful. Several critical reviews in newspapers and magazines have felt that Mohan Kumar is perhaps Khushwant Singh's alter ego, "an uncomplicated man whose only demand is uncomplicated sex." (Bhatia, 6) It is also felt that "the protagonist is not so much Mohan Kumar but his burgeoning sex drive." (Bhatia, 6) Whatever the interpretation, the style is racy and lucid and with few digressions. The novel begins with Mohan Kumar, a successful businessman in Delhi being jilted by his wife Sonu who is described as "quick-tempered, possessive and wanting attention all the time." (5) The hypocrisy of the urban elite and their penchant for social gossip is also exposed. After his wife returns to her parents's home, Mohan Kumar is unable to visit the posh clubs because of "the gossip in his large circle of friends." (8) There are snide remarks at the club bar and even pertinent queries about whether Sonu was out of town. Mohan tries to counter such retorts by women like Usha Malhotra with aggressive counter-attacks like, "And how are your husband and boyfriend getting along." (8) The hypocrisy of the social elite is shown when Mohan Kumar ruminates about their own married life. None of them are living a life of marital bliss.

> He knew that not one of his circle was really happy in his or her marriage. They just got along. And grumbled. Not one of them had the courage to call it off. To hell with the bloody lot! (8)

The hollowness in the social life of Delhi's elite is thoroughly exposed. They are shown as creatures of comfort, insecure and over-competitive. Their life styles are seen as comfortable but monotonous:

> The clubs or parties we went to were useless. We met the same kind of people, who drank the same kind of liquor, indulged in the same kind of small talk and bitching. All trapped in the meaningless quest for money, creature comforts and hankering for social respectability. (195)

The author thus shows how the nouveau riche and urban elite fritter away their lives in banalities. Modernisation is reflected only in consumption, not in civic consciousness or mutual respect of other human beings. Dipanker Gupta echoes similar sentiments in *The Telegraph* when writing about Punjabi culture's dominance in India. He says that for most of them, the end product of Westernisation is "a heightened drive for consumption." (12) Khushwant Singh's novel, like the popular fiction of Shobha

De, shows how the baits of money, fame and status entrap human nature and make people selfish and materialistic. The society, which Mohan Kumar inhabits, is the changing society of Delhi. The people are products of a unipolar world and a post-Manmohanomic resistance to cultural values. By proving instances of the lifestyle of the characters of the novel, Khushwant Singh makes us mentally cognizant of the play of forces of cultural politics that have penetrated into every little aspect of Indian life.

The first section of the novel deals with the estrangement from his wife and then describes Mohan Kumar's lusty efforts to set up a more flexible arrangement for his physical needs. This search for a suitable live-in partner is an audacious plan as he advertises for a paid companion to share his bed. The protagonist realises the audacity of his venture and how it would shock middle class sensibilities and hurt his estranged wife, in-laws and their family. He is also worried that "it might not fit the parameters of the matrimonial columns and might be turned down by the advertisement departments." (11) His choice of the two all-India dailies in which to insert the advertisements and the rejection of *The Hindustan Times* and *The Hindu* as being too conservative, reflect Khushwant Singh's awareness of the newspaper industry. After much contemplation the advertisement is carefully worded. Sexual desires are camouflaged. He is in search for respectable companionship, the concept of "living together," an increasingly common feature amongst men and women in Europe and USA.

Whilst in search of a suitable partner, Khushwant Singh makes his protagonist parody several institutions of arranged marriages in India, such as matrimonial advertisements in newspapers:

> The matrimonials were caste-obsessed, fair-skin obsessed, money obsessed and, with the exception of widows and divorcees virginity-obsessed. (10)

So Mohan Kumar decides to cock a snook at such attitudes and inserts an advertisement clarifying the need for a live-in companion for a mutually agreed time-duration. He realises that such advertisements in a tradition bound country would scandalise and shock friends and relatives. However in his search for suitable women companions, Mohan Kumar is an iconoclast and defies conventional norms. Before there is a response to the advertisement, Mohan Kumar has an amorous relationship with his sweeperess or 'jamadarni.' Her assets are "her ample behind" and that "she was also full-bosomed and had a narrow waist." (15) The relationship with Dhanno is very clandestine. The other servants are sent on long errands. This relationship is amply described in the chapter entitled 'Dhanno.' This is a trend that Khushwant Singh follows in this novel, naming the chapters after the women he has made love to. The book becomes a catalogue of the nine women he beds. Nine of the chapters are named after these various women, as a tribute to their diversity. Renowned literary critic Makarand Paranjape in his review of the book makes a snide remark about the wide choice of lovers: "Kumar's choice reflects a certain eclecticism or political correctness, when it comes to sexual partners. Of the eight on display one each is African-American, Kashmiri-Pakistani Muslim, Dalit Hindu, Hindu Brahmin, Tamilian Christian, Goan Roman Catholic, Sri Lankan Buddhist and an unnamed woman of easy virtue in Bombay." (4) The wide range of lovers is not just political correctness or promoting the spirit of national integration but an attempt by the author to parody the Indian, particularly North Indian obsession with 'fair-skinned' women as the best choice for a wife. The matrimonial advertisements of all our leading newspapers are every Sunday filled with monotonous regularity of the demand of fair-skinned brides. The wide choice of lovers is thus the author's sly comment that women of various hues and cultures can be equally desirable. In fact Khushwant Singh deliberately portrays the Tamilian Mary Joseph, the Goanese Molly Gomes and the Sri Lankan diplomat Susanthika Goonatileke as dark-skinned. Susanthika even tells Mohan: "I'm not much to look at. Too dark and too skinny for the tastes of most Indians." (264) The author thus insinuates that many North Indians are victims of tradition and cultural stereotypes that to be fair is beautiful.

Mohan Kumar's defiance of this tradition is evidence in his

brief but passionate relationship with his sweeper's wife Dhanno. The descriptions of lust and making love are another instance of the insatiable sexual urge of Mohan Kumar. The sexual encounter is described thus:

> Each time Mohan made love to a new body, it was like exploring a new landscape. Women were much the same in their essentials but enchantingly different in detail. Dhanno's body had a musky odour unlike his wife's which always smelt of French cologne. (23)

Critics have commented on Mohan Kumar's relationship with Dhanno as just mere carnal desire and lust. This is true but Khushwant Singh is also using this affair to expose yet another cultural stereotype. Mohan feels that sex with a sweeper's wife would be most fulfilling based on gossip and rumour from his college days in India. The author shows that Mohan's response is typical of the average Indian male.

> He recalled his college days in India. One of the boys had told him those sweeper women made the best lovers; they were uninhibited, wild and hot. Apparently there was no better antidote for sore eyes than sex with a sweeperess. (16)

The relationship is also the author's comment on the loose and fickle morality of many so-called pious men in urban India. As Mohan recalls, "Such master-servant liaisons were not uncommon. Poorly paid menials welcomed second income and their spouses were not very particular about infidelity provided it brought in some money." (16) Again the author is quite realistic about such relationships.

The lust for lower class women and their well-proportioned bodies has been recorded earlier in Indian English fiction. Rohinton Mistry in his collection of short stories entitled *Tales from Ferozesha Baag* writes about lustful desires for a 'gunga' (the common name for a sweeper woman in Bombay) by a respectable middle class man. There are frequent references to this trend in his tale "Auspicious Occasion" in which the owner of the house Rustomji is attracted by his sweeper woman Gajra who is described as "young and luscious," "quite pretty and voluptuous." (9) He describes her burgeoning breasts as "two prime Ratnagiri mangoes, juicy and golden smooth" (9-10) and prays to God for a vision of the nipples of her breasts. He finds her movements like "bending her knees, thighs apart, patting her behind to smooth her fabric" (10) very erotic. Rustomji also has fantasies about his 'Gunga,' Gajra just like Mohan Kumar has for Dhunno. They both feel lustful towards these working women. The only difference is that Mohan Kumar makes the appropriate advances and beds Dhunno whilst Rustomji's desire remains in the realms of fantasy. It must be admitted however that Mistry's usage of language whilst describing such sexual fantasy is much more subtle and humorous.

In African literature also there is an instance in which an unusual sexual relationship is described. The reference is to Buchi Emecheta's novel *Gwendolen* (1989). In this powerful absorbing story with many dimensions, Emecheta handles the theme of incest with great tact and pity. The protagonist Gwendolen is seduced as a teenager by her Granny's friend, Uncle Johnny and her own father Winston Brillianton. The unusual aspect of a father making love to his teenaged daughter occurs during the two-year period when his wife Sonia is away in Jamaica. He cannot control his physical urge just like Mohan Kumar in the absence of his wife finds Dhanno irresistible. Earlier he had not even noticed Dhanno. In Emecheta's novel, the actual love making, the father's lust, Gwendolen's shame and subsequent pregnancy are described with a lot of sensitivity and subtlety. Her Greek boyfriend Emmanuel is wrongly blamed for making Gwendolen pregnant. Trying to preserve her father's honour, Gwendolen runs away from home. Before the child is born, Winston commits suicide. This leads to a further estrangement between the mother and daughter. Gwendolen has to bear the stigma of being an unlucky, unwanted child and the cause of misfortune. It is only after Gwendolen's daughter is born that Winston's role in seduction becomes obvious. Emecheta handles the theme of incest and its ramifications vividly but with great sensitivity in this her tenth novel. The ramifications of lust are described subtly by Emecheta in *Gwendolen* and with saucy impertinence by Khushwant Singh in *The Company of Women.* Both the novelists adopt a modernistic attitude to the male protagonists who are unable to control their lustful desires. The psychology of the individual is examined instead of just presenting the lusty men as evil incarnate. Both Winston and Mohan Kumar become victims of lust. Winston commits suicide in shame and Mohan dies of AIDS, so both these authors provide a moral element also.

Scenes of lust abound in *The Company of Women.* After the episode with Dhanno, Mohan has a brief but blissful relationship with Sarojini Bhardwaj, the Professor of English from Rewari, who responds to his advertisement. Sarojini is a victim of an unhappy marriage and is also yearning for company and sex like Mohan. The sexual encounters with Sarojini are not frenetic like with Dhanno. Instead Mohan feels "elated, powerfully macho and grandly overpowering." (48) Dhanno and Sarojini are his mistresses after the break up of his marriage. However his initiation to sex took place as a student at Princeton University in the USA. His first relationship was with an Afro-American girl Jessica Brown, a tennis champion at the University. She seduces him to make love and he lost his virginity at the age of twenty. At Princeton University, Mohan Kumar's reputation as sexually attractive and virile increases because he has, as one of his American friends puts it, "The biggest doodah in the world." (90) After Jessica, Mohan went on the rampage, "like a stud bull in a herd of cows on heat. I lost count of the girls I bedded the following spring and summer." (95) He also has a bizarre experience with a woman who is older than him, a Kashmiri Muslim Yasmeen whom he met in a class of comparative religion. This is a fascinating experience as Mohan and Yasmeen become friends after a fierce debate in their class about the theory and practice of Hindu and Islamic rites. The author's conclusion is also interesting. Mohan realises that the copulation "had somehow drained out whatever anti-Muslim and anti-Pakistan prejudices I had imbibed during my school and college years in India." (113) Maybe Khushwant Singh in his typical irreverent manner is implying that relations between these two South Asian neighbours would be more cordial with more people-to-people contact. For as he says, "It was not love but lust that proved to be great healer." (113)

The framework of the novel is very fascinating. It opens with a third person narrative about Mohan Kumar entitled "The Secret Life of Mohan Kumar" (Pages 1-75). The novel ends with a similar section called "The Last Days of Mohan Kumar." (277-94) The bulk of the narrative is in first person, which gives it more immediacy. The entire second section called "The Memoirs of Mohan Kumar" (83-250) are in first person. This entire section is a flashback of his youth, aspirations, relationships with his father, life of love and lust at Princeton university, homecoming, marriage, honeymoon, failed marriage and other love affairs.

A writer called Khushwant Singh supposedly writes the framing sections. This writer as the fictitious character Kumar claims is a friend of his. Now what does Khushwant Singh achieve by this device of making himself a character in his own novel? One major objective, which it achieves, is shifts in narrative voice. Another objective that the author achieves by this device is distancing. This bifurcation of the narrative prevents readers from thinking this novel as autobiographical or mere senile fantasies. It justifies what Khushwant Singh admitted in an interview with *The Hindu* that the idea for the book emerged when he heard of a man who indulged in various liaisons after a broken marriage.

The homecoming, the arranged marriage with Sonu and the subsequent honeymoon are discussed in first person in the second section. In these chapters, Khushwant Singh is at his satirical best. The over-protectiveness of Mohan Kumar's father, the lack of finesse in the marriage advertisement, the girls of marriageable age on display and crass vulgarity of the nouveau-rich are all scathingly exposed. The protagonist Mohan is quite scathing about opulence of his future in-laws. "They had everything I disliked about upstart Punjabi families. Pots of money but no class. I had seen enough evidence of that in their sitting room. Black marble, white marble walls, chandeliers more appropriate in the lobby of a hotel than a private home." (136) A society that believes largely in externals and glamour is shown. Mohan's father despite the garb of religion, frequent visits to Hardwar and to temples and gurudwaras is enamoured by Rai Bahadur Lala Achint Ram because of his wealth. "He's one of the wealthiest Punjabis in Delhi: sugar mills, cinema houses, bungalows, farmlands." (127) The marriage is agreed to for contrasting reasons by Mohan's father and Sonu's father Lala Achint Ram.

> Father was obviously looking forward to a matrimonial alliance that would raise his status in society. Lala Achint Ram was keen to have an 'America-returned,' highly educated boy as his son-in-law to add respectability and sophistication to all the benefits of wealth that he already had. (139)

Mohan Kumar is keen on the marriage because of sexual fantasies "about deflowering Sonu, the haughty little memsahib, and having her in bed whenever I wanted." (139) The protagonist provides a lucid insight about why he opted for marriage with a family whose lifestyle, pretentious behaviour and lack of class he abhorred. He shows that the desire for sex was the propelling force that led him to marriage and not romantic notions of love. In fact he considers love as an elusive concept which does not necessarily lead to a happy marriage. Mohan says:

> I weighed the pros and cons of marriage. To me sex was the more pressing need, than love or companionship. For too long we have been fooled into believing that the basis of a happy man-woman relationship is love. Love is an elusive concept and means different things to different people. There is nothing elusive about lust because it means the same thing to all people: it is the physical expression of liking a person of the opposite sex. . . . Love cannot last very long without lust. Lust has no time limit and is the true foundation of love and affection. (138-39)

Later in this section there are also some interesting insights into cross-cultural encounters. Mohan, after years in USA, is aghast at the formalities associated with marriage, like astrologers examining horoscopes of both the bride and bridegroom.

> I was suddenly transported from a world in which men and women bedded each other if they so desired into another where they sought the guidance of palmists, astrologers and soothsayers before taking off their clothes. I decided to go along with everything my father wanted. Perhaps I should not have, but I hate discord and unnecessary complications in life. (140)

The problems of starting a business, "running from one government office to another" (144) and the effectiveness of bribes to get things done, all trademarks of Delhi are lampooned in this section of the novel. The wedding itself becomes an occasion for Rai Bahadur to "display his wealth and high connections; ministers, governors, judges, senior bureaucrats and over a thousand others of the elite of the city." (147) The ceremony itself becomes an ostentatious display of wealth. The author terms it a charade or a "garish display of opulence." (147) The dowry is on display.

> Stacks of expensive Banaras and Kanjeevaram saris, gold bangles, a diamond necklace, diamond ear studs and a diamond nose pin. Capping them all was a brand new Mercedes Benz decked in flowers in which I was to take away my bride. (148)

Whilst describing the wedding scenes, Khushwant Singh parodies the crass consumerism, ostentatious display of wealth, name dropping and desire to be close to politicians of Delhi's elite. Lala Achint Ram asked the "most senior Union minister who was at the wedding—the Finance Minister—to hand me the keys of the car. It was as dazzling a display of wealth as any I had seen." (148) The author here is cleverly showing how older values have subsided and display of material success becomes paramount as a new hedonistic entrepreneurship has taken India by storm. Dipanker Gupta in his article entitled "Nor'westerly winds" has depicted some of the features of such a society. He lists them as, "To succeed materially, to be worldly wise, to live beyond one's means—Culture and arts of the past no longer count in their own right." (12) Yet there is another dimension to this novel. It is not just social satire. The scenes of religious fervour and harmony at Hardwar are depicted with great feeling. Even the sceptical Mohan Kumar is enamoured by the experience. Here Khushwant Singh depicts the spiritual element in Indian society, which is shown as all abiding. The influence of the soothing atmosphere of these scenes of devotion has a permanent impact on Mohan Kumar. He is magnetically drawn to the scenes of immersion in the Ganges. Later in the novel he keeps returning to the Har Ki Pauri ghat at Hardwar.

After the marriage, events are predictable. There is an expensive ten-day honeymoon at a new hotel Timber Trail Heights in the Shivalik Hills on the way to Shimla. After the birth of their first child, a son, the bickering starts. Sonu, accustomed to the ways of her parents's home, finds it difficult to adjust with a self-confident and self-sufficient husband like Mohan Kumar. There are frequent quarrels, over the naming of the child, the selection of servants and furniture. Both are temperamentally different and being strong-willed refuse to adjust. Mohan is a strong-willed individual with a zest for life. Sonu who is used to being a memsahib in her earlier home feels unwanted. She feels she has no role to play and becomes sullen. Her constant refrain is "without consulting me, without telling me." Mohan has also not tried to win her confidence but has tried to dazzle her with wealth and material comforts. The conflict between Mohan and Sonu is one of tradition versus individualism. Years in USA have made Mohan individually self-reliant. For him self-reliance, the willingness to try new things and innovate is of much greater importance than privileges of birth. Sonu remains a cultural hybrid immersed in a world of tradition but also desiring the wealth and comforts of the hedonistic society. She wants to play the typical role of a conventional housewife, in charge of household affairs. She finds her territory threatened by the self-reliant and self-confident attitude of her husband. The author also cleverly exposes a long-standing belief in Indian society that children help to cement a marriage. Musing on this belief Mohan says,

"However my experience does not support the belief that this (birth of a child) also reduces the tensions of a marriage. On the contrary the birth of our son had produced more discord than harmony." (193) The young boy reacts to the quarrels by turning to Mohan's father for company. When the old man moved permanently to his ashram at Hardwar, the young Ranjit clings to the company of his ayahs. This makes the possessive Sonu more frantic and envious and she "fired one ayah after another on the flimsiest of excuses; she steals my things, she is very lazy, she spoils the child, and so on and so forth." (194)

Thus the marriage drifts apart despite the birth of Ranjit. Sonu keeps nagging and needling Mohan and he either ignores her or keeps out of her way. Indifference and intolerance gradually lead to the break-up of this marriage. Break up of the family and marriage, especially in the wealthy stratum of Indian society is a theme, which is often seen in the fiction of Shobha De also. In his perceptive essay, "Family and Marriage in *Socialite Evenings*" Subhash Chandra writes that "these hoary institutions of family and marriage have come under tremendous strain in the modern times, primarily in the Western culture, and also in the rich stratum of the Indian society." (143) In his article, Chandra shows how "*Socialite Evenings* presents a picture of the institutions of the family and marriage obtaining in the wealthy classes of Indian society." (143) Commenting on the reasons for the disintegration of these institutions, Subhash Chandra cites sociologist Charles Cooley and says: "One of the major causes of the disintegration of family is the rampant promiscuity in family relations. Another factor is lack of a set routine of work and excessive leisure among women of the richer classes which becomes a chief cause of the restless, exacting, often hysterical spirit harassing to the owner and everyone else, which tends towards discontent, indiscretion and divorce." (143) Some of these symptoms can be applied to Khushwant Singh's novel also. Sonu has excessive leisure, becomes restless, suspicious and hysterical which makes harmony in marriage very difficult. Another reason cited is that they hardly have any sex. Mohan, who has a strong sexual drive, thus looks for other avenues. An unexpected partner is his wife's nurse, the Tamilian Mary Joseph. Mohan justifies the liaison by stating that "the body's needs come above religious taboos and notions of morality." (177) Mary Joseph's reasoning was also simple, "only one life to live." (177)

This novel has been criticised for being an expression of the libidinous acts of the protagonist Mohan Kumar. However the novel has a wider appeal and is not a mere recapitulation of the sexual fantasies of an author in the twilight of his career. Whilst describing Mohan Kumar's sexual exploits, the author also ridicules and upsets the apple cart of many patriarchal institutions and conventions. For instance Mary Joseph narrates the incident of how the padre of her village church had a sexual relationship with her. The padre is shown as being in the throes of a dilemma, being torn by the demands of the flesh and the demands of his profession. So he expresses sorrow after making love and indulges in a farcical act of repentance.

> After he finished he asked me to pardon him and made me pray with him to Jesus to ask his forgiveness. Imagine no, still naked and sweating and kneeling on the floor and praying to God! He made me feel worse than a prostitute who did it without asking for money. Tell me, saar, is it a sin to do it with somebody you like. (181)

By such a candid confession, Mary Joseph comes across as a much more honest character than the pretentious priest and social elite of Delhi. So, such scenes of lust are not just shocking pornographic details, but a technique to tumble sexual taboos and chauvinistic attitudes towards man-woman relationships.

Mohan's relationship with the masseuse from Goa, Molly Gomes, represents yet another bonding of lust. However Molly's cheerful nature is also a stark contrast with the suspicious attitudes of Sonu. Molly helps Mohan relax. Molly is a very fascinating character. Her complexion is coffee and cream and she is described as being "short, stocky and dark" (214) and a "natty little chatterbox." (217) Yet in her attitude to men and life, she is like one of Shobha De's liberated women, fully aware of her sexuality and sensuality. She resembles Aasha Rani, the heroine of Shobha De's novel *Starry Nights*. Like Aasha Rani, the lively

Molly tries to shatter patriarchal hegemony in society. Aasha and her sister Sudha, highly seductive stars of the tinsel world of Bollywood display disarming nonchalance in their torrid sexual affairs. Aasha Rani breaks all sexual taboos with gusto. However it is not for mere carnal pleasure. Sudhir Kumar in his perceptive essay, "Artist as Vamp: A Feminist Approach to *Starry Nights*" says, "She [Aasha] and the likes of her enthrall and enslave the males and become 'successful.'" (191) Molly is similar to Aasha, conscious of her radiant charms and physical attraction. When Mohan compliments her on her figure, she boldly says, "Want to see what I really look like?" (228) She then proceeds to take off her clothes and stand naked before Mohan. "She slowly turned around to show me her behind as well. I had never seen a naked woman before. I tried to grab her in my arms but she pushed me back and said I couldn't till she'd seen what I had hidden behind my clothes." (228) In bed she is described as an artist of sex. During her first night with Mohan they make love thrice on the carpet near the fireside. The depiction of the sexual scenes is quite sensual.

> She nibbled the lobes of my ears, pressed her thumbs into the backs of my shoulders, ran her fingers over my belly, middle, thighs and shins, down to my feet. She rubbed my toes and insteps. Not a part of my body did she leave untouched. It was relaxing, soothing. (221)

The sunbathing, oil massage and love making on the terrace are also sensually described. The climax is the most prolonged "that either of us had experienced in our lives." (247) Molly describes it as a unique experience. She says, "this kind of love-making in which every part of your body makes love to every part of your partner's is a once-in-a-lifetime experience." (246)

Her attitude like Aasha Rani is very frank and she admits that the sexual act enables her gain power. Talking about her work as a masseuse in Goa she says: "It was while working in five star hotels that I occasionally agreed to have sex with some foreigners. I didn't enjoy it very much. I felt dirty at first when they pressed dollar bills into my hands after they had finished, but after a while it seemed normal; I didn't feel like a whore." (223) She has chucked up her marriage to a foreigner because he could not satisfy her sexually. Like Aasha Rani, Molly also has no hang ups about religion. Aasha Rani was willing to get converted to a Muslim in order to marry her sweetheart Akshay Kumar (Muslims are allowed four wives and Akshay was already married). Similarly Molly says, "I go to church only to please my parents—all religions teach you to be good and honest so what is the big deal about being Christian, Hindu, Muslim or Parsee!" (214) Sudhir Kumar in his perceptive essay writes that Shobha De's heroines "demolish the mythical and iconographic images of woman imposed by patriarchal structures." (197) Molly is not playing the role of the mythical, dutiful wife or seductress. She is aware of her sexuality and uses it to gain power and control. Later in his essay Sudhir also says that "Shobha De's heroines protest against the massive oppression and exploitation carried through various patriarchal ideological constructs manifest in history, philosophy, culture and arts." (197) Molly is like a heroine of Shobha De's fiction. She is also trying to break the shackles to attain full liberation. In this relationship, Mohan Kumar is also attempting to liberate himself from the shackles of a society which is full of sexual constraints and restrictions. His relationship with Molly is the most satisfying. The physical and mental pleasure of this relationship leads to change in thinking of both Molly and Mohan. They both realise that freedom of will is more important than all the sexual taboos imposed by society and the hypocritical man-woman relationships that prevail amongst Mohan's friends and contemporaries.

Molly's life story also exposes yet another cherished institution of middle class India, the extended family. The vivacious Molly vividly describes how as a fourteen-year-old, her uncle, her mother's younger brother, seduced her. Here again lust is seen as all-pervasive. "He sat down on the sofa pulled me onto his lap and started kissing the back of my neck and my ears. I could feel his prick getting stiff and large against my bum. He began to fondle my breasts, then squeeze them roughly." (229) With his sharp eye for detail and piercingly accurate characterisation, Khushwant Singh explores the world of passion, romance, fantasy and hard reality of each character. For many of the women reality is harsh. This is evident in the cases of Mary Joseph, Molly Gomes and the Sri Lankan diplomat Susanthika Goonatilleke or Sue. The so-called guardians of morality seduced this trio of women, Mary by a priest and both Molly and Sue by their uncles. As Sue tells Mohan at Hardwar, "My own uncle, my father's younger brother. The usual thing, you know, a close relative whom you trust." (266) This bold exposure is typical of Khushwant Singh. He is exposing the humbug attitude towards women of middle and upper classes of India. In theory women are supposedly elevated and worshipped as life giving forces but were often treated as objects of lust. As in the case of both Molly and Sue, it is members of their family who are the seducers that cause distress. The author thus implies that Mohan's experiment with short-term companions is no more bizarre than the religious and moral codes imposed on Indian society. The novel shows that these codes do not prohibit adults from having sex whenever and with whomever they wish. It only weighs them down with guilt, deceit and disgrace. Mohan's discovery that lust is the true foundation of man-woman relationship is thus seen as valid. Talking to Samita Bhatia, Khushwant Singh says, "Being an iconoclast I write very openly about such things." (7) In the same interview the author also frankly admits that depiction of sex increases the popularity and appeal of a novel and subsequent sales. He says, "Most authors write candidly about sex. Shobha Dc and Arundhati Roy do so as well . . . A novel minus sex is a damn dull novel." (7)

Sex, friendship and the desire to develop a new image are the motivating factors in the relationship between Mohan and Sue, the second secretary in the Sri Lankan High Commission. Before the start of the clandestine relationship with Sue, the Sri Lankan diplomat, Mohan is enmeshed in a dilemma. He has been branded as a 'lafanga'—a no good loafer who consorted with women of loose character. "Sonu succeeded in giving me the reputation of a compulsive womaniser." (251) At this stage of his life, Mohan feels both lonely and the loss of normal human dignity. Mohan realises that he is trapped.

> I could not think of a way out of the impasse because I needed sex on a regular basis, with a change of partners every few months. I did not relish the idea of visiting brothels or having call girls who serviced many men every day; my woman had to be exclusively mine for the time she was with me. (252)

So, at this juncture, the clandestine meetings with Sue are a perfect antidote for Mohan. He finds solace in these meetings because Sue is clever and alert and he can discuss several topics like difference between Hinduism and Buddhism with her. Their friendship develops during the visit to Hardwar. They both physically desire each other. This desire is described in purely physical terms and without any expression of endearments. It is the relationship of two mature adults who enjoy carnal pleasure and the secrecy of their relationship to avoid gossip. The lust is described as, "our bodies craved to be locked into each other, her yoni ached to receive my lingam—the cosmic union!" (273) Both have no hang ups about sex. In fact Sue says, "Sex is the greatest thing in a human life. The more varied it is the more enjoyable." (267) So they meet regularly at weekends at Mohan's house. The secret meetings went on for two years and the code name for these dalliances was 'Operation Colombo.' Besides the physical and mental satisfaction, the relationship with Sue led to a change in image for Mohan Kumar. As the meetings are clandestine, the upper crust of society did not know of this infatuation. Hence, as Mohan writes, "my image changed from that of a sex maniac who paid all kinds of women for their services to a man of impotent respectability." (278) When Sue departs for New York, they keep in touch via the telephone. They even corresponded regularly. Gradually however the romance fades away. Within six months of her departure, Sue wrote and informed Mohan that "she was engaged to marry a fellow Sri Lankan diplomat posted in Washington and we should stop writing or calling each other on the phone." (275) The letter saddens Mohan. We now get a psychological insight into the changing nature of Mohan's demands. Previously when his mistresses departed, Mohan would look for other partners. Now with age he has mellowed. It took him time to get reconciled to her loss. Their relationship had ended with some symbolic romantic gestures. He had put a pearl necklace around her neck and slipped a gold ring with sapphires on her finger. He feels lethargic when Sue departs. Even the desire to go to Hardwar has ceased. As he says, "the two persons with whom it had come to be closely connected in my mind—my father and Sue—had gone out of my life." He gives up the room at Hardwar. He now likes to spend more time with his children Ranjit and Mohini. Feelings of emptiness and restlessness overcome him. Signs of age and changing temperament.

The third section of the novel entitled "The Last Days of Mohan Kumar" (279-96) is brief. The protagonist Mohan Kumar loses his sexual urge. He tried tonics and went to health clubs for different kinds of massages, Kerala, Ayurvedic and Swedish and "simple massage by pehalwans [wrestlers]." (279) He felt a little better but it did not reactivate his libido. During a business trip to Bombay, Mohan rediscovers his manhood after an affair with a woman brought to the hotel room by the bearer. The discovery that he had not gone kaput revives his confidence and he again lives life to the full. However the sexual relationship without a condom in Bombay proves fatal. Blood tests show that he is HIV positive. When Dr. Malhotra informs him of this he becomes morbid. "The prospect of dying a horribly painful death continued to haunt him day and night." (292) He was also concerned that his children would have to live with the stigma of "having a parent succumb to a sexually related disease." (293) For nearly two years after the dreaded verdict was pronounced Mohan led a relatively healthy and outwardly normal life. He eschewed sex. However after a virulent cold, Mohan developed symptoms of TB in his lungs and contacted AIDS. He becomes philosophical and reads the *Bhagavad Gita* and recites the Gayatari mantra from sunrise to sunset. However, overcome by remorse and fear, he takes thirty sleeping pills (Calmpose) in one night and as the author says, "puts his head on the pillow and closes his eyes." (296)

The end is sudden and abrupt. Purabi Panwar writing in *The Pioneer* raises certain pertinent questions: "But why does Mohan

Kumar, the main character die of AIDS at the end of the novel? The end is so very abrupt and dissatisfying and hardly in keeping with the general mood of enjoyment in the book." (8) Reacting to this criticism, Khushwant Singh tells Purabi with his usual candour, "I did not know how to kill him. This seemed a fitting end to reckless philandering." (8) Seen in such a context it seems a realistic ending. However a moralistic context to a brisk tale of philandering and defying traditions does seem awkward. Shiela Reddy in her review says, "and if his death is abrupt, his demise begins the day he loses sex drive several years before he commits suicide, chanting the Hindu hymn to life's splendour." The ending could have been more imaginative. But at least Khushwant Singh has not resorted to maudlin sentimentality in the conclusion. It is terse and brief.

Newspaper reviews of Khushwant Singh's novel have not been complimentary. *The Company of Women* has been described as either pornographic or a bad piece of writing or puerile fiction or a swan song gone wrong. Khushwant Singh however remains unperturbed. Talking to Samita Bhatia, the veteran author says, "It's all part of the game. A swan song doesn't have always to be a lament." (6) However in another interview, Khushwant Singh has said, "I must confess I was reluctant to have this book published. I felt it would not be acceptable." (Padgaonkar, 1) Khushwant Singh had originally called this novel, "The Fantasies of an Octogenarian" and intended it to be an attempt to catch up with lost time. The Author's Note contains the following disclaimer. "As man gets older, his sex instincts travel from his middle to his head. What he wanted to do in his younger days but did not because of nervousness, lack of response or opportunity, he does in his mind." (vi) However such is Khushwant Singh's deliberately cultivated image of a man obsessed with sex and Scotch that critics have over-reacted to the scenes of sex and fantasy. There is also more to the novel than Mohan Kumar's periodic relationships and liaisions with different kinds of women. Khushwant Singh admits that the novel reflects the current paradox of Indian society, the opening up to liberal and Western values, which is also matched with growing intolerance. He says, "the book reflects what is happening around us. At one level people are earning quick money and indulging in ostentatious living and a lot of pretence about moral standards that no longer exist." (1) Reacting to the general consensus that the book is about sex in all directions the author says that people expected serious or philosophic fiction from him because of his age. However he claims to be multi-dimensional and certainly not one-track which has enabled him probe many areas in this novel and write about many subjects in the past. He has also admitted that the motivations for all his novels have been obsessions. He tells Samita Bhatia, "At different stages in one's life one has different obsessions—which can be funny or tragic." (6) His first novel, *Train to Pakistan*, was penned when the horrifying communal violence that accompanied the Partition was uppermost in his mind. Later his second novel, *I Shall Not Hear the Nightingale*, was largely based on a family involved with the Quit India Movement of 1942 and it was during the phase in his life when he thought a lot about politics and the national movement. An obsession about his hometown Delhi was serenaded in his most widely acclaimed novel to date, *Delhi*. The author has explained that "later in my old age, fantasies became an obsession." (Bhatia, 7) So his latest novel, *The Company of Women* reveals the sexual fantasies of an octogenarian. The inspiration for this book was Muriel Spark's *Remember You Must Die,* a novel set in an old people's home. Spark had some hilarious anecdotes to reveal about the sexual fantasies of old people. In contrast Khushwant Singh returns to his youth to create these fantasies.

The author has admitted that scenes of sex are essential in a novel. He says that uninhibited writing on sex in Indian English fiction was started by Shashi Tharoor. In his work *The Great Indian Novel*, Tharoor was explicit about Draupadi being bedded by her five brothers. Shobha de and Arundhati Roy have also written with great candour about sex. Now it is to be seen if the depiction of sex in Khushwant Singh's novel is mere pornography or is it sensuous. Some of the scenes with Molly and later with the Sri Lankan diplomat Susanthika Goonatilleke or Sue are quite sensuous. The attention to detail in the oil massage scene on the terrace of Mohan's house and prying at Sue's body whilst taking a dip at Hardwar are scenes which are quaint, unusual and arouse interest. They are not just scenes of explicit erotic material with the singular purpose of arousing the reader sexually. The emphasis is not just on anatomical details and the sex act itself but on human relationships and defiance of tradition. Another question that arises is what type of fantasy is celebrated in this novel, his first novel in 10 years as his publishers Penguin have billed it. Initial critical acclaim has been harsh. Many critics consider *The Company of Women* as the fantasies of an author in the twilight of his career. The novel has been criticised as just the irresistible urge of an old man to share his fantasies. However Khushwant Singh has clarified this criticism by saying that he is recreating the fantasies of youth. The reaction to Khushwant Singh's work has been varied.

Celebrated sports editor G. Rajaraman has felt that this novel is an indication that Khushwant Singh's writing skills are on the wane. Rajaraman raised the question that "After *The Company of Women*, it is hard not to ask: Why does Khushwant Singh not put his pen away in the remotest corner of his cupboard?" (6) Using analogies from sports, Rajaraman says that this novel makes evident that Khushwant Singh is past his prime. He compares Khushwant Singh to an ageing champion who is struggling to fight the passage of time. Continuing with this comparison Rajaraman says that just as a champion should quit when the body is aching and the limbs are creaking, similarly an author should quit when the muse of creativity is on the decline. He considers this novel as puerile fiction and the work of an author who has lost much of his celebrated creativity. In his article, "Khushwant, Save us your Fantasies," Rajaraman says, "It is an entirely grim book, making for sad reading. There does not seem to be any room for joy, except the temporary sort that the protagonist Mohan Kumar experiences with a variety of women—from his wife to the maid, from the Kashmiri-Pakistani to the Goan masseuse, from the Tamil Christian to the seductive Sinhalese diplomat, from the African-American co-ed to the demure professor from Rewari. Sadly there is no joy even when he is with his children." (6)

Noted critic and creative writer Makarand Paranjape says, "His sizzling new novel is easy to read and just as easy to forget." (4) He considers this book as the work of "senile fantasies." (4) Paranjape is critical of the episodic and loose-structured plot, the lack of thematic or philosophical depth and repetitive events. He is particularly critical of the dull and lack-lustre style: "Even when his characters are climaxing together, Singh's style remains limp and flaccid, failing to rise to the occasion" (4)

Dileep Padgaonkar also feels that *The Company of Women* is not successful as an erotic novel. |He stresses that to write about erotic passion, the author must use language very subtly. His complaint is that Khushwant Singh has not handled language with grace and subtlety in his fourth novel, *The Company of Women*. He has even belittled Khushwant Singh's claims as a writer of pornography. He says, "Any reader exposed to the multiple orgasms in the fiction of Jackie Collins or Harold Robbins or even more to the sexual acrobatics described in pornographic literature or on the internet would be forgiven for believing that Singh has taken him for a ride." (1) Padgaonkar feels that Khushwant Singh's work is not of the same calibre as the treasure troves of erotic writings of James Joyce, Henry Miller, D.H. Lawrence and William Burroughs. He feels the major difference is the usage of the language. According to Padgaonkar the use of language of Joyce, Lawrence and others was subtler in their depiction of the emotional and spiritual aspects of relationships. Padgaonkar however does admit that Khushwant Singh like the celebrated Western authors uses eroticism to undermine convention and strike at the old order. Padgaonkar also complains that Khushwant Singh's novel does not fully use the rich vocabulary of eroticism. He says that Vatsyayana the author of the classic Kama Sutra "devotes thirty-four aphorisms to the kiss alone, lists 84 basic pictures of copulation and enumerates a large number of love-marks and vocal sounds that enhance passion during love making." (1) Several love sounds are listed such as sobbing, cooing, moaning, groaning, humming, hissing, clucking, chirping, quacking, mewing, braking, mooing, roaring and bellowing. This criticism of Khushwant Singh's novel is justified, as the vocabulary could have been more stimulating. Padgaonkar also feels that the protagonist Mohan Kumar is not a bold rebel defying the sexual taboos of society but a "banal erotomaniac." (1) This is a psychiatric term, which refers to an individual wholly pre-occupied with sex and possessed of a compulsive and insatiable desire for sexual activity.

Like Shobha De's provocative novels *Starry Nights* and *Socialite Evenings*, Khushwant Singh's work *The Company of Women* will also be subjected to various critical appraisals. However it must be admitted that Khushwant Singh's work like that of De reveals pictures of a society in transition. Shobha De's novels show the hypocrisy, degenerated values, double standards both of the celluloid world and celebrities of the higher social strata. Khushwant Singh's novel depicts similar traits in the life-style of the upper middle class and the affluent in consumerist Delhi. Money, power and sex dominate the lives of the characters of De's novels and Khushwant Singh's *The Company of Women*. Both these authors depict the rapidly changing consumerist society in urban India in which traditional values are getting eroded and the meek do not inherit the earth. Shobha De's novels are not a treatise on sex and have a more profound meaning. The same can also be said of Khushwant Singh's latest novel. Shobha De's heroines depict modern women's search for identity in a male dominated society. Similarly Khushwant Singh's protagonist Mohan Kumar discovers that a single man or woman can either have sex or human dignity. They cannot have both. Mohan also realises that lust is the true foundation of man-woman relationships. Being a recent victim of an arranged marriage Mohan experiments with different partners. *The Company of Women* for all its explicit sex, is not the work of a hasty or angry young author. Khushwant Singh does not either rage at the absurdities of society or cloak his lust with the romance of love. There is no anger, hatred, romance or self-pity in Mohan Kumar who fully understands that life is too precious for such self-indulgences. This is the attitude of a mature author. Just as Shobha De's novels are a protest against the established patriarchal order of society similarly Khushwant Singh's novel parodies the sexual taboos, hypocrisy in man-woman relationships and the crass consumerism of the high society in the rapidly changing metropolis of Delhi.

Works Cited

Bhatia, Samita. "In the Company of Khushwant," *The Telegraph Magazine*, 17 October 1999, 5-9.

Behal, Suchitra. "Old yes, but 'dirty' no," *The Hindu*, 19 September 1999, xiv-xv.

Chandra, Subhash. "Family and Marriage in *Socialite Evenings*." Dodiya, 142-48.

De, Shobha. *Starry Nights*. New Delhi: Penguin, 1991.

Emecheta, Buchi. *Gwendolen*. London: Flamingo, Fontana Paperbacks, 1990.

Dodiya, Jaydipsinh, ed. *The Fiction of Shobha De*. New Delhi: Prestige, 1999.

Gupta, Dipanker. "Nor'westerly winds," *The Telegraph*, 20 August 1999, 12.

Kumar, Sudhir. "Artist as Vamp: A Feminist Approach to *Starry Nights*." Dodiya, 187-99.

Mistry, Rohinton. *Tales from Ferozsha Baag*. Ontario, Canada: Penguin, 1987.

Padgaonkar, Dileep. Lead article in *The Sunday Times of India Review*, 10 October 1999, 1.

Panwar, Purabi. "Confessions of an old teenager," *The Pioneer*, 25 September 1999, 11-12.

Paranjape, Makarand. "Khushwant Singh's One-Night Stand," *The Indian Express*, 19 September 1999, 4.

Pathak, R.S. "Feminist Concerns in Shobha De's Work: A Study in Attitudes," Dodiya, 34-50.

Rajaraman, G. "Khushwant Spare Us Your Fantasies," *The Hindustan Times Magazine*, 3 October 1999, 6.

Reddy, Shiela. "The Truth About Dirty Old Society," *The Hindustan Times Magazine*, 10 October, 1999, 7.

Sen, Sarbani. "The De Debate: Cultural Politics and De's Novels." Dodiya, 21-26.

Singh, Khushwant. *The Company of Women*. New Delhi: Viking Penguin Books, 1999.

Suroor, Hasan. "Khushwant Singh's great fling," *The Hindu*, 3 October 1999, X.

Verma, Pavan. "Provoking people has become part of my character," *The Hindustan Times*, 3 October 1999, 6.

The Nausea and the Aroma of Sex: Khushwant Singh and D.H. Lawrence

O.P. MATHUR

> Relationship is threefold. First there is the relationship to the living universe. Then comes the relationship of man to woman. Then comes the relationship of man to man. And each is a blood-relationship, no mere spirit or mind.[1]

Relationships, according to Lawrence, are 'vital' and not 'mental,' 'bodiless' or 'dead.' They should be pulsating with life and meaning. The very titles of the last novels of D.H. Lawrence and Khushwant Singh, *Lady Chatterley's Lover* and *The Company of Women*, point to two different types of sexual relationships. The former presents a vital, individualized woman, with all the ambience of a 'dead' life with her semi-paralysed husband, finding her fulfilment in a lover, who too, with her, awakes into life and vitality. *The Company of Women* has its root not in 'vital' love for an individual but just 'companionship' with a series of women for the sake of a planned, transient sex. A relationship which Lawrence, however, would certainly have called 'dead' because of its treatment of women as sexual objects for a momentary, physical, businesslike relationship of pleasure for money.

Sex, sharing the Divinity's joy of creation, is highly sacred, fully sanctioned by religion and society. The Christian bridegroom says to the bride, "With my body I thee *worship*." (Emphasis added) The Hindu scriptures too have gone to the extent of including the act of procreation as the first of the sixteen 'Sanskars' or rituals of life, for it marks the very beginning of all individual lives. The features of sex as a part of life are, according to Lawrence, marked by tenderness (which, incidentally, was the title he had initially thought of for his novel), fidelity and a desire to marry and beget children. These features are closely paralleled in Hindu scriptures which, in addition, allow eight types of marriage including 'Gandharva vivaha' in which love and sex precede social and religious sanction. Incidentally, Connie's love and sexual relations with Mellors in *Lady Chatterley's Lover* might be said to fall under this category, for her marriage with Clifford is null and void on account of disablement. But the affairs of Khushwant Singh's Mohan Kumar with one woman after another are nothing but unalloyed sin. The religious importance of the life-long togetherness of man and woman, reinforced by mutual share and care and a joint bringing-up of children, creates an emotional communion so deep that it suffuses their being and often percolates to the soul, sometimes accompanied by a wish to be together even after death, whatever be the form of such existence.

Though conscious of the whole religious and social dimensions of sex and of the profoundly uplifting ways in which it has been treated directly or allegorized into love for God, it is surprising that a Sikh like Khushwant Singh, who wrote an authoritative history of the Sikhs and even renounced his award after 'Operation Bluestar,' comes close to churn this sacred subject into pornography and attempts to render "bullshit into art form" as he has himself put it.[2] Is it only because "sex sells better than Sikhs"[3]? But he is already a married man, who in his eighties could not be expected to stoop to such a level. The book has certainly earned plenty of notoriety for him, and he has been variously nick-named as 'King Leer,' Sexual Caesar,' 'The Litterateur of Lip,' 'Kisswant Singh,' 'Kissmet' (i.e. he kissed whoever he met), 'the gland old man of Indian life and letters' and 'the Puck of Indian literary scene.'

Khushwant Singh himself wrote about his dilemma in a significant Introduction to *I Believe*, an anthology of statements of their personal beliefs made by a number of well-known Indians, front-ranking in their respective fields.

About this time I had grown into manhood and began to

> fall in and out of love with girls I met. Like all young men I cherished the illusion that somehow life's problems could be solved through a perfect mental, emotional and physical equation with a woman. How futile and frustrating it was.[4]

In his dilemma he called himself "an agnostic as well as a Sikh,"[5] after approvingly quoting from Robert Browning:

> All we have gained by unbelief
> Is a life of doubt diversified by faith
> For one of faith diversified by doubt,
> We called the chess-board white, we call it black.

Though he led what he calls "a disciplined life,"[6] Khushwant Singh's subconscious is reflected in his work as is the case with every writer to a greater or lesser extent.[7] His words that reveal an unjustifiably low and depressing view of mankind are perhaps true, if at all, only of persons like himself: "no matter how happily married a couple is, the thought of adultery is never out of their minds. The opportunity may never come but in their fantasies they are adulterous."[8] A resort to the idea of 'fantasy' seems to be Khushwant Singh's only shield to defend a pornographic literary novelist like him. He declares in an interview that it was through his protagonist Mohan Kumar that he had expressed his fantasies[9] on which there could be no censorship. But why publish such fantasies at all? His defence that "Provoking people has become part of my character"[10] is hardly satisfying, for it further provokes the question: why display the dirty linings of your undergarments for public gaze, for it may do more harm than good by tickling their imagination to translate such fantasies into reality. Such 'blue literature' may do further harm by spreading the cult of hedonism and atheism as its natural corollary. Here is their Mephistophilean 'leader' serenading them: "I don't believe in a maker and he won't ask me a thing when I die, I'll die and that's it. There's no after life. There's nothing further. Death is a full-stop."[11]

Luckily for him, there is no Ayatollah Khomeini among

Sikhs. Flying in the face of most literary writers, Khushwant Singh declares: "Love is an ephemeral and divine concept, it doesn't last; lust lasts."[12] Partly controverted by his own *Train to Pakistan,* this approach seems to be the footstool for the portrayal of unnatural sex with a hermaphrodite in *Delhi* and the more 'respectable' one in the octogenarian's fantasy in *The Company of Women* which ambivalently portrays a protagonist, hedonistic, but not atheistic, devoid of any illusion, innocent of the sacredness of sex. Mohan Kumar is a smart, successful and sexy businessman the early and closing periods of whose life are described by an objective narrator, closely resembling the author, while the thoughts, ambitions and activities of the rest of his life constituting its most important period are narrated by the protagonist himself in a completely honest and truthful manner which does not conceal anything or attempt to mystify the reader. After his initiation into the 'mysteries' of sex by a number of women in America, Mohan Kumar, having realized his sexual prowess, is transformed into a sex-hungry millionaire. His marriage with a vain and self-centred woman, coming from a family proud of its newly acquired wealth, fails after he has spent thirteen of the best years of his life in his patiently trying to find a satisfactory equation with his wife. Divorce follows inevitably and again Mohan Kumar finds himself a 'free' man, a highly respected millionaire craving for the satisfaction of his ravenous sexual hunger, symbolized by an 'amazingly oversized organ, whose frustration with his married life makes him discard the idea of a second marriage or keeping a permanent concubine or passing a more or less celebate life as a widower. He has now no alternative but to have respectable women, one after another, whom he can pass off as his relatives or temporary guests. What a fall of the pristine and sexually innocent Indian youth who had gone for higher studies to America!

The core of the novel consists of Mohan Kumar's varied acrobatic sexual encounters with a number of such women who are as different as possible from one another in their stations in life, physical characteristics, sexual preferences, in addition to their belonging to different regions, one of them even being a Sri Lankan diplomat. All this is sufficient material for the octogenarian author's fantasies which, unlike a normal man forgetting or not talking about them, he lovingly puts on paper with his over-Puckish pen. He is fully in his elements at last, and his fantasies, run wild over the female body—'above, around, between, below.' The responsibility for the degeneration of the personality of Mohan Kumar and his decline from a pure youth into a sexual debauch lies firmly with his academic environment in America and the social environment in India.

The portrayal of the industrialised Western culture exercising a corrupting influence upon the traditional life of the East, presented with touching sympathy, is comparable to Lawrence's contrast between the 'vital' life in an environment natural in more ways than one and the urban, mechanical life represented by Lord Clifford. Mellor's work as a gamekeeper brings him close not only to nature but also to the breeding and upbringing of little creatures, while for Lord Clifford producing a child is just a mechanical activity for a woman devoid of any emotional content and to be forgotten as soon as the child is delivered. Connie naturally feels suffocated in such an atmosphere where she is expected to produce an heir for Wragby Hall after a transitory sexual relation with a man as repulsive as Michaelis. The backdrop of the industrialized society is common to both novels, but while in *Lady Chatterley's Lover* Connie is lucky in finding her fulfilment, there is no such escape route for Mohan Kumar whose predisposition to sex has been aroused by several girls in America to such an extent that he is unable to control it in the rest of his life. A successful marriage could have saved him. But the vanity of the newly-rich flows in the blood of his wife, and his in-laws do not trust even a rich man like him to take proper care of their daughter. His wife herself disdains Mohan Kumar's affectionate old father for whom he has the highest affection and respect. The seeds of tragedy are there and they fructify, as we have seen, into a serial concubinage. Mohan Kumar is overpowered first by the sexual freedom of the Western world and then by the undigested materialism and consequent snobbery of the Westernized segment of Indian society.

Largely in consonance with the domestic and social backgrounds in the two novels are the ways in which physical relations and their deeper connotations are presented, specially by D.H. Lawrence. The deliberately transient relationships in *The Company of Women* are just physical, business-like, temporarily emotional, if at all, and totally unrelated to the depth of the personalities of either the protagonist or any of the procession of his concubines. They give and receive pleasure, not happiness:

> Each time Mohan made love to a new body, it was like exploring a new landscape. Women were much the same in their essentials, but enchantingly different in detail. But lust was also an aspect of love—perhaps its most important constituent. When mental and emotional companionship were not available, it was as good a substitute as any that a man could want.[13]

It is but fair to both the novelists and to the reader to give a relatively presentable specimen of a part of the first and almost the best of such encounters with a regular concubine, virgin and incidentally a lecturer in English:

> 'O God, you will split me into two,' she said clasping him by the neck. She was fully aroused. In a hoarse voice she whispered urgently, "Ram it in.' He did as he was told. She screamed, not in agony but in the ecstasy of a multiple orgasm. She had never experienced it before nor believed it was possible. Her body quivered, relaxed. (48)

But both parties know that their parting is inevitable, for in the words of Omar Khayyam quoted by the lady lecturer:

> The bird of time has a little way to go.
> And lo! the Bird is on the wing.

This applies to all such affairs of Mohan Kumar, but since this is the first, he is full of tears of regret as she too is, and they even publicly kiss each other passionately in the railway compartment in the disdainful gaze of all the other passengers.

The affairs that follow are more mechanical and much less

emotional, if at all. The last affair with the Sri Lankan diplomat is almost a purely business-like proposition, for sudden transfers are a part of her job. Into such a life of which "each minute be with pleasure past," as a poet puts it, it is very occasional for any cerebration to enter. Among the few such points where somewhat deeper dimensions of sexual relations briefly flash upon some characters, one is where a catholic nun, Mary Joseph, one of the protagonist's concubines, defends sex as higher than morality and our concepts of sin on the ground that "body's needs come above religicus taboos and notions of morality" (177) or "How can such a nice thing be sin?"

Against these momentary glimpses of a few relatively unimportant and somewhat 'heretical' morality, D.H. Lawrence builds a comprehensive vision of sex which even a clergyman like the Bishop of Woolwich called something "essentially sacred" and the last two pages of *Lady Chatterley's Lover* as "a most moving advocacy of chastity."[14] Another clergyman Purbendary Hopkinson regarded the novel as "a book of moral purpose."[15] At the trial, the literary critics were a chorus of praise. Helen Gardner's profound deposition is fairly representative: "The sexual scenes are the core and heart of the book's theme and meaning."[16] Practically every critic has agreed with Lawrence's own comment in his 'Apropos' to *Lady Chatterley's Lover* in which he called it "an honest, healthy book," for "the restoration of a phallic language was the means chosen in Lawrence's last novel to bring this about."[17] Perhaps some similarity of this sort of trans-physical consciousness of love with the purely emotional communion is between the boy Krishna and the Gopis in Hindu mythology. But for Lawrence physical sex is the foundation on which "phallic consciousness" is built, gradually deepening and transcending sexual communion into what K.K. Sharma calls "spiritual consummation."[18]

In *Lady Chatterley's Love* this gradual deepening is portrayed with sophisticated suggestivity. The love between Connie and Mellors begins quite naturally with the tear of Connie at the sight of small chicks reminding her of her "female forlornness,"[19] the frustration of her maternal instinct. And with her tear "the old flame shooting and leaping up" (119) the loins of

Mellors. Nature animate animates their love. It is in this unique manner that the dawn of love is portrayed with such tenderness for the lower life in the lap of nature. From Connie's "tormented, modern woman's brain," "a great cloud" is lifted in "a kind of sleep." (126) Her first sexual communion with Mellors follows soon after the beginning of this 'tenderness':

> Then with a quiver of exquisite pleasure he touched the warm, soft body, and touched her navel for a moment in a kiss. And he had to come in to her at once, to enter the peace on earth of her soft, quiescent body. It was the moment of pure peace for him, the entry into the body of the woman. She lay still, in a kind of sleep, always in a kind of sleep. (121)

Gradually with each succeeding communion she achieves more and more of self-realisation, self-fulfilment and self-confidence. The description of one such intercourse consisting of multiple orgasms blooms with sheer poetry of ecstasy, cosmic and sublime in its increasing reaches of primordial symbolism:

> And she felt him like a flame of desire, yet tender, and she felt herself melting in the flame, she let herself go. . . . But it came with a strange thrust of peace and a ponderous, primordial tenderness, such as made the world in the beginning. . . . She dared to let herself go, everything, all herself, and be gone in the flood. . . . And it seemed she was like the sea, nothing but dark waves rising and heaving with a great swell, so that slowly her whole darkness was in motion, and she was seen rolling in dark, dumb, mass . . . till suddenly, in a soft, shuddering convulsion, the quick of all her plasm was touched, she knew herself touched. The consummation was upon her, and she was gone. She was gone, she was not, and she was born: a woman. (180-81)

Such passages are the reverse of pornography, focussed only on the feelings of the lover and with the implied assertion of sex as the key to life, to spiritual regeneration or rebirth, "serious matters"[20] which justify Lawrence being called a Puritan. Tenderness, fidelity and a desire to marry and beget children, as we have seen, are essential to Lawrentian sex, as they are in *Lady Chatterley's Lover.* But in *The Company of Women*, the last two are carefully avoided while the first two are superficial, transitory and so without much significance. It is obvious that Khushwant Singh has made no attempt to propound any 'philosophy' of love in this novel except that lust is love, and his portrayal of this type of 'love' begins and ends in the purely physical.

But the average reader of *The Company of Women* may miss much (if he just keeps wallowing in descriptions of physical sex and does not try to go deeper into the interplay of heredity and environment in the character of the protagonist, a tragic figure rooted in tradition but corrupted by circumstances. His pious father's training strengthens his Hindu roots, making him recite the Gayatri Mantra and perform Surya Namaskar every day. He recites the Gayatri Mantra even before unpacking his luggage after reaching Princeton for higher studies. Having imbibed the quintessential teaching of Hinduism (Ahimsa and Tolerance), he stoutly defends his faith against the onslaughts of a Pakistani class-fellow Yasmeen: "All I say is try not to injure anyone's feelings. The rest is marginal." (105) He is thereafter haunted all night by the 'magical scene' of the holy Haridwar with the moon and a star reflected in the calm river, and, as he says, "it was to recur in my dreams for the rest of my life." (130) However, these sacred memories do not quite cleanse his mind of libidinous desires, and though he is cajoled, almost forced into sexual relations perhaps, the underlying consciousness of being a sinner all along is apparent from his first encounter, that with Jesica, to the last one with a Bombay prostitute who deservedly infects him with H.I.V., leading to his nemesis, the tragic catastrophe, arising from his fatal flaw of an obsession with sex. A heavy overdose of a tranquilliser, with a recitation of the Gayatri Mantra with the swallowing of each pill, makes him enter into eternal sleep, with the rhythms of the mantra singing him to his rest. Mohan Kumar is both a willing sinner and a willing victim of his sins. Thus if we can overlook the numerous sexual acrobatics, we can be more sensitive to traditional Indian undertones running through the novel, the protagonist's deep-rooted affection and gratitude for his father for whose sake he had returned from America, (45) and after whose death he, full of grief, undergoes all the religious rituals including the immersion of his ashes at Haridwar for the peace of his father's soul. Thus the novel can yield at least a few choicest slices of morality, and respect for religion and tradition to a sensitive person, adult and mature in his outlook towards sex.

Both D.H. Lawrence and Khushwant Singh seem to suggest a misguided approach to sex, one directly and the other inversely and by implication Lawrence through relatively minor characters like Clifford and Michaelis, and Singh through his very protagonist Mohan Kumar with no other character to illumine the path to true sex, while Connie and Mellors illustrate the right key to life and human regeneration.[21] In Singh, Sex pure and simple is the hero, while in Lawrence it is "the holiness of heart's affections, and for sex as a part of that holiness, not as a hole-and-corner affair of dirty post-cards, strip teases, and pin-ups."[22] In both the novels individual and societal concerns have been attempted, in *The Company of Women* more directly than in *Lady Chatterley's Lover*. In fact, social concerns figure prominently in many of D.H. Lawrence's novels. But in *Lady Chatterley's Lover*, they seem rather to be relegated to the background, though they are very much there. To conclude, Khushwant Singh's protagonist caught in the Mephistophilean trap of superficial and promiscuous sex leading him straight to the fate of Faustus, conveys only a limited message, while in Lawrence Connie and Mellors do so through their own slow and gradual realization of the true depths of sexual consciousness. The comparison between these two novels approximately illustrates Richard Hoggart's distinction between the two types of sex: "Body without mind is brutish; mind without body . . . is a running away from our double being. Lady Chatterley and the gamekeeper each unconsciously seeks relations in which tenderness, physical passion, mutual respect all flow together. So this novel describes much more than physical sexual relations."[23]

Sex in *The Company of Women* is largely confined to the

physical side through the tragic decline and fall of its protagonist on account of his obsession with sex and the impact of a newly industrialized 'culture' saves it from being "brutish." *Lady Chatterley's Lover,* on the other hand, opens up new parameters of sexual relationship which broaden out, as we have seen, into a comprehensive vision for the regeneration of mankind through, what he calls "phallic reality" which is "beyond sex."[24] Khushwant Singh himself did not rate his novel very high. Its remaining "on top of India's best sellers' list for over four months" is an indication of the average reader's taste.[25] Khushwant Singh's descriptions of sex are not 'sacred,' not to be compared with the uplifting sculptures carved outside temples like those of Khajuraho and Konark, while D.H. Lawrence is described by Sri Aurobindo as a philosopher, poet and saint, "Yogi who had missed his way and come into a European body to work out his difficulties."[26]

NOTES

1. Quoted in Julian Moynihan, "*Lady Chatterley's Lover,* the Deed of Life," in Mark Spilka, ed., *D.H. Lawrence: A Collection of Critical Essays* (Englewood Cliffs: Prentice Hall, 1963), p. 72.
2. Quoted in Karan Thapar, "Keep kicking, Khushwant, we like it," *The Hindustan Times,* 3 Oct. 1999, p. 4.
3. Bachi J. Karkaria, "Just Ask for KS," *The Sunday Times of India,* 3 Oct. 1999, p. 14.
4. Khushwant Singh, ed., "Introduction" to *I Believe* (New Delhi: Orient Paperbacks, n.d.), p. 8.
5. *Ibid.,* p. 10.
6. Suchitra Behal, "Old yes, but 'dirty' no," *The Hindu,* Sunday, 19 Sept. 1999, p. xv.
7. Albert Mordell, *The Erotic Motive in Literature* (New York: Collier Books, 1962), Chapter V.
8. Suchitra Behal, p. xiv.
9. Shoma Chaudhri, "I'm not a dirty old man," *Outlook,* 4 Oct. 1999, p. 66.
10. Pawan K. Varma, "Provoking people has become part of my character," *The Hindustan Times,* 3 Oct. 1999, p. 6.

11. Karan Thapar, p. 4.
12. Madhu Jain, "We've Had So Many Donkeys as PM" (an Interview with Khushwant Singh), *India Today,* 10 Aug. 1999, p. 54.
13. Khushwant Singh, *The Company of Women* (New Delhi: Viking, Penguin Books, 1999), pp. 23-24.
14. "Summing and Verdict" on the trial of Penguin Books in Old Bailey, London on Nov. 2, 1960 (Appendix to D.H. Lawrence, *Lady Chatterley's Lover*) (New York: Grove Press, 1960), pp. 377 and 378.
15. *Ibid.*, p. 380.
16. *Ibid.*, p. 372.
17. Quoted in Frank Kermode, *Lawrence* (Suffolk: Fontana/Collins, 1993), pp. 132 and 133.
18. K.K. Sharma, "Censorship and Freedom of Mind: Some Reflections," in K.K. Sharma, ed., *Censorship and Literature* (Delhi: K.K. Publications, 1998), p. 128
19. D.H. Lawrence, *Lady Chatterley's Lover,* with an introduction by Richard Hoggart (Harmondsworth: Penguin Books, 1961), p. 188,
20. Frank Kermode, p. 136.
21. *Ibid.*
22. Richard Hoggart, Introduction of *Lady Chatterley's Lover*, p. xiv.
23. *Ibid.*, p. viii.
24. Frank Kermode, pp. 122 and 125.
25. Khushwant Singh, "Farewell to 1999," *The Hindustan Times,* 1 Jan. 2000, p. 19.
26. Quoted on the Inner Title Page of Chaman Nahal, *D.H. Lawrence*: *An Eastern View* (Delhi: Atma Ram, 1971).

Lust for Life or Zest for Life?: A Study of *The Company of Women*

D.K. PABBY

By interrogating the theme of Khushwant Singh's latest novel *The Company of Women* in a polemic manner, I am trying to understand and analyse the complexity of this novel which has been pejoratively categorised as a 'popular novel,' 'pulp novel' or 'pornographic novel' by some reviewers. The novel undoubtedly contains some elements of *erotica* as well as *exotica*; and that is what makes it an extremely interesting but meaningful reading. Having been written at the ripe age of eighty-five by one of our first-rate novelists writing in English, it is churned out of the writer's varied experiences and intimate and scholarly knowledge of different branches of knowledge. 'Sex' remains the chief point of reference throughout the narrative, but it is not there for the heck of it—it does lead to exposition of two points of view to cope with the complexities and ironies of life especially in an evolving society like that of India. In this context, Khushwant Singh's words in the author's note acquire an additional undercurrent of meaning:

> As a man gets older, his sex instincts travel from his middle to his head. What he wanted to do in his younger days but did not due to nervousness, lack of response or opportunity, *he does it in his mind.* I started writing this novel when I was eighty three. I finished it in eighty five. An equally apt title for it could be: 'The fantasies of an octogenarian.'

The fact that Khushwant Singh finally retained the title *The Company of Women* in preference to the former, is indicative of the true character of the novel or still better the main focus being on 'hetrosexuality' rather than just 'figments of my senile fantasies.'

It has to be acknowledged that the learned readers of literature will find the plot of the novel 'simple and linear.' But soon the complexity and seriousness behind the facade of simplicity of plot becomes perceptible to the sensitive and objective reader. Several layers of the thematic meaning, undercutting satire, subtle irony, stylistic experimentation in narrative strategies, etc. start unfolding themselves once the reader looks at the protagonist Mohan Kumar's sex adventures with uncoloured vision and unbiased mind. In line with the narrative strategies of the modern psychological novel, *The Company of Women* opens in a dramatic manner making a very meaningful use of the 'flashback technique':

> For Mohan Kumar, it should have been a day of rejoicing. It was not. He had looked forward to it for twelve years. His wife had at long last decided to leave him; despite the months of acrimony that had preceded it, she had agreed to give him a divorce provided she had custody of their two children. He was so anxious to get his freedom, that besides the two children he agreed to give her whatever else she wanted in the way of alimony: jewellery that he and his father had given her, furniture, pictures—anything she named. She wanted nothing. She seemed as eager to get rid of him as he was to get rid of her. That afternoon she had packed her things and driven away to her parents's home. She had not bothered to say goodbye. The children sensed that this was not just another visit to their grandparents. They embraced and kissed him before running out to get into their mother's black Mercedes. The car had shot out of the gate with unnecessary speed; she had made sure the children have no time to turn back and wave goodbye. Mohan should have been celebrating his newly won freedom from his nagging, ill-tempered wife. But as he sat in the balcony of his double-storied bungalow, his feet resting on the railing, smoking a Havana Cigar, *he felt empty inside*

> *and shrouded in loneliness.* There was all-pervading silence. No screaming of children fighting with each other . . . their squabbles had often irritated him. Now he missed them. The house suddenly had far too many rooms, and the night too many hours. He was weary. (3-4)

A close reading and careful analysis of the opening paragraphs reveals several things:

1. The plot will be episodic in character.
2. The character of the protagonist will be round and psychologically-complex.
3. Strength of passion, lust, self and freedom override all other considerations for not keeping traditionally-arranged marriage going on somehow in spite of marital discord and incompatibility .
4. Equality of gender is fast becoming a reality, socially acceptable.
5. The children become the worst casuality and have to face traumatic dilemmas when the separation finally becomes a legal reality as much as during the processing of the case.
6. Poignant reality of separation from the partner, though apparently providing freedom or relief to the male, does cripple him somewhere inside when the feeling of 'emptiness inside' and 'loneliness' or alienation make their presence felt.
7. The pleasant and enjoyable squabbles of children get replaced with 'weariness.'

The next few pages in the first chapter titled "a new beginning" present a critical retrospect on highlighting the typical middle-class mentalities such as an arranged marriage of an America-returned young Hindu Punjabi through matrimonial columns of an English newspaper and the easy way in which Mohan Kumar has allowed himself to be offered for sale and finally agreeing to marrying Lala Rai Bahadur Achint Ram's daughter Sonu as he had made the highest bid. However, after the birth of their first child, a son, difference in temperament of the two begins to surface and Mohan discovers that Sonu was not only quick-tempered and possessive, she also did not like the presence of his old father in the house which was a sort of gift from her father. As Mohan had progressed in his business of exports, he bought himself a bungalow of his own with a garden in Maharani Bagh. This he thought will keep Sonu and his father out of each other's way. But he was proved wrong and his father, sad and diminished, finally shifted to an ashram in Haridwar. Though he was not given to introspection, he does ruminate over love, marriage and sex life like an amateur philosopher. In the seventh year of their marriage, they had a daughter born out of loveless relationship. Even this did not bring them any closer and their quarrels became endemic which coupled with the real culprit 'gossip' finally resulted in their divorce. Mohan's changed situation demanded new solutions and the Princeton-educated young man in his forties comes out with an idea of inserting an advertisement in *The Times of India* "seeking a live-in companion for a mutually agreed time duration. Willing to pay air fare to Delhi and back and Rs. 10,000 per month for expenses. Free board and lodging in comfortable home with three servants and chauffeur-driven car. Religion no bar. Relationship to be without strings attached on either side. If interested, enclose photograph and bio-data. Correspond box no.__________." (11) This method of Mohan, making a 'new beginning' in a purely western-oriented style and the response that he receives, do mirror the new-emerging sociological phenomenon in the upper echelons of the society in which people are financially comfortable and believe in an Epicurean or rather Hedonist way of life. Like his creator, very clear minded about the main basis for a Man-Woman relationship when he says (just before deciding to marry in Lala Achint Ram's family which he was convinced 'lacked a sense of class' in spite of being stinkingly rich):

> I weighed the pros and cons of marriage. To me sex was more pressing need than love or companionship. For too long we have been fooled into believing that the basis of a happy Man-Woman relationship is love. Love is an elusive concept and means different things to different people. There is nothing elusive about lust because it means the

> same thing to all people: it is the physical expression of liking a person of the opposite sex: Cuddling, kissing, and fondling leading to sexual intercourse. Love cannot last very *long without lust*. Lust has no time limit and is the true foundation of love and affection. (137-38)

The question that may be validly raised in this context is whether physical and sensual pleasure is the only source of happiness to a person? The answer will reflect the person's basic orientation from days of his childhood, the environment he is exposed to during the formative years; and pleasant and unpleasant real life experiences thereafter. Khushwant Singh is thus indirectly raising some significant sociological questions that are relevant in the evolving of a 'progressive-minded and permissive society.' The evolving of such a society, shorn of sham-morality, double dealing, deception and confidentialities and above all the general hypocrisy may actually usher the society into a newly-defined era of healthy relationships without any hang-ups and guilt-complexes. The process of evolution of such a society is certainly a slow one that will acquire parameters of respectability after a long drawn period of several turbulences and ups and downs. With more than a dozen TV channels relaying Western-music programmes and some serials too oriented accordingly, and becoming very popular especially among the adolescent youth, Mohan Kumar's perceptions sound quite prophetic in the years to come. The novelist here is implicitly making a plan for a more open, more permissive and more tolerant society in matters of sex-related societal norms. In the chapter titled "Susanthika," Mohan Kumar avers:

> After I got my divorce, I felt that I had been freed of Sonu and could lead my life the way I wanted to. I had not reckoned with her vindictiveness. Whenever I went to the Gymkhana or the Golf Club, I would sense a change in the attitude of my friends and their wives towards me. They stared at me as if they were seeing me for the first time. The men made simple remarks calculated to hurt or irritate me. . . . Sonu was undoubtedly responsible for the gossip

> (of my prospective marriage with a physiotherapist from Goa, Molly Gomes). Her servants must have got to know from mine that a woman who passed for a lady doctor was staying with me. My sour ex-wife would not miss any opportunity to making my life public. . . . Sonu succeeded in giving me the reputation of a compulsive womanizer. Although many young women eyed me with a mixture of desire and curiosity, I know they would never have the courage to step out with me. In their parents' eyes I was simply a lafunga—a no good loafer who consorted with women of 'loose character.' *It was the loss of human dignity that bothered me.* There was nothing dirty in what I did, but their looks and remarks made me out to be a filthy sex-maniac. Gradually, I stopped going to the clubs and turned down invitations to parties. I stayed at home, drank alone, listened to music or watched TV. I wallowed in the misery of one whom no one loves. For a time I quite enjoyed my loneliness. (251-52)

Mohan also wonders whether his experiment of taking on mistresses on a short-term basis has been successful and ruminates: "It might have been if Sonu had put me out of her mind and stopped resenting me. On the other hand if it were not Sonu it could have been someone else, male or female, who resented my having a good time. But what was the alternative to the clandestine affairs I had been having? How could I openly have a woman companion whose parents, brothers, sisters, ex-husbands would accept her having an affair with a divorced man and not get upset with her? I could not think a way out of the impasse because I needed sex on a regular basis. . . . I also realised that the sort of relationship I sought with women made me a social outcast. I did not like that. *I wanted to regain respectability*, but how was I going to do that in a society which could not accept my enjoying intimacy with unattached and willing women?" (252) These are obviously complex sociological questions having a psychological bearing for a society that is passing through a phase of transition and is struggling hard to retain its conventional value-system in the wake of onslaughts of Western ways of life through multimedia and the process of globalization.

Coming back to the narrative, we find that the ending of the novel has been brought about in a very post-modernist manner. While bragging about 'the rediscovering of his manhood,' Mohan is blissfully ignorant about having contracted a fatal illness while having sex without a condom with an un-named bai in a Bombay hotel. The irony and seriousness of the situation dawns on him when Dr. Malhotra, a highly qualified America-returned doctor now practising in Delhi, tells him that his blood sample has tested him HIV positive, but assures him: "We can control HIV and prevent it growing into full-blown AIDS for many years. You don't have to worry about longevity. You can have a full span of life—another ten or twenty years. But no more sex." (290) When the doctor left, a pall of gloom enveloped Mohan as there was no one he could turn to for comfort. But he acknowledges that he had only himself to blame for what had happened to him. More than the prospect of dying, a horribly painful death with AIDS, the fear of being treated as a pariah by the world and his own children thinking badly of him haunted him day and night. Once again Dr. Malhotra's words provide him the much-needed solace: "No one need know. So far, only I know you are an HIV+VE case—not even my laboratory staff know in whose blood they have detected the virus—and I'm under oath not to divulge the ailments of my patients." (291) Having been comforted thus, Mohan had his last will and testament made after consulting his lawyer over the legal terminology providing adequately for all those who had looked after him but the major portion of property, the company, the jewellery, etc. went to his two children Ranjit and Mohini. It was after about two years of relatively healthy and outwardly normal life, eschewing sex, that symptoms of TB in the lungs and AIDS were detected. He tried to take the verdict manfully, reciting Gayatri Mantra and reading his father's copy of the *Bhagwad Gita* from time to time. Much of what he read in it made sense to him but the passages on death and re-birth confused him. And one night, after vomiting blood, he understood that his fate had been decided. While contemplating suicide with the help of thirty sleeping pills, the question of what his children would make of it all troubled him for a while, but composing himself like a stoic, he felt that they would perhaps be better off without him and besides, he had ceased to matter to them already. While gulping thirty pills of Calmpose one by one each with recitation of a Gayatri Mantra, it was the image of his father, alone and content by the Ganga in Haridwar, that came and clung to his mind. Thus with tears sliding down his face, Mohan put his head on the pillow and closed his eyes.

Reviewers like Makarand Paranjape have found much fault with the loose, episodic and reductively repetitive structure of the novel as well as its abrupt and unconvincing ending. But it seems that both the structure of the plot and the ending are fashioned so with a deliberate design as is signified from these words of Mohan Kumar:

> To fight the feeling of emptiness and the restlessness that came upon me in the evenings, I took to recording the events of my life. This is what you have read—not exactly as I put it down, because I've asked my writer friend, Khushwant, to tinker with these words a little; I am no writer. He can do what he likes with these pages; I have been comforted by the memories of the women I have loved in my own way. That much is enough. (296)

Khushwant Singh with the help of his protagonist, though in his usual nonchalant and casual manner that he employs in his weekly columns, does want to shock the readers out of their conventional attitudes, biases and taboos about sex which he holds and rightly so to a large extent to be a natural urge. Journey of Mohan Kumar from his adolescent days to his final good-bye to this world, also brings out very poignantly the essential loneliness of man with which every individual has to contend. With recurrent commentary on the life-style of Mohan Kumar's widowered father, juxtaposed against his own diametrically opposite one, the perspective of two alternative ways of life also emerges. One of these relates to the Epicurean philosophy of life in which "pleasure of the self is the one good and our innately sought goal, to which all other values are subordinated."[2] This is contextualized through the happenings in Mohan's life. The second is illustrated through his father's conventional but simple middle-class Hindu's passage to life with the help of a philosophy of asceticism which is defined as: "Asceticism may be characterised as a voluntary, sustained and systematic programme of self-discipline and self-denial in which immediate sensual gratifications are renounced in order to attain some valued spiritual or mental state."[3] In addition to this, the novel through the character of Mohan's wife Sonu whom he finds very nagging, bitter and jealous and juxtaposing it against that of the so-called liberated ones like Jessica Browne, Sarojini Bhardwaj, Yasmeen, Mary Joseph, Molly Gomes and Susanthika, who go to bed with Mohan Kumar without any qualms of conscience, raises significant open-ended questions about gender-equality, male and female sexuality, marital discord, nuclear families, etc.

The Company of Women thus operates on a much wider canvas than what its title very apparently and naively seems to suggest: very briefly the novel basically celebrates a strong passion for life as also life's vagaries in all its variety; and the mere lust for life, at least at some levels, gets transformed into an enthusiastic zest for life. Finally, the experiment of alternating the use of first person and third person narrative with the purpose of fine tuning the process of 'distancing' of the author from the protagonist, has definitely added another dimension to the richness and complexity of the novel. The concluding part of the novel does seem to make a definitive statement in favour of the need for balance and moderation rather than excesses and obsessions in all walks of life and more particularly with reference to physical indulgence and reckless gratification of sensual desires.

NOTES

1. Khushwant Singh, *The Company of Women* (New Delhi: Viking, Penguin India, 1999), "Author's Note."
2. Edward Craig, ed., *Routledge Encyclopedia of Philosophy* (London & New York, 1998), Vol. 3, p. 340.
3. *Ibid.*, Vol. 1, p. 517.

In Defence of Khushwant Singh

RANGANATH NANDYAL

Sex plays a vital role in life. It is an integral and indispensable part of life. The relationship between the two sexes is something that cannot be ignored or treated in a haphazard manner. The Great Transcendentalists, who were ardent admirers of Indian culture, did not frown upon sensuous pleasures. Emerson realized the importance of the soul as well as the body. "See, hear, smell, taste etc. . . . while these senses are fresh and pure," said Thoreau.[1] Commending the Hindus for their frankness in discussing sex, he wrote: "we are so degraded that we cannot speak simply of the necessary function of human nature. In earlier ages, in some countries, every function was reverently spoken of as regulated by law. Nothing was too trivial for the Hindu law giver, however offensive it may be to modern taste."[2] He was, unlike many, not shocked by Whitman's *Leaves of Grass*. "I am the poet of the woman the same as the man," proclaimed Walt Whitman in "Song of Myself."[3] When he sang of the body in "One's Self I Sing," he did not ignore any part of it:

> Of Physiology from top to toe I sing.
> Not physiognomy alone nor brain alone is worthy
> For the Muse, I say the Form-complete is worthier far,
> The Female equally with the Male I sing. (303)

Rejecting all conventional modesty, he declared:

> Welcome is every organ and attribute of me, and of any man
> Hearty and clean,

> Not an inch nor a particle of an inch is vile, and none shall
> Be less familiar than the rest." (303)

He vindicated the body and made it a compeer of the soul:

> I have said that the soul is not more than the body
> And I have said that the body is not more than the soul. (315)

In "A Backward Glance O'er Travel'd Roads," he averred: "*Leaves of Grass* is avowedly the song of sex . . . the espousing principle of those lines . . . gives breath of life to my whole scheme that the bulk of the pieces might as well have been left unwritten were those lines omitted . . . the lines I allude to, and the spirit in which they are spoken permeate all *Leaves of Grass*, and the work must stand or fall with them." (319) Moreover, it was through the body that Whitman tried to transcend the body. He looked upon sex as something integral with and conducive to spiritual evolution of man. He said:

> O I say these are not the parts and poems of the body
> only, but of the soul,
> O I say now these are the soul. (321)

As an inheritor of the Great Transcendental Tradition, Henry Miller not only admired Eastern culture but also acquired the Eastern attitude towards sex. Regarding the frankness of Miller in describing sex, Karl Shapiro wrote: "it is possible that he is the first writer outside the Orient who has succeeded in writing as naturally about sex on a large scale as novelists ordinarily write about the dinner table or the battlefield."[4] It is very interesting to note here that the attitude towards sex of Khushwant Singh—who met Henry Miller in London—[5]is similar to that of the American transcendentalists and that of ancient and medieval Indian thinkers and writers.

II

When the ancient Indians thought a thing worth doing they did it well without reservations of any kind. Their questioning mind probed into the secrets of sex with the same frank, open-minded thoroughness which characterized their approach when dealing with philosophy and religion, astronomy and medicine. To them sex was a normal function of nature. They were neither puritanical about nor afraid of discussing or describing sex. With this bent of mind, they enquired into the mysteries of sex to help mankind to lead a better and fuller life. Treatises like *Kamasutra* and *Ananga Ranga* are the products of their intense research. Kama (desire), according to ancient Indian thinkers, is one of the Purusharthas, the ideals of life, the other three being the Dharma (righteousness), Artha (wealth) and Moksha (salvation). The expression Kama includes the pursuits of the worldly pleasures, the pleasures of the flesh and the senses. "There is a prevalent idea," proclaimed Radhakrishnan, "that the Hindu view concedes no reality of life, that it despises vital aims and satisfactions, that it gives no inspiring motive to human effort. If spirit and life were unrelated, spiritual freedom would become an unattainable ideal, a remote passion of a few visionaries. There is little in Hindu thought to support the view that one has to attain spiritual freedom by means of a violent rupture with ordinary life. On the other hand, it lays down that we must pass through the normal life conscientiously and with knowledge, work out its values, and accept its enjoyments. Spiritual life is an integration of man's being, in its depth and breadth, in its capacity for deep meditation as well as reckless transport. Kama refers to the emotional being of man, his feelings and desires. If a man is denied his emotional life, he becomes a prey to repressive introspection and lives under a continual strain of more torture. When the reaction sets in, he will give way to a wildness of ecstasy which is ruinous to his sanity and health."[6]

Moreover, to the ancient Indian mind, sex is neither immoral nor moral, but it is amoral; and what is fundamental and justified in life is also fundamental and justified in art. Discussions of sex and sexual activities or descriptions of male and female anatomies are rampant in ancient Indian sculpture as well as literature. Khajuraho and Konark temples are glaring examples of erotic sculpture in India. Numerous examples are present in Indian literature. Sri Veda Vyasa described Sri Lalita as follows: "Nabhyala vala romalilataphala kuchadvayi" (These two breasts are the two fruits growing on the creeper-like hair which springs from her deep navel); "Kamesa jnata Saubhagya marda voru dvayanvita."[7] (The symmetry and smoothness of her thighs are known only to Kamesa.) Kalidasa, in his *Kumarasambhava* gave graphic description of Parvati's body:

> Vrittanupurva cha na chatidirghe Janghe
> Subhe sristavatastadiye
> Sesanganirmana vidhau vidhaturlavanye Udpadya ivasa yatna.[8]
> (The creator, after he had fashioned her beautiful thighs, not very long, rounded, symmetrical, had to make an effort, as it were for the production of excellent beauty, when forming her other limbs).

> Anyonya Mutpidayadutpalachyah
> Stanadvayam Pandutaha Pryvriddham
> Madhye yasthasyam Mukhastha Tasya
> Mrinal Sritrantaram Pyalabhyam.'[14]
> (Of her, the lily-eyed one, the two breasts, yellowish white, have black nipples and pressing against each other, were so rounded that it was impossible to find between them as much space as could be occupied even by lotus-fibre).

Further in the eighth canto of *Kumarasambhava*, Kalidasa described the sexual enjoyment of Siva and Parvati with a gusto and frankness which was not surpassed by even Casanova:

> Tam Vilambitapaniya mekhalamuduhajjaghana bhara duwaharm. (163)
> (Carrying her, whose girdle was hanging loose and who was heavy to bear on account of the weight of her hips.)

> Varumula nakhamargaraji Bhisthdehbanam
> Mritavilochano Marah
> Basanah Prastitilasya Samyamam Kuruatim
> Priyatamamavarayat. (164)
> (His eyes being captivated at the moment by the series of nail marks at the root of her thighs, Siva prevented his beloved as she was tying up her garment which had become very loose.)

Even in the stotras of Sri Adi Sankara, references to big breasts and heavy hips are often found.[9] Sri Jayadeva in his *Gita Govinda* described vividly the beautiful body of Radha and the exciting love-play between Radha and Krishna. Phrases like "Nitambhavati" (woman with heavy buttocks) "Pinapayodhari" (woman with big breasts) are not infrequent in the narration of this enthralling kavya.[10]

III

If one closely studies Khushwant Singh's *The Company of Women*, one would arrive at the conclusion that Khushwant Singh not only followed but toed the line of the great Indian writers from Veda Vyasa through Kalidasa to Jayadeva. For instance, the following description of a love play between Mohan Kumar and Molly Gomes is vivid and reminds the reader of Kalidasa's *Kumara Sambhava*: "She effortlessly slipped my organ into her vagina . . . only the twitching and milking of my organ assured me she was wide awake. It was blissful; it was prolonged. We took turns being on top of each other. . . . I began to pump into her. She crossed her legs behind my back and heaved up each time I plunged down. . . . We climaxed together. . . . Her legs loosened their grip on me."[11] Khushwant Singh's knowledge of *Kamasutra* and *Ananga Ranga*, it seems, came to his help while describing the scene of love play between Yasmeen and Mohan: "She sat astride my middle; spread her ample frame over me and directed my phallus into her. She was wet and eager and my penis slid in easily. Her breasts smothered my face. She held each in turn and put its nipple in my mouth, urging me to suck it. She kissed me hungrily and noisily on my nose, lips and neck, leaving her saliva on me, while she heaved and thumped me with her huge buttocks." (110) Examples of this type are available in *The Company of Women*. A close study of these scenes vis-a-vis *Kamasutra* or *Ananga Ranga* will be interesting.

Further, a blend of the sexual and the religious is undeniably a characteristic of ancient Indian culture. All yagnas are based on the ideas that Mithunikarana would lead to spiritual bliss. Sexual intercourse is Agnihotra.[12] "They direct the observance and performance of mithuna as a religious rite or part of a religious rite. (Taitreya Aranyaka, IV, 75; X, 62, 67; Aitreya Aranyaka, 1, 2, 4, 10; V 1, 5, 13) and they direct that Mantras are to be observed during the observance of the rite. (Rigveda, V, 82, IX, 85, 37) One of the articles of faith of the Vaidik people therefore was, the sexual union led the way to bliss hereafter and must be performed in a true religious spirit to ensure spiritual welfare."[13] Mithuna as a religious rite has a place in the *Vamadeva Vrata, Mahavrata*, and *Saubhagyakanda* of the *Atharvana* Veda."[14] Besides, the worship of Siva in the form of lingam[15] is prevalent in Indian society. The tantriks, moreover, believe that through some sexo-yogic asanas *Kundalini*—the psychic force lying dormant in the human body—can be raised from *Muladhara Chakra* to *Sarhasrara Chakra* and some spiritual heights can be reached in the process.[16]

As an Indian scholar and voracious reader, Khushwant Singh must have been knowledgeable about spiritualisation of sex, though there is no internal or external evidence to prove that he tried to attain supraconsciousness through sex. The juxtaposition of references to religious practices with sexual encounters occur frequently in *The Company of Women*. These are: (i) Mohan Kumar's recitation of the Gayatri Mantra, his visits to Haridwar and the banks of the Ganga and his indulgence in sex with Sushanthika in Haridwar (264-68); (ii) Sarojini going through her ritual of lighting agarbatties and invoking the blessings of Goddess Saraswati and having propitiated her patron goddess, her waiting for Mohan's return from office to have sex with him (53-54); (iii) Yasmeen slipping out of bed and saying her morning namaaz after a satisfying sexual session with Mohan Kumar (112); (iv) Having come to know that he was afflicted with HIV, Mohan reciting Gayatri Mantra from sunrise to sunset and reading *The Bhagavad Gita*. (294) These religious references in sexual contexts should be examined keeping in view the tradition of blending the sexual with the spiritual in Indian thought.

IV

Ancient Indians gave paramount importance to truth and sincerity in human life. 'Satyameva Jayate' (Truth will triumph) proclaim the Vedas. To be truthful to oneself and to be sincere in whatever one does is to be moral. In other words, according to ancient Indians, immorality is the breaking of one's own integrity. Khushwant Singh too, like ancient Indians, tried to be sincere in executing his duties as a writer. His primary aim was not to shock the susceptibilities of the respectable but to report what he believed to be the whole truth about the nature of man through the depiction of his protagonist Mohan Kumar.

In his video-interview for IGNOU, Khushwant Singh honestly admitted: "Even at this age, I have a wicked eye. I fantasise many things and as an octogenarian I can't practise them."

Great thinkers all over the world have proclaimed that the human being is a combination of angel and animal and a spirit imprisoned in flesh, a descent of divinity into materiality.[17] Khushwant Singh's provocative novel *The Company of Women* and the adverse criticism on it remind us of the age old conflict between the flesh and the spirit and importune us to ask ourselves whether it is really any deplorable inconsistency for a human being to be both angel and animal with equal devotion. Is it not possible in other words, to be mystic and sensualist with out actual contradiction? *Sahṛidayas* should answer this vital question.

NOTES

1. Quoted in Walter Harding, *A Thoreau Handbook* (New York: New York Univ. Press, 1959), p. 133.
2. Henry David Thoreau, *Walden* (New Delhi: S. Chand, 1975), p. 54.
3. Walt Whitman, in *American Literature of the Nineteenth Century* ed. William J. Fishe et al, p. 321.
4. Karl Shapiro, "The Greatest Living Patagonian," in *Start with the Sun: Studies in Cosmic Poetry*, ed. James E. Miller Jr. et al (Lincoln: Nebraska Press, 1960), p. 201.
5. During a video-interview done on Khushwant Singh for IGNOU, Khushwant Singh told the author of this article and Namita Gokhale that he had met Henry Miller in London and had read *The Tropics*.
6. S. Radhakrishnan, *Eastern Religions and Western Thought* (1940; rpt. Delhi: Oxford University Press, 1975), p. 450.
7. R. Anantha Sastry, trans., *Lalita-Sahasranamam* with Bhaskara Raya's Commentary (Madras: The Theosophical Publishing House, 1976), Sloka 34, p. 54; Sloka 39; p. 55.
8. M.R. Kale, ed. *Kumara Sambhava of Kalidasa* (New Delhi: Motilal Banarsidas, 1981); Canto 1, verse 35, p. 13.
9. Sri Adi Shankara in *Tripura Sundari Stotra* speaks of Her Nitamba (buttocks) as *Nitamba-Lita-Bhudaram* (excelling the mountain in greatness).
10. See Sri Jayadeva, *Gita Govinda Kavyam* (Madras: Vavilala Ramaswamy Sastrulu). Also in the Telugu *Prabandhas*—the most popular form of poetry in the 16th and 17th centuries—references to buxom breasts (Uttunga Kochapalil), big buttocks (Nitamba), heavy hips (Jaghana), and trunk like thighs (vuruvu) are rampant; a vivid description of the first meeting of the hero and heroine for sexual enjoyment (Prathama Samagama) is present in every Prabandha.
11. Khushwant Singh, *The Company of Women* (New Delhi: Penguin Books India, 1999), pp. 221-22.
12. Satapatha Brahmanam, XI, 6.2.10 & III, 22 in Sir John Woodroffe, *Shakti and Shakta* (Madras: Ganesh, 1951), p. 104.
13. Also, Woodroffe averred: "There is nothing 'foul' in this except

for people to whom all erotic phenomena are foul. 'This is a very indecent picture' said an elderly lady to Byron, who retorted, 'Madam, the indecency consists in your remarks.'" *Shakti and Shakta*, pp. 133-34.

14. *Ibid.*, p. 138.
15. The *lingam* has the form of the male member very magnified and it stands on a platform which is ritualistically called the Gauripatta (slab of Gauri or Parvati) and it is a representation of the vulva. Moreover, as Alex Wayman said in *The Buddhist Tantras*: "The worship of Divinity under sexual emblem is very ancient in India, presumably as old as the Mohenjodaro civilization, which is usually held to be pre-Aryan. *The Buddhist Tantras* have numerous references to male and female deities, and the later class of that literature called the Anantara Yoga Tantra is pervaded with sexual symbolism." Alex Wayman, *The Buddhist Tantras*: *Light on Indo-Tibetan Esotericism* (New York: Samuel Weicer), p. 164.
16. In this regard, Colin Wilson said: "The body can be made drunk with its own vitality far more easily than the intellect or the emotions with theirs. Many men have experienced the feeling 'I am God' in a sexual orgasm." Colin Wilson, *The Outsider* (London: The Pan Books, 1978), p. 113. Also the following statements of Acharya Rajneesh are worth considering in this context: "man got the first luminous glimpse of Samadhi—the non-cognition contemplation—in human history during the experience of intercourse only" and "It is imperative to know Kama if you want to reach Rama." *Sex to Supraconsciousness* (New Delhi: Orient Paperbacks, 1978), pp. 43 and 128.
17. As Alan W. Watts said: "Psychologists with a slant to materialism therefore argue that mysticism is nothing but sublimated sexuality and frustrated fleshliness; whereas they maintain that the love-imagery is nothing but allegory and symbolism, never to be taken in its gross and animal sense. But is it not possible that both parties are right and wrong, and that the love of nature and the love of spirit are paths upon a circle which meet at their extremes? Perhaps the meeting is discovered only by those who follow both at once." Alan W. Watts, *This Is It and Other Essays on Zen* and *Spiritual Experience* (New York: Pantheon Books, 1967), p. 119.

Attitude to Love and Sex: A Study of *The Company of Women*

BHAGABAT NAYAK

After a decade long silence, Khushwant Singh, a 'dirty old man' and a 'rollicking sardar' has stirred up a real hornet's nest with the publication of *The Company of Women* (1999). He is India's most famous iconoclast, agnostic and eccentric; a man with an unerring tendency to injure sensibilities, and with a penchant for controversies for his attitude to love and sex. As a lawyer, bureaucrat, a visiting lecturer to prestigious universities in India and abroad, a frequent television interviewee, a former M.P and India's most talked about journalist, irreverent columnist and editor, Singh is a multi-faceted personality. Advancing age has not mellowed him down; rather, it has brought back his youthful sensuality under the influence of wine and in the company of women.

In an assessment of the novel, Samita Bhatia writes in *The Telegraph Magazine* how Singh explains with a wave of his hand, "At different stages in one's life one has different obsessions—which can be funny or tragic." (6) So *Train to Pakistan* (1956) was penned when the violence that accompanied the partition was uppermost in his mind. His second novel, *I Shall Not Hear the Nightingale* (1959)—which went unsung—was largely based on a family involved with the Quit India Movement of 1942. Another obsession, his home town, is portrayed in the novel *Delhi* (1989). But his most powerful obsession with love and sex finds expression in his latest novel, *The Company of Women* (1999). In an exclusive interview to *The Sunday Times of India* on the writing of the novel Singh states:

> A novel comes out of an obsession. I was just obsessed with this idea. I heard about a man in a similar situation as I had placed my protagonist. His own daughter told me that after her parents' marriage had broken down, each time he took her out he had a different woman with him. He was going around with all kinds of women. That gave me the idea that instead of being saddled with one person, I should allow my hero to have a succession of women all of whom he would finally discard. None of those relationships worked out though it is difficult having periodic liaisons. This is just a story though.

He also writes in his author's note to the novel "as a man gets older, his sex instincts travel from his middle to his head." It appears what he wanted to do in his younger days but did not do because of nervousness, lack of response or opportunity, he does in his mind now in his old age. The novel is a selection of memoirs of this octogenarian which he camouflages as real characters and the men and women portrayed here are no more than 'figments of his senile fantasies.'

Responding to the charge of deliberate obscenity, Singh told a journalist, "I have been deliberately misunderstood by many people who have not bothered to read the book. . . . I have used four-letter words. Perhaps the text is racy, bawdy and has a lot of sex. That is me. And that is also a lot of people." (7) Some of the well known writers like James Joyce, Henry Miller, D.H. Lawrence, Anais Nin, Appolinaire, William Burroughs Write, Kamala Markandaya, Shobha De and Arundhati Roy write most candidly about love and sex. "A novel minus sex is a damn dull novel." (Bhatia, 6) Their concerns went well beyond descriptions of sexual acrobatics. It is not so much their eroticism that is remembered but how they made use of language and of eroticism to undermine convention and strike at the old order that matters.

Singh knows that good literature shuns obscenity. But he has the realization that whatever he writes becomes 'acceptable' and 'saleable' because of his reputation as an editor and writer. He says candidly, "Anything that I published—whatever rubbish it may have been—sold well." His attitude to love and sex is spontaneous and he can amalgamate the experiences like reading Spinoza, falling in love and smelling the dinner cooking, in the manner of John Donne. But unlike Donne, he transmutes the personal experience of the lover into an affirmation about the nature of man. Going through the novel we can assume that Singh has expressed his attitude to love and sex in order to create a taste by which he can be judged. His attitude to love is subjective and has enough experience to realize love's many moods—from cynical to the idealistic and ecstatic to Osho Rajnish's philosophy. Love for him is both 'fair and brown.' Assessing love as a human will and ill, he presents it as an essential element in human mind. At the same time he recognizes it as a trivial and mundane affair in the experiences of Mohan Kumar and Susanthika, a Srilankan Buddhist girl for whom it was a kind of salvation in the form of a romantic idealization in the post modernistic era.

Khushwant Singh's *Train to Pakistan* is a 'realistic epic' on the eve of the independence day and partition situation in Indian history. In the novel Singh has narrated two pairs of lovers and beloveds—Jugga and Nooran and Hukum Chand and Haseena Begum. While the former pair's love is platonic, the latter's love is sensual and mundane. In presenting the characters, Singh expresses his "robust and vigorous pre-occupation with sex" (Shahane, 29) that symbolizes a 'dominant motive' in physical and spiritual sense. In *I Shall Not Hear the Nightingale*, "Singh's obsession with sex results in exercises in copulation involving major characters as well as minor in practically every chapter." (Naik, 220) Singh has presented the finer qualities and sensibilities of a woman in Sabhrai who bears with all "tenacity and purity of her faith, and this evokes the respect and admiration of everybody." (Iyengar, 503) On the other hand "Champak is little more than a bitch, and the novel describes at some length her exercises in sensuality." (Iyengar, 502) Singh sketches these two women but his Sabhrai becomes the radiance of faith and this is the reason why she almost 'steals' the novel. In *Delhi*, he expresses the power of love and lust in the characters of Taimur, Aurangzeb and Nadir Shah: "this unholy trinity primarily stands for the love of power, religious fanaticism and lust for wealth—the banes of politics in modern India." (Dhawan, 204) In the novel, "society enters history and history enters into society." (Zeraffa, 11)

Singh's 'passion for women and love for scotch' is expressed in the character of Mohan Kumar in *The Company of Women*. Mohan's adoration of sex and hypnotic power of love mesmerizes the strong and powerful sentiments of different women who come in contact with him. Singh's description of sex in the book is very significant and it is love and sex that dominates. The theme of the novel has made it high as an erotic one for all practical purposes and for its obscenity, pornography and erotica. It is felt that the purpose is voyeuristic and the novel aims at sexual stimulation. On the launch-function of his novel he pecked on the cheek of Maha Qazi, the daughter of Pakistan High Commissioner in India, Ashraf Jehangir Qazi. When a storm began to brew, he asserted that it was a grandfatherly peck. Whatever may be Singh's motive for writing the novel, it seems to me that the book generates feelings of love and romance, linking sexual passion to societal concerns. The novelist has emphasized anatomical details and the sex-act itself. The novel reminds us of Vatsyayana's *Kama Sutra*, and at times offends our finer sensibility.

Mohan Kumar's erotic passion and sexual drive is the central theme of the book. In describing Mohan's sexual trysts with different women Singh expounds how "no other people have expounded on the entire range of sexual activity as exhaustively as the Hindus." (*The Sunday Times of India*, 10 October, 1999) It appears that Singh might have incorporated the description of Mohan Kumar's sexual drive from Bhartrihari, Kalidasa and Bhavabhuti, the Poet-Philosophers of ancient India. Every religion forbids extra-marital relations for obvious reasons. Mohan Kumar's pre-marital relation in America had prompted him to continue extra-marital affair in India. His preference for the nudity of sex is almost an inborn instinct which he fails to overcome.

Mohan Kumar's marriage with Sonu was of "bodily compulsions" and they had "usually loveless sex." (6) He was of the impression that marriage deprived him of the company of other women which he had during his education in America. He was bit Lawrentian in his ideology of love, sex and women and dreamt the 'rainbow' of his past. Newness in sex and discovering the body of a woman each time gave him sensual pleasure failing which he would have felt life as an epitome of boredom and tiredness. His sex urges were unsatiable and full of fantasies. He did not like to make it a routine affair with his lifelong companion. His adolescent desires convinced him that occasional adultery would not destroy a marriage even though it was a sin.

Mohan's love and sex life can be divided into three stages, pre-marital, marital and extra-marital. At first when he fell in love with Jessica Brown, the tennis champion of Princeton, he says, "I went to her room. She greeted me with a lusty French kiss" (92) and "I fell on her greedily." (93) Again Yasmeen Wanchoo, a self-possessed, bigoted Pakistani Muslim lady who had an aversion for Hinduism and India, said to Mohan:

> Wouldn't it be nicer if we settled Pak-India problems this way rather than by abusing each other and fighting? (110-11)

After a sex bout, she admitted that it was a sin. In the second stage Mohan enjoys his married life with Sonu. Following a bitter divorce, he continues his third stage of making love with a series of women. He got involved with Dhanno, a sweepress and mother of three children. Singh makes it clear how "so called untouchable women were in fact the most touchable" (16) as is evident in the master-maid relationship. Sarojini Bhardwaj, an English teacher of Govt. College for women, came in contact with him through a matrimonial advertisement. She was "sexless but brainy" (51) but in her first encounter with Mohan:

> She screamed, not in agony but in ecstasy of a multiple orgasm. She had never experienced it before nor believed it possible. Her body quivered, relaxed. . . . Then a fit of hysteria overtook her. She clawed Mohan's face and arm and chest and began to sob. I'm a whore, a common tart! I'm a bitch; she cried. Mohan held her closer and reassured her, You are none of those; you are a nice gentle woman

who has not known love.' (48)

After Sonu's departure with her children to her father's house Mohan made love to Molly Gomes of Goa, a trained nurse of physiotherapy and a masseuse in star hotels who says to him: "nothing in life gives a greater sense of fulfilment than the satisfying coupling of male and female." (222)

Susanthika Gunatilleke, the second secretary to the High Commission of Sri Lanka, was a Buddhist. The highly intelligent, young and animated and a feather weight of sexual passion met Mohan at Haridwar. In their meeting they started kissing each others' hands with soft laugh, "like signing an India-Sri Lanka peace Treaty" (264) and their love-talk was expressed in the code words "Operation Colombo." (271) Susanthika could not stay long in India. In order to fulfil his 'sex drive' and 'sex fantasy' he examined the postures of naked women in *Playboy* and *Debonair* and went to Bombay in search of Molly Gomes. He has the last sex encounter with a 'bai,' a Maharashtrian prostitute in a hotel who regenerates his old sex. Shortly after this, he is detected with HIV positive and gets his 'nemesis and rest' before attaining fifty.

Sex with a new woman was pleasurable to Mohan. Studying the human instinct Singh writes how "it got less and less exciting when repeated with the same person." (76) The passion for sex continues in toto, from a 'Maharani to Mehtarani.' When Mohan enjoys sex with Mary Joseph, she justifies her adultery: "only one life to live, sex is important," (177) and when it is denied it becomes more important and "body's needs come above religious taboos and notions of morality." (177) If this is true "how can such a nice thing be sin." (182) A woman like Mary can say "for me this was heaven." (182)

The denouement of Mohan's career in love and sex is really shocking. Mohan had everything in life—knowledge, status and money but he lacked morality. His love's labour was full of lust. Singh has pointed an accusatory finger at him. He calls him a "Muhammad Ali of sex" (251) and presents how his love and relationship with many a woman was not sanctioned in any religion. Mohan bedded many women and paid money to some of them. He says to Molly, "You are worth a lakh of rupees every-time." (249) Like Iago, love for him, is 'the lust of the blood and permission of the will.' There is also another side to his love. While he is in heated argument with Yasmeen Wanchoo, Singh compares his love with that of Lord Krishna, the eternal lover, a living consciousness among Indians and epitome of love who "had over one thousand mistresses; his life-long companion was not his wife but his aunt, Radha." (98) Yet, people worship him and "no one dared to call him a womanizer." (71)

Sex is not a taboo for Singh. Rather he has described it as a passion and a need of the body. As a puritan he has belittled love in the novel and the nemesis of Mohan presents Singh as a moralist. Singh shows the incompatible relationship and maladjustment between wife and husband in a contemporary millionaire's family. But narrating the love and sex experiences in Mohan's life, Singh has taken love and sex from sensual to celestial.

The novel presents love as a Shavian 'life force' not with the purpose of making man a 'superman' but rather a 'sub-human.' It presents lust and amorousness in love which cannot make the 'marriage of true minds.' The novelist presents Mohan's love in morbidness and colours it with 'lust' through his descriptions. The novel appears almost like a series of Video-Cassettes on man-woman relationship. Of course at last Mohan realizes that the sort of relationship he sought with women made him "a social outcast." (257) At the time of death, Mohan reads the *Bhagwad Gita* and gets satisfaction with Lord Krishna's line, 'For one who dies, birth is certain.'

Molly Gomes and Susanthika are abused by their close and immediate relations and undergo traumatic sensual experiences. Though the novel appears to be strictly for adults, Singh has concluded it with a message to sex maniacs in every society—"Avoid free sex and get rid of AIDS." The deep meaning is highly suggestive and the discerning readers are free to draw their own conclusions. Therein lies the merit of the book.

Works Cited

Bhatia, Samita. "In the Company of Khushwant," *The Telegraph Magazine*, 17 Oct. 1999.

Dhawan, R.K., ed. "Khushwant Singh's *Delhi*: A Gloss on History." *Indian Literature Today* (New Delhi: Prestige, 1994).

Iyengar, K.R. Srinivasa. *Indian Writing in English* (New Delhi: Sterling, 1985).

Jung, Anees. "Man Not the Faith," *The Times of India Sunday Review*, 18 March, 1990.

Naik, M.K. *A History of Indian English Literature* (New Delhi: Sahitya Akademi, 1982).

Padgaonkar, Dileep. *The Sunday Times of India*, 10 Oct. 1999.

Shahane, Vasant A. *Khushwant Singh* (New York: Twayne, 1972).

Singh, Khushwant. "A Novel Comes out of Obsession," *The Sunday Times of India*, 10 Oct. 1999.

____. *The Company of Women* (New Delhi: Viking, 1999).

Zeraffa, Michel. *Fictions* (Harmondsworth: Penguin, 1976).

A Case for *The Company of Women*

SUBHASH CHANDRA

The intention of this essay is manifest in the title itself—I wish to defend the novel against the adverse criticism that has greeted it in the form of reviews. I will not invoke any of the current literary theories, which is the vogue in literary-intellectual circles—'theory' is believed to lend weight and substance to the argument which, often enough, is not only accepted (something uncritically, paradoxically), but appreciated in proportion to the obfuscation injected, into the discussion. My defence will be as subjective, and impressionistic, as the criticism of the novel and since all (mis)readings are considered equally valid/invalid, ever since the "death of the author" (thanks to Roland Barthes), I do not feel overly uneasy, at the prospect of the essay seeming a bit partisan.

Singh has reportedly felt hurt (he shared his feelings with two interviewers) at the negative responses that his latest novel has evoked, but in fact, Singh himself is responsible, at least partly, for this negativity, because part of the criticism (and the more trenchant portion of it) concerns the blatant portrayal of lust/love in the series of sexual encounters Mohan Kumar, the protagonist of the novel, undertakes. I would like to quote Singh's comment on himself, in an interview to Ashok Chopra, on the occasion of the release of his earlier historico-fictional work, *Delhi*, in *The Hindustan Times* (Sunday Supplement; 14 January 1990, p. 2): "I am a dirty old man, I will remain a dirty old man and I will write as a dirty old man." This statement, coupled with the prolific reference to breasts and buttocks in the Malice column, has created a particular kind of image of Singh, which he now seeks to undo—perhaps in the wake of the hostile reception of *The Company of Women*. He tells Suchitra Behal (*The Hindu*, 19 Sept. 1999): "Since I laughed loudly, praised good looking women and the wine I drink, people choose to call me that ('Dirty Old Man') . . . it hurts." Why should it hurt when people call what he called himself? But this is beside the point for the purpose of my discussion. What I want to foreground here is that the criticism of the book has been structured to a large extent by the image Singh has, over the years, built for himself which, perhaps did quite well for him as a journalist/columnist, lending spice to his writings and making them sensational and more saleable, but which seems to have become the Albatross around the neck of his novel. Let us see how?

A great deal of antipathy stems from the critics' inability or desire to separate the author from the narrator and the hero of the book which, in turn, leads to blurring of the perception of the personality of Mohan Kumar and certain other aspects of the novel. This line of thinking is contained in Suchitra Behal's question: "Did writing this book come to you naturally, considering its theme? Makarand Paranjape, an outstanding and perceptive critic and scholar, falls prey to the temptation of interchanging the author with the protagonist and, therefore, writes a damning response to the novel: "A man, it is said, is known by the company he keeps. In the case of Mohan Kumar, the protagonist of Khushwant Singh's new novel, the company is almost entirely female. The book is a catalogue of the women he beds,—well, at least those he considers worthy of mention. These number nine, including his wife." (*The Indian Express*, 19 September 1999). Behal's and Paranjape's are the representative examples of criticism of the novel on this particular point. Paranjape's comment makes Mohan Kumar to be a sex-maniac, whose sole purpose in life is to seek sexual gratification, to complete exclusion of everything finer in life.

Let us examine the narrative. We are told that when Mohan Kumar joins Princeton University on scholarship, he is a virgin. His fighting shy of bathing naked with other hostel boys, and his considering the question from one of the boys—who had felt amusedly shocked at the size of Mohan's 'doodah'—whether he had ever "put that inside a pussy,"—as vulgar, introduce to us a Mohan Kumar who is a typically, middle-class Indian boy, representative of the Indian culture. But then he begins to go out with girls—as is the practice at Princeton.

The two noteworthy things in his relationship with Jessica Browne (a black girl—a sophomore, one year his senior at the university are that it is Jessica who invites him to have a game of tennis with her (she is a good tennis-player), while he expresses his diffidence, as he is a novice at the game and the second that it is she who takes the initiative for consummating sexual intercourse with Kumar: "'Want to see what I'm really like?' she asked. And without waiting for answer she slipped off her blouse and skirt. . . . I had never seen a naked woman before." (92) Jessica's amused assurance that "We'll soon take care of that," to Kumar's statement that he is a virgin, is emblematic of the American culture, where virginity (whether of boys or girls) is regarded as an anachronism. True to her word, as Mohan tells us, "She took me to her bed, pulled me above her and directed my thing into her." (93) The other sexual experience Mohan Kumar has (and these two are explicitly mentioned in the novel) is with Yasmeen Wanchoo, a Pakistani woman married and with three children, and much older than himself. It is important to consider how the sexual relationship comes about with Yasmeen. Here is a physical description of Yasmeen: "She had nut brown hair, large gazelle eyes and was fighting a losing battle with fat. She had a double chin, her arms had sagging flesh and there were tyres developing about her waist." (100) No sex appeal, in short. And Mohan Kumar is expectedly not attracted to her sexually. In fact, his acquaintance with her starts on a frictional note because of her virulent attack on Hinduism, which angers Kumar, even though he is not a devout Hindu. And the discordance continues in their several discussions, since she is a bigotted Muslim and a fanatic believer in the supremacy of Pakistan's military prowess. So, there is hardly any likelihood of "sex" entering their relationship. But it does. Not because of Kumar's innate lasciviousness, but because Yasmeen almost begs for it. And he gives it to her in charity as it were. Kumar is being truthful when he informs us: "I swear I had nothing more on my mind than spending a pleasant evening with Yasmeen," (107) and then goes on to tell us how it happened. We have no reason to doubt his version, because he is not, by any means, an unreliable narrator. In Kumar's words:

> Then she held my hands in hers and looked into my eyes *till I had to lower my gaze, embarrassed.* Suddenly, she put her arms round my neck and said, 'It is our last evening together. Make love to me. Something to remember you by for the rest of my days.' *To say that I was shocked would be an understatement.* This was the last thing I had expected of the evening. . . . But she did not give me a chance to protest. *She took me by my hand and led me to the bedroom.* (108 emphasis mine)

Is this the man who is accused of being focussed only on sex? Undoubtedly, he has a series of sexual contacts with scores of other girls during his stay in America, but that is part of the American cultural milieu—the boys and girls frequently change their dates and sexuality is uninhibitedly considered a part of the relationship. No moral strings are attached to sex. So Mohan Kumar practises the American cultural norms during his stay.

The next phase of Mohan Kumar's life is depicted in India after his return to Delhi in the chapter "Homecoming." The novelist, intentionally, as if anticipating the criticism against Mohan Kumar, introduces certain crucial details. Mohan was offered, while still at the University, highly paid jobs by multinational corporations. He was also offered a lecturer's job in the department of Mathematics at Princeton itself. He could have stayed on there—in the easy atmosphere of the States, "with all the creature comforts it provided," and where dating and bedding were the norms—if the sole purpose of his life had been to enjoy sex. But let us hear Mohan: "I did not have a sense of belonging to the country or its people. I was Indian, belonged to India, wanted to make my mark in India and nowhere else." (114) Mohan is different from those who continue to stay on in the States and who have women—American, European immigrants and Latinos to "cook, keep house and warm their beds." So, it is clear that he wants to settle down to a different kind of life and that he can do in India. Obviously, sexual gratification is not his top priority.

Like any other Indian boy, he accepts his father's decision to get him married—though he protests at the process of scrutinizing girls (with their families) and then their being rejected by father. He feels bad for the rejected girls, for their humiliation, which speaks of his sensitivity and decency. Finally, the marriage is gone through and, like any other normal young man, he looks forward to regular sex and later a family, which would give him emotional support and companionship. But Mohan Kumar gets neither. After the initial burst of sex between Sonu and him, she goes almost frigid and worse, the frigidity is accompanied by her cantankerous, carping nature for ever finding fault with Mohan, flaunting her parents' financial status, and insulting the simple, unassuming, fair-minded, but self-effacing father of Mohan Kumar. The father is eventually driven away from his son's home (even though his grandson Ranjit is extremely fond of him) to Haridwar, where he lives for the rest of his life, a subdued, sad and unhappy man. To top it all, Sonu has a jealous, suspicious nature—accusing Mohan of sexual liaisons with every woman he talks to in a pleasant manner. Nothing can please Sonu, nothing can put her in good humour. The exasperation of Kumar, who has purchased a sprawling bungalow, got it decorated aesthetically and filled it with all kinds of gadgets to please his wife, is symptomatic of the bitterness that is in store for him in the years to come with Sonu: "Is there anything I do which pleases you? I've done all this to make you happy. All the thanks I get is a barrage of criticism?" (174)

What pushes Mohan Kumar into illicit sex is the long abstinence forced on him by his frigid wife who first abides by her mother's admonitions not to have sex during pregnancy for six months and later takes refuge under her gynaecologist's advice: "The doctor said no sex till I have weaned the baby. After six months I will start giving him milk from a bottle and some solids like Farex. *Then we'll see what we can do.*" (176, emphasis mine) What kind of response is this? The tone is patronizing and the intention is to postpone cohabitation, probably even after the baby is weaned away. What does a normal, healthy young man do in such circumstances? Perhaps the institution of prostitution is sustained by women like Sonu—who deny their husbands the compulsions of the natural urge. Mohan Kumar does not visit a prostitute, because he regards that understandable. But he beds Mary Joseph, one of the two wet nurses, who is as starved of sex as Kumar as she has been away from her husband in Kerala.

Apart from Sonu's frigidity and nagging temperament (for ever on the prowl to pick holes and create a fight), her mother-fixatedness (or parent-fixatedness) is another disintegrative element which destroys their marriage. A mere cold and fever make her rush to her parental home and stay there, till she is compelled to join Kumar. And she leaves her parents, rather reluctantly. Then it is the pregnancy which confines her with her parents, as they suggest she have the baby while being with them. This is not all. Her discharge from the nursing home takes her back again to the parents, where she would have gone on staying indefinitely, had Kumar not been firm in his stance. She comes away, but the parents remain reluctant to let her go. "She knew I meant business," says Kumar. "She told her parents. Very reluctantly they agreed to let her go." It is important to note that driven by the desire for the company of his wife and child, Kumar had been visiting her at his in-laws, their rude, arrogant and contemptuous behaviour notwithstanding. Always ready to create a fracas, and exasperated by Kumar's silences, Sonu mentions divorce. Emboldened by Kumar's quietness on the issue she presses for it the next time. He agrees.

Then we witness Kumar's efforts to satisfy his sex drives. An advertisement in the newspaper, for purely live-in relationships on certain terms, quite decent, in fact, to the female partner. Kumar could be criticized for not allowing any of these relationships to mature into a lasting one. Or he could have thought of a second marriage, anyway, being an eligible, wealthy man. But he does not. The reason for his not marrying again is clear enough: the bitterness caused by Sonu is enough for a life time. One cannot castigate Kumar for the live-in relationships, for the present sociological scenario is in a ferment even in India. With the exposure to the Western cultural paradigms through the satellite channels, the institution of marriage may be redefined and the future definition may validate this type of living arrangements.

Excessive focus on sexual morality has relegated to the background some of Kumar's praiseworthy qualities: he is a self-respecting man who insists on starting his own business, a decent man, who does not force himself on Sonu for the initial few days, as she is scared of sex, a generous employer, whose staff are (both at the office and at home) happy with him, and above all an honourable man, who does not believe in seducing his friends' wives, and who keeps the terms of the contract, when his live-in partners are with him. And to say that he is devoid of emotions is not quite correct. He feels tenderly towards Sarojini, whose eyes well up with tears, at the time of her departure; he is truthful, when he tells Molly: "I think I'm falling in love with you," and when Susanthika is going away, he earnestly pleads: "You will keep in touch, won't you?"

The novel at the deeper level is much more than mere sexual bondings between Kumar and his women. It, in fact, constitutes search for happiness on the part of the protagonist. He seeks it within the institution of marriage and after the marriage fails, he strives for it outside marriage. Happiness remains a chimera for him and so it is perhaps for human beings at large.

The novel, above all is not devoid of poignant moments. Kumar's father missing his wife at the proud moment of his son being back from the States, having topped the University in the professional course, and his tears wetting Kumar's hands, who does not know what to say, is a moving moment. And so is the fond relationship between the grandfather (Kumar's father) and the grandson, Ranjit, who loves his grandpa. Kumar's father decides to leave for the ashram in Haridwar in the interest of marital peace between his son and Sonu. I would like to quote the relevant passage: "Father was ready with his luggage when I reached home that afternoon. Baby Ranjit was asleep. My father gazed at the child's face for a long time. He could not hold back his tears. He murmured a silent prayer as he left." (187) The shimmering beauty of the Ganges at the time of the Arti in the evening, when "temple bells started clanging," when the priests "came down the steps of Har Ki Pauri, as if in a majestic procession," and pilgrims placed leaf-boats with flowers and lit oil lamps in them on the stream and the dark river reflected a "myriad quivering light" is a memorable experience for Mohan Kumar as well as the reader.

The novel can be faulted for its abrupt ending, as pointed out by Purabi Panwar in her review in *The Pioneer* (25 September 1999). The endings generally pose a problem to novelists, we are told by E.M. Forster, who goes on say that marriage or death are the devices often employed. Marriage has already taken place. Leaving Mohan Kumar to carry on would leave the novel inconclusive, and diffused. Hence this alternative.

Feminists would be on solid ground on the point of representation of woman as vamp—Sonu not being endowed with one redeeming characteristic. The novel is from the male point of view and the author could be arraigned for misogyny, for painting the woman black. But then if there can be *ecriture feminine*, why can't there be *ecriture masculine?*

The novel needs to be approached neutrally in order to be enjoyed fully.

Laughter, Criticism and Self-Fashioning: The Essays of Khushwant Singh

PRAMOD K. NAYAR

Khushwant Singh has titled his collection of writings *Not a Nice Man to Know*[1] (1993). In his opening remarks ("Seeing Oneself") he reiterates this claim. (5) This paper seeks to demonstrate how Singh's writings dismantle his own claim. I propose to show how Singh's text becomes a staged discourse which contradicts and deconstructs his prefatory statement about himself. For my purpose I have focussed on Singh's use of humour for self-fashioning. From a study of the language of his comic discourse I draw certain conclusions about his "Self." The paper is thus divided into two sections. The first analyzes the anatomy of wit in Singh's journalistic essays. The second part unravels the representations of the self which the reader gleans from such a reading. Obviously, one of the assumptions of the paper is that even so-called "paraliterature" can be useful to understand the figure [of the writer] in the carpet [of his/her works], to borrow Henry James's famous formulation. The essays selected are those which contain humour.

I

Khushwant Singh's essays prepare us for the laugh with great subtlety of technique. Singh employs the anecdotal form of the essay. The anecdotes to follow are framed in the opening section of the essays. This framing is achieved through bits of information handed out to the reader. We note, for example, Singh's serious opening tone of "Doomsday in Yogiland." After telling us about a rare astronomical conjunction, in very specific terms, he uses miscollocation. Singh writes: "On the evening of 3 February 1962 to be exact, at 5.35 p.m.—eight planets *joined forces* in the Capricorn and *declared war on the world.*" (91, emphasis mine) Here a set of phrases used to describe one thing is associated with something else (planets do not declare war!) We are then told of the efforts made by the "Sadhus" of India to avert disaster as a result of this cosmological event. The image of war is re-employed: "The battle was on. Wicked planets versus the holy men of Hindustan." (91) Here, the anecdotes to follow are framed as the description of a miracle, or battles, and so on.

In "Going Gaga over Yoga" Singh begins with a description of Swami Dhirendra Brahmachari: "Although everyone will admit that he looks every inch the picture of a sage of ancient times, many disapprove of his frequent appearances on television." (111) Or, in "New York on $17 A Day" the essay opens with the cabdriver's question: "This your first time in New York?" Singh meditates before he answers. He thinks: "What kind goes down better with an American cabby—The innocent abroad or the experienced traveller? I opt for innocence." (153)

Singh's strategy in these kinds of opening is to provide a signal for the later anecdotes. The framing and the signal has to be ambivalent, so that the humour can be subversive. Singh's opening passages seldom herald humour. We have already noted the specific details recorded in "Doomsday in Yogiland." A tone of scepticism is deliberately introduced in the lines following the description of Swami Dhirendra Brahmachari in "Going Gaga over Yoga: "Not everyone approved. . . ." Singh's remarks are thus suggesting a polyvalency of the signs. The Swami's physique may be interpreted as denoting the positive effects of Yoga, or the unascetic-like physique of an ascetic. This polyvalency is at the heart of future developments of the joke.

A second move occurs in the opening sections. This is the orientation of the joke. The orientation generally refers to the thematic preoccupation of the joke.[2] For example, we are oriented towards the subject of the article: superstition, make-believe, Yoga, a fellow journalist (in "Prabha Dutt") and so on.[3] Orientation also contributes to the reader's expectation which is deliberately kept ambivalent. This can be illustrated by noting Singh's piece of information on Swami Dhirendra Brahmachari:

"Other yogis, envious of his success, call him the Rasputin of New Delhi." (111) Through such a use of antonomasia we are awakened here to the negative qualities of this Yogi.[4] The reader is now prepared for the full anecdote. She awaits, necessarily in the dark, for what is to be revealed.

At this point of the narrative, the formulaic pattern of the joke is employed. Types and characters provide this pattern: superstitious believers, bossy women, fake Gurus, an innocent abroad. Such a typification informs and shapes the reader's response. This response is due to the substructure of the anecdotal essay.

The reader of Singh's writings—middle class English educated Indian (usually)—is aware of the bare details, or the type, of the anecdote. This awareness of generic details is more or less universalised in Singh's essays: India's veneration of holy men (and holy cows, as Singh adds), false gurus, bossy women, the vastness of the American continent etc.

Typification in Singh's essays relies on the reader's awareness of generic substructures. His descriptions tend towards either ecphrasis or hypotyposis.[5] The set description—ecphrasis—may not be true to detail, or may be exaggerated and/or modified intending to entertain. Such ecphrasis can be found in Singh's descriptions of the Yoga ashram (112), Yogic system of diagnosis (113), or a New York hotel room (155). There is also hypotyposis—realistic description—which is almost always combined with ecphrasis in Singh. The hypotyposis is meant to attract our attention to the object described. Examples are numerous in Singh. In "Doomsday in Yogiland," Singh writes of the result of various rituals performed to ward off evil: "The issue between the priests and the planets was fiercely contested. On the evening of 5 February, the moon deserted the conjunction in the Capricorn and the enemy were in full retreat. The battle was won." This rather exaggerated and excursive description is soon followed by a very realistic narration: "In these forty-eight hours and twelve minutes India literally burnt hundreds of tons of precious clarified butter, rice, coconut and other edibles. At least a million dollars passed from the pockets of the credulous to base Brahmins . . . the loss to the nation owing to the stoppage of work during the 'crisis' totalled thirty-five crores of rupees." (92)

A similar example of hypotyposis as revealing the comic pathos is found later on in the same essay. We are told that Maharaja Ranjit Singh's astrologers "consulted . . . the horoscope, put their heads together and assured him he had at least another ten to fifteen years to go. Four days later, the Maharaja was dead." (94) This hypotyposis following upon ecphrasis brings out both the pathos (of economic loss) and the comedy (of self-deluding superstitious people) simultaneously. The humour emerges with a sense of outrage, as in the above example.

The generic substructure of the anecdote is elaborated into a "context" by the narrator. Singh recounts his experiences for the reader. A transition is thus being made. When Singh speaks of being "cheated [by taxi drivers] in England, France, Italy, Egypt," (153) or the death of a favourite subordinate colleague (17) he is particularising a recognisable experience. The universality of events is now located *within* the personal experience of Khushwant Singh. Thus the substructure of the anecdote helps the reader identify with the particularity of Singh's experience. This is the "context" (the word here is obviously used in a broad sense) of the anecdote.

In Singh's essays, anecdotes grow out of one another. Yet they all link together, as a good narrative should. To demonstrate this technique of Singh, I propose to dismantle the structure of his travel essay on America.

We are given a series of events, as they happen to Singh. This series is linked with itself, as Walter Nash requires of the anecdote, (66) by a short anecdotal phrase or comment. In the episode of the taxi cab, Singh counts his money. He discovers he has little left if he pays $ 2.25 to the cabdriver. Singh writes: "I make a quick calculation. A quarter tip for the cabby. And if I walk in with my valise, I'll avoid the hotel commisionaire!" (154) This economic crisis imagery is the link into the next episode—that of the hotel. Singh writes: "I make the reception desk without loss of money." (154) The hotel episode again closes on a similar image: "New York Sightseeing offers me a choice of fourteen tours ranging from $ 4.50 to twenty-six dollars. Even the cheapest would leave me with a little over five dollars for the evening. . . . I cross out sightseeing." (156) The theatre episode ends without a direct mention of money (Singh is careful not to misuse, or abuse, his strategy). Yet the economic metaphor persists. The episode ends thus: "Now I feel as if I *owned* Times Square, New York, the whole of the United States of America. I re-enter the bar with a *proprietary* air." (159, emphasis mine) The following subsection ("What Country You From") also ends with an economic metaphor: "Where in this great city can one *spend* a couple of cold winter hours for *nothing*?" (162, emphasis mine) And then, the essay itself closes thus: "It is obvious to me that New York can be done in under seventeen dollars a day but it is not fun. I decide to cut short my stay." (163)

Having noted the linkages of the anecdotes the reader draws up the "paradigms of the total theme." (32-33) These are: poverty, the desire to see and know, and the incompatibility of the above two. Humour is located in such a recognition.

The final stage of our analysis is locating the locus of the joke. The locus, Nash informs us, is the word or phrase which clinches the joke. (34-35) This locus is indicated through a debunking of established, believed in or romanticised "truths." In the remarkable essays "Holy Men and Holy Cows" and "Going Gaga over Yoga" Khushwant Singh's brilliant wit is adequately demonstrated. During his meeting with a certain Swami Ananda in "Holy Men and Holy Cows." Singh provokes him by referring to another (similar) "Sadhu." Swami Ananda explodes into filthy abuse of this other Swami. In what is clearly one of the loci of the anecdote, Singh writes: "I was alarmed at the language. Swami assured me: 'Ours is a religion of purity and love. We can't have frauds among us.'" (107) Singh adds a little later: "It became a game. The score for loving everyone was five, 'bloody buggers' won by a margin of seven." (107)

In "Going Gaga Over Yoga" Singh ends a section with Swami Dhirendra Brahmachari's vituperative denouncing of another Yogi. Then Singh comments drily: "One of the benefits claimed by Yoga is an equable temper and a sweet tongue which does not lend itself to speaking ill of anyone." (118)

The essay on Japan ends likewise. Singh has lost his passport, travel documents and money. An Indian official in Japan tells him: "Japanese taxi drivers never take anything. It could be the passenger who took your place." Singh comments, in a clear indictment: "Maybe the person who hired the cab after me and took my money was another Indian." (176) The locus of the joke thus provides the criticism, punchline or revelation to the reader. It rounds off the anecdote in connection with the orientation, framing, substructure, context and description, and total themes.

It now remains to be seen how Khushwant Singh's wit is relevant and useful to delineate his "Self."

II

I believe that Singh opens his book with a staged discourse about himself, a misrepresentation. "I am not a nice man to know," he announces. (5) I suggest that this exordial remark, like the orientation and signal of the anecdote joke, is a narrative strategy. It attempts to precondition our response even before our reading his text.

The essay's prime unifying feature, Graham Good notes in *The Observing Self* (1988), is the self. The "wholeness" of the experience the essay represents is thus held together by this concept of the self.[6]

Throughout the collection of experiences, we perceive the events through Singh's gaze. The essays are, as we noted before in the case of the particularising feature of the anecdote, a personal recounting. We are thus able to obtain his views, judgements and moods. Our reaction to his humorous asides and remarks help us understand this self-fashioning.

In his obituary piece on Prabha Dutt, Singh tells us that in the early stages of their relationship he was "overawed by her presence and the viva-voce test she put me through." (17) She regarded him the way "an insect collector would examine the latest beetle in his collection." (17) Then, he writes: "[Prabha Dutt] did me the honour of treating me as her father-in-office." (17) He ends the piece by praising her as a "gusty" journalist for whom he had great respect. (18-19) From the humour of the opening section, to the end, Singh fashions a self which is progressively more clearly demarcated. He does not come across as a specimen beetle, or an incompetent editor or a scared boss. Rather he is a well-respected father figure. The humour, directed against himself, plays a major role is this re-fashioning.

In his piece on Japan he describes how he ogles the lady assistant of the Director of the Non Theatre Association. (172) This prelude-to-pass atmosphere is however adroitly reversed. Singh writes: "The lady assistant with whom I have not exchanged a word has conveyed to me . . . that she has never encountered a more intelligent foreigner." (172-3) The lascivious-Sikh role he projects has just been undone by the lady herself!

There is no flippancy to Singh's wit. Though he opens anecdotes in a serious manner, it is *humour* itself that brings about a serious image of Singh. There is a great deal of the "responsible journalist" tone in his humour. A few examples of this apparently contradictory self-image prove my argument.

In "Doomsday in Yogiland" Singh's opening epideictic discourse of exaggerations and descriptions preface his contemptuous demolishing of the superstitions. This is a responsible act for a journalist read by about 4,00,000 Indians (which was the approximate number of *The Illustrated Weekly* readership). Singh comments, with a hint of reproach, "Some educated Indians are sceptical about the claims made by astrology but they bow to astrological prediction in some form or the other." (93) He ends the paragraph with an ironic query: "What greater homage could 500 million people pay to the 'Science' of astrology?" (94) The journalist Singh, with his peculiar combination of humour and serious reporting, is revealing the sad truth of India's "educated" class.

In "Going Gaga over Yoga" a similar responsible self is visible behind the narrator of witty anecdotes. We are told of the commercial benefits accrued by Yogis through their Yoga ashrams. The ashram of Swami Dhirendra Brahmachari occupies "about 12,000 square metres of land in the *heart of the capital.*" (111, emphasis mine) The London *Observer* captions an article on Yoga, "Cash Vibration" referring to the profits raked in by the Yogis who, by definition, are to observe vows of celibacy and poverty. (119)

I believe that Singh's humour is only the proverbial tip of the iceberg. It suggests a flippant, not-so-serious self. However, as the reading demonstrates, Singh's "hatred" (as he mentions in the opening remarks [4-5]) is towards falsehood and hypocrisy. He comes across as a journalist who is revealing the pathos of "progress"—corruption, human mortality and poverty—through humour. This is a far-from-casual journalist-self. Singh's humour paints him as a responsible, caring and deeply commited person who hopes to educate people through laughter. Khushwant Singh is, then a very nice man to know.

NOTES

1. Khushwant Singh, *Not a Nice Man to Know: The Best of Khushwant Singh*, ed. Nandini Mehta (New Delhi: Penguin, 1993).
2. Walter Nash, *The Language of Humour: Style and Technique in Comic Discourse* (London: Longman, 1985), pp. 34-35.
3. This style of orientation in the opening section is reminiscent of James Thurber's.
4. Antonomasia is a trope where a proper noun is replaced by an epithet. A good example would be the "bard" for Shakespeare. Other indirect descriptions are also used—official address instead of the name, or a famous proper name attached to another person believed to share some quality associated with this name. In this case, Singh's linking of the name of the notorious Rasputin to Swami Dhirendra Brahmachari is the use of antonomasia to awaken us to possible not-so-nice qualities of this man.
5. Ecphrasis was the set piece in the Alexandrian neo-rhetoric of second century A.D. Its object was to describe, with little constraints of verisimilitude. Hypotyposis, on the other hand, had to impart a realism to representation. It was rhetorical ploy to add what Roland Barthes describes as "the lustre of desire" to any object, event, place or person. For a discussion of these rhetorical modes see Roland Barthes, "The Reality Effect," *The Rustle of Language*, trans. Richard Howard (Oxford: Basil Blackwell, 1986), pp. 141-48.
6. Graham Good, *The Observing Self: Rediscovering the Essay* (London: Routledge, 1988), p. 8.

Women and Men in My Life: Autobiography through Cameos

SUBHASH CHANDRA

The title of the book positions women first and then men. And even though the work is about men, too, with whom Khushwant Singh came into contact and interacted, the picture on the front page shows only three women surrounding the writer. Anyone who has regularly and closely read Khushwant's Malice columns would be fully aware of his penchant for the lascivious and salacious and anyone who has read his story "The Bottom Pincher," published in the *Illustrated Weekly of India* several years ago, would be familiar with the no-holds barred titillating descriptions of the rhythmically and tantalizingly moving rounded buttocks of women. His unique method of reviewing a book focusses more on the vital statistics of the female writer than the contents of the work. Why?

It is a deliberate strategy. He has consciously cultivated this stance. He delights in promoting the image of the dirty old man for himself. He is astute enough to know that everyone enjoys a bit of sex, covertly, and even though some "proper" people may condemn him for practising obscenity, they feel titillated and enjoy it. Sex sells. And so does Khushwant Singh. He commands a large readership, in various languages (his Malice column is translated into several regional languages). The sales of *Delhi*, the historical novel by Khushwant Singh, were phenomenal. The release of *Women and Men* was waited for by the public with baited breath. After a minor hiccup in the form of a law suit against the book, the book got to the reading public. The court case ironically gave a fillip to the sales of the book, which got free publicity and did not do any harm to the writer who, in any case, seems to thrive on controversies.

However, it is not only sex that makes his works eminently readable. At the deeper level, his writings contain linguistic finesse, ideological stance, search for truth, and metaphysical statements. His books offer an enlightened discussion, and dispassionate analyses of issues and rational probings into matters of political, social and religious importance. They successfully effected shifting of readers' horizons. His *Train to Pakistan* dramatizes the ennobling power of love, which can transform a confirmed lout Jugga into a person capable of saintly sacrifice. *I Shall Not Hear the Nightingale*, a Sahitya Akademi award winning novel by Khushwant Singh, portrays the expansiveness of Sabhrai's motherly love which grows to include her son's friends into its fold ignoring the risk to her son's life. The novel *Delhi* presents the chequered history of Delhi in a colourful and entertaining manner, besides possessing literary attributes. *Women and Men in My Life* (New Delhi: UBS, 1995) delves into human nature by closely observing, analyzing several eminent women and men whom the writer happened to befriend. The work brings out the inherent instability and the shifting nature of human relationships, and also underscores the fact of the mortality of humans—a fact which is well known to all of us, but which we, in our daily life, tend to forget.

The death of Devyani Chaubal, a film critic, "fat, full of life, malicious gossip, mimicry and zest for life," (10) the painful suicide of Indrani Aikath Gyaltsen who had a "soft gentle voice," and the death-wish of Ghayoorunnisa Hafeez who having lived a full, and happy life is reduced to asking, "why does not Allah listen to my prayer and send for me? I don't want to live any longer," (32) provide potent examples of the mortality of humans and their essential loneliness and sadness.

There is something fortuitous and mysterious in the ways people come close to each other, become intimate friends, sharing the most intense moments of joy and sorrow and then inexplicably drift apart, getting separated by geographical or emotional distance, becoming cold and apathetic. The writer does not offer any explanation for this phenomenon, but underlines this feature of human relationships in several of his write-ups. One of the instances in Khushwant's relationship with Dharma Kumar. In spite of the writer's desire to continue the contact, the two did not meet. Says the author, "Thereafter, whenever we met we promised to ask each other over for a meal. But neither of us has done so." (48) The experience gets repeated in Khushwant Singh's relationship with Prema Subramaniam, who he came to ardently admire as "the most lovable woman in my life." The writer shared some intimate and enjoyable moments with Prema, who was in Madras and who would write letters to him running "into 30 pages with writings on the margins. . . . To my weekly letter of a few paragraphs she could send four to five a week." (73) And what was the fate of this beautiful relationship? Prema had to follow her husband to America where he and the other members of the family had settled. The following words of the writer reveal the tender and lingering sadness caused by the inevitabilities of life: "Last year Prema resigned her job with Higginbothams and left for New York. There is little chance of my seeing her for the next five years. Her letters have become shorter as she has to write on air-letter forms. She still keeps sending me gifts. But I expect with the passage of years they too will get scarcer." (74)

Any budding writer could profitably read *Women and Men* for the fine and vivid descriptions of people—their physical and mental attributes. Khushwant Singh seems to have a keen sense of observation, which enables him to capture the total personality of the subjects he writes about and the innate sense of humour and wit he is endowed with is reflected in his judgement and evaluations of people. I would like to give some examples. About Dharma Kumar, Khushwant Singh says: "She was more animated than any woman I had met: her eyes sparkled; her toes twitched; her hands were restless. She was an excellent mimic and delightfully malicious." (43) This is how he describes Kamna Prasad: "She was a couple of inches taller than me. Long, lustrous, jet-black hair falling down to her hips. Neither very fair nor very dark but light *cafe-au-lait* complexion. Beautiful neck, middle-sized bosom, very slender waist with her flat belly, displaying her belly button and unusually broad hips, designed to accommodate a brood of children." (62) And this is what he has to say about Rita Devi Verma: "I noticed she had high cheek bones, the same as some eastern people have. No make-up, no jewellery, fair skinned, tall, slender and beautifully proportioned with a long neck, full bosom, slender waist and long legs. She looked more like a professional model than a housewife living in a middle-class locality like Sujan Singh Park." (86)

The complexity and diversity of human nature is also brought out in *Women and Men*. What makes men and women behave in strange ways and adopt devious methods which at times boomerang, causing problems for themselves, is entirely beyond the scope of human comprehension. Indrani Aikath Gyaltsen's consuming passion for fame as a literary genius and money led her to indulge in plagiarism. She reproduced verbatim several pages in her second novel, *Crane's Morning* from a novel, *The Rosemary Tree*, published about twenty years ago. The publisher of the latter novel sent notice to Penguin Viking, the publishers of *Crane's Morning*. The constant fear of being exposed as plagiarist, and facing ignominy caused depression in her, leading to her eventual suicide (A warning to the upcoming writers—there is no short cut to fame and money). In Gopal Das Khosla, we have an example of a person possessing a self-destructive streak. His impracticality is revealed in his complaining to the then Home Minister about the financial irregularities committed by A.N. Bhandari, his Chief Justice in the Punjab High Court with whom he was not getting on well. Expectedly, Bhandari told Khosla that "it was not a nice thing to do." But no harm was caused to Bhandari who bided his time. Later Khosla's antipathy towards S.K. Sikri (later Chief Justice of the Supreme Court) impelled him to write a defamatory piece in his column Grimm's Fairy Tales in *The Tribune*. Apart from an apology, which the Sikris made him tender after a prolonged court case, Khushwant Singh suspects that Khosla lost his elevation to the Supreme Court on this account. Khosla was meant for bigger positions, but he himself queered his pitch. Prem Kirpal, who rose to be the Head of the Cultural Division of UNESCO, Secretary of the Ministry of Education, and the kingpin of the chain of Delhi Public Schools, had a funny (hilarious) dimension to his personality: he wanted to get close to women and yet invariably either managed to spoil the relationship or consciously ran away when the D-day came. When he was not getting anywhere with Priobala (Mangat Rai's elder sister), Khushwant Singh told him that "some women responded to action and he should simply grab her in his arms and kiss her." (159) Prem dutifully reported Khushwant Singh to her verbatim. She was incensed and called Khushwant Singh a rascal. The next episode was still more funny. Having come intimately close to a South Indian lady colleague of his, Prem Kirpal got his father's approval to the wedding for which the date was actually fixed. "Prem disappeared from Delhi and sent her a telegram saying he had broken his leg and the marriage would have to be postponed indefinitely. For a few days he even had his leg put in plaster." (140) However Prem's compulsiveness made him continue with his incorrigible habit of making passes at women. Often it is within the means of people to be generous and hospitable, but they act close-fisted and stingy. The author rightly divids people into "givers" and "takers," "suckers" and "spongers." He narrates the sponging habits of no less a celebrity than Chetan Anand—the film-personality—and tells us how Chetan went on inviting himself to the writer's home and enjoyed his hospitality for months on end back in Lahore. But not even once did he ask Khushwant Singh over to reciprocate his hospitality. We all are familiar with such types in our own lives—people who suddenly vanish into the loo at the appearance of the bill in a restaurant.

Why are some men more successful than the others in the matter of securing the love of women? There could be diverse factors, but Khushwant Singh narrates one which seems to play a vital role in the matter of love. The story of Chetan's success with girls reveals to a large extent the inherent nature of girls. Not that the strategy could be uniformly applied with equal results, but what Chetan did in order to worm his way into the heart of the young beauties has a psychological dimension to it. Khushwant Singh tells that Chetan was an inveterate philanderer. So much so, that he succeeded in "winning the heart of the most sought after girl in the university, Uma Chatterjee. Though she was a Christian, defied her parents and agreed to marry a Hindu boy who till then had no job." (102) Khushwant Singh threw a party to celebrate their engagement and Chetan, in the presence of his fiancee, flirted outrageously and shamelessly with other girls present. They got married, had two children, but Chetan's rakishness proved too much for Uma who left him for Alkazi. "Chetan shacked up with a Sikh girl young enough to be his daughter." (102) What was the secret of his success? Chetan would put on his overcoat in the month of June, and with a stubble on his chin and a single flower in his hand, he would call on his girl-friend. Inevitably, she enquired about his wearing the coat in that hot weather. He would reply: "This is all I possess in the world," and he would then present the flower to the girl. It worked. Make a girl feel sorry for yourself, and you have won half the battle. It is a short emotional distance from there. Even though a lot has been written about male chivalry, protective instincts constitute the strongest part of the female psyche. That explains why very often so many ordinary-looking nincompoops walk away with pretty and charming girls. Their under-doggishness does the trick for them.

In *Women and Men*, Khushwant Singh tells us about the quirks, queernesses, predilections, prejudices, eccentricities, secret desires and the ambiguous and inexplicable attitudes of a large number of people, but there is an airy reticence about himself. Readers of the Malice column expected some frank, even damning confessions from the writer in his autobiography. There is nothing of the sort. Khushwant Singh comes out to be a person, who has been manipulated, taken advantage of, admired and sought after, but his image remains a laundered one, his feet of clay remain hidden. To this extent, the book falls short of the genre of autobiography.

Nonethless, the book remains a significant piece of creative writing. It confirms that Khushwant Singh is the master of the anecdote. He weaves an engaging story around the most trivial of incidents and succeeds in holding our attention. And since all of us are at some level of consciousness Scheherazade's husbands, we immensely enjoy reading *Women and Men in My Life*.

Viewing the Other Woman in Khushwant Singh's Short Stories

ALESSANDRO MONTI

In Khushwant Singh's "A Punjabi Pastoral" a blossoming girl, drawing water at a well in a scanty attire plus two pitchers, saves the day for a depressed American missionary and a bored Sikh communist who are visiting a secluded village in Punjab, where the former has started social cooperation between the Sikh majority and the few Christian converts. Apparently you cannot change the Indian ways of life, since the two visitors find the Sikh leader drunk, whereas the Christian converts have merrily relapsed into the darkness of Hinduism, However, the vision of a rustic beauty dispels any impending gloom:

> Suddenly Hansen stopped talking. He sat up straight as if electrified. From Moola Singh's courtyard emerged a girl, barely sixteen, with two pitchers balanced on her stately head, she came towards the well where we were sitting. She wore a man's striped shirt. It has no buttons in the front and made a V formation running from her neck down to the middle of her flat belly. On either side, the V was mis-shaped by her youthful breasts.[1]

"A Native Woman Drawing Water at a Well" might be another title for Khushwant Singh's short story. Wells are obviously a key site in Orientalist and post-Orientalist texts, because of their easy association of feminine beauty with learned reminiscences. As a genre piece, also pictorial, the conventional icon of women fetching water bares (if I am allowed such a word) the self-conscious forays of the colonial male, gazing into the forbidden field of exotic voyeurism. To achieve respectability, albeit spiced with the pleasant vision of scantily clad dusky beauties, items of biblical landscape are often added to counterbalance the well-rehearsed sign of the Oriental scenery, the half-naked woman caught in her privacy, Such is the case, for instance, of the anonymous Victorian missionary reporting back from his Indian agenda, *via* the ancient Palestine. He blurs deliberately (in a "tableau de voyage" labelled *Women fetching Water from a Well*) the Eastern scenery into an amalgamated biblical trope, cobbling together the Middle East and India on the common ground of their atemporal consistency with everyday life as depicted in the Old Testament. He writes, when it comes to wells and lasses

> We saw a band of young girls going to a well with their pitchers on their shoulders, who appeared among the most beautiful of their sex we saw in the East. They had slight and elegant figures, a native grace of mien and air, added to which the tasteful drapery of their light simple attire, the dark tresses that fell in wild luxuriance over their necks and shoulders.[2]

The hackneyed biblical concordance of the Victorian traveller is aptly mirrored by the missionary in the short story, who cites a most famous verse from the *Hebrew Melodies* by Byron, "She walks in beauty, like the night," thus positing an embarrassing equation between the image of graceful innocence evoked in the poem by the feminine presence ("Where thoughts serenely sweet express/How pure, how dear their dwelling place") and the vision of the Other woman as a coloured and brown Venus, whose presence is specifically inscribed into a distanced past or space, either biblical or belonging to the Orientalist script.

As a matter of fact, the patronizing gaze of the male intruder at the well constitutes a whole body of textual Oriental fantasies. Women balancing pitchers on their stately heads are undoubtedly the exotic domestic counterpart to the naughty Eastern wench, the odalisque (a "nautch-girl," in colonial India) or the inmate of the harem. However, both types of represented women (either housewives or something else) share a high state of undressing, their nudity (or half-nudity) being an unmistakable sign of Otherness and imagined verisimilitude. For instance, an engraving (*Vandaersker*) by the Polish/Danish artist Elisabeth Jerichan-Bauman (travelling to Africa and the Middle East) shows two women with the usual pitchers, their appearance ranging from a teasing transparency of dress to the unconcealed exposure of the body.

Another short story, "Maiden Voyage of Jai Hind," features a farcical passage to India and an Indian "Lothario"[3] who gazes, or rather peers, into the wrong cabin. This narrated event mishandles with a revenge the orientalist stereotype of the feminine lazy body in the nude, focalizing a white woman (a wife and a mother, to boot) into an object of illicit desire. The naked body of the English lady lying on her berth for the gaze of an Indian peeping Tom is directly suggestive of the picture of a reclining nude odalisque, a "Maya Desnuda," as the writer points out, rather than a real creature in flesh and bones. The unsavoury situation deploys a further connection with well rehearsed instances of prurience, the stolen vision of the white naked body being a must of the decadent travelogue in India or in other exotic countries.

To quote a case in point, the Italian poet Guido Gozzano, on a quick tour of the subcontinent at the beginning of our century, manipulates in his text an extensive corpus of discursive and pictorial fantasies, masquerading the European woman he meets as white slaves being raped by brown Indians or kept in well stocked "zananas," for the imagined pleasure of the Western visitor, who indulges in the pleasurable fantasy of being a Mogul king.[4] This wild fantasizing highlights with its exotic flavour the vision of the "grandes horizontales" which haunt the domestic interiors and landscapes of the contemporary European painting, such as Manet's *Olympia* and the slightly puzzling *Déjeuner sur l'herbe*.

In the latter picture, the luscious and titillating detail of the naked woman on display represents an indirect Orientalist scenery, whose basic structure is reminiscent of frozen harem pictures "where the location simply provides a new setting for a single or group nude with the added pleasure of seeing the forbidden."[5] Analogously, the porthole in Khushwant Singh's story allows a full exhibition of a private space redolent of lazy sexuality and scenically organized as in an Orientalist painting, for the benefit of an absent and extraneous viewer. This inevitably brings into question to what extent the viewing position of the gazer implicates him in the prurient imagined scene.

To avoid the overt sexual innuendos usually associated with the subject, the Victorian code of aesthetics and morality forbade every visual connection between the English woman and the lecherous gaze of the dark skinned man. It is well known how the contentious picture *In Memoriam* by Patron, 1868, was thought too revolting for description, since "in the original version 'Maddened Sepoys hot after blood,' as *The Times* put it, were bursting through the door," into a room crowded with English women and children.[6] *In Memoriam* "was designed to commemorate the Christian Heroism of the British Ladies in India during the Mutiny of 1857, and their ultimate Deliverance by British Prowess." In the final version Paton replaced the sepoys with a party of Highland soldiers entering the room to rescue the women and the children.

In "Maiden Voyage of Jai Hind" the cluttered space detailed by Patron is defused into the jumble of a small cabin, Khushwant Singh foregrounding the image of a displaced Cleopatra, reminiscent of the domesticated orientalist references Charlotte Bronte adopts to reshuffle the tropes representing odalisques.[7] Given these traits, the scene in the cabin is also obviously de-representative of the suffocating melee of female nudes Ingres exhibits in his *Turkish Bath*, almost epitomizing all the feminine postures a male viewer might dream of. In this connection, Khushwant Singh deploys a full exposure of the body, including front and back visualizations of the reclining lady.

Being grounded on a "bed trick," since the intruding gazer blunders into the privacy of a cabin while pursuing an affair, the story also re-enacts the small intrigue typical of the Anglo-Indian situation comedy, in the circumstance revolving around a more complex encounter, suggesting at least an infringement of the ethnical borderline.

The whiff of miscegenation which taints the grotesque act of gazing (since the blundering Indian is after a blonde Swedish beauty) is forelighted in "Black Jasmine," a story endorsing the flawed stereotype of the black woman being sexually too active. Making her body available through unveiled display, the black woman poses herself as a fetished object, a forbidden fruit to be savoured with awe and perverted delay. The excess of her body, its raw sexual attractiveness (the represented black woman is an assemblage of tropes making an Other of her, from her "very black and oversized nipples," to the "fuzz of her pubic hair" and "her wanton negroid body odour"), pre-empt the scene of any possible glamour, arousing in its stead an ambiguous mixture of overloaded desire and troubled repulsion, which eludes either satisfaction or refusal.

This mode of perceiving the body of the female black Other, as it were an object of estrangement, transcribes the male impulsions into the items of an unhinged logic, which suspends recognition and enforces fear, in spite of desire. Such measures of protection against the excessive availability of the other pose a paradox, since they displace metaphorically the unveiled body, by erasing the voyeuristic desire because of the pangs of revulsion it causes and by representing it as a possibility of distanced or delayed off desire.

To cope with the uncrossable identity of the Other woman, the text deploys disturbed suggestions of racial stigma and forebodings of unlikely sexual transgression, both items being summed up by the adjective "black" given in the title of the short story. In this connection the text needs a measure of sexual protection against the excessive availability of the "Black," whose difference in skin and behaviour requires the reassuring agency of a "deshi" name, Jasmine. However its redeeming quality easily yields brackets to ambivalence and devoluted meaning, Jasmine being mispronounced into "Yasmoon." This uneasy transition unveils a further possibility of derogative translation in the title of the short story, the adjective "black" concealing the disapproving "hubshi," a word of historical origin but still in use, meaning an inferior and almost animal-like race of men.[8] The clash between the scented jasmine and the disturbing presence of the oversexed and lecherous "hubshi" marks the transition from the sequestered and safe space of the "zanana" to a field open to sexual competition and displaying the involvement of the male onlooker—no more an external gazer of exhibited nudity but a character inside the picture.

NOTES

1. Khushwant Singh, *The Collected Short Stories* (New Delhi; Ravi Dayal, 1989), pp. 44-45.
2. Anonymous, *The Indian Mirror: Illustrations of Bible Truth Drawn from Life in India* (London: Nelson, 1878), p. 26,
3. Meaning a rake, a seducer, from Rowe's play *The Fair Penitent.*
4. Guide Gozzano, *Verso la cuna del monde—Lettere dall'India* (1917, EDT: Turin, 1998).
5. Reina Lewis, *Gendering Orientalism* (London and New York: Routledge, 1996), p. 112.
6. See C.A. Bayly, ed., *The Raj—India and the British, 1800-1947* (London: National Portrait Gallery Publications, 1990), p. 241.
7. Charlotte Bronte, *Villette* (1855; Harmondsworth: Penguin, 1985), pp. 275-76.
8. More correctly "habshi," from the Persian. Originally an "Abyssian," now a "negro."

Khushwant Singh's Short Stories: Our Exciting Literary Property

PRADEEP TRIKHA

The short story for Khushwant Singh has been more successful than the novel, poetry or drama because as he says, it has "its roots in tradition."[1] Writers in India adhere to a set of rules and above all "the standard is uniformly high and popularity unrivalled."[2] Singh first established his reputation as a writer though *The Mark of Vishnu and Other Stories.* Since then he has become India's one of the most celebrated and widely read journalists. He has been billed as "clever," "intelligent" and "exciting" in one way or another. His style is original, his material realistic and varied. He has declared that his "roots are in the dunghill of a tiny Indian village."[3] A large majority of his stories have a characteristic note of "a rather heavy handed satire"[4] on several aspects of Indian life. Singh has four volumes of short stories to his credit—*The Mark of Vishnu and Other Stories* (1950), *A Voice of God and Other Stories* (1951), *A Bride for the Sahib and Other Stories* (1967) and *Black Jasmine* (1971) which have appeared in *The Collected Short Stories of Khushwant Singh* (1989). He captures wide range of themes, aspects and comic ironies of Indian life including bureaucracy (e.g. 'Man How the Government of India Is Run!'); democratic election procedures (e.g., 'The Voice of God'); anglicized Indians (e.g., 'A Bride for the Sahib') and Indians abroad ('Mr. Kanjoos and the Great Miracle'). There are stories about sex (e.g., 'Black Jasmine' and 'The Rape'). In 'The Mark of Vishnu,' 'The Memsahib of Mandla' and 'Death Comes to Daulat Ram,' Singh concentrates on supernatural and folklore. He also deals with issues like 'love' and 'memory' in 'A Love

Affair in London' and 'The Portrait of a Lady.' Apart from having craftsmanship and perception, Singh has a sense of self-criticism which he uses to reveal comedy of life. Endowed with "special powers of insight and organisation,"[5] he experiments on a variety of fronts. His belief in the tradition of realism encourages other writers to follow his school of the short story. In order to validate the assertion, let us analyze some of the stories.

II

'Karma' is a story of Sir Mohan Lal, an anglicized Indian, who thinks too high of himself, looks down on his fellow Indians because they are "inefficient, dirty and indifferent." He is waiting for the train in a first class waiting room at the railway station, orders for a small drink, looks forward to a warm conversation with an Englishman. The train arrives, he settles himself in the compartment, suddenly two British soldiers barge in, they throw out his belongings and luggage on the platform. He protests in Oxford accent but nothing happens, the train goes. The crux of the matter is that anglicised Indians unnecessarily ape the West, they must respect their own culture otherwise they are left with a handful of dust in their endeavour to imitate others. This they do at the cost of losing their self-respect, individuality and identity.

In stories like 'Mr. Kanjoos and the Great Miracle,' 'A Bride for the Sahib' and 'When a Sikh Meets Sikh,' Singh expresses his concern about how Indians abroad misrepresent India so much that they often become a butt of ridicule. They aspire to accomplish their parsimonious motives. 'Mr. Kanjoos' is a story of a family—Mr. Kanjoos, his wife and two children. He alongwith the narrator ('I') was nominated as a member of an Indian delegation to an International conference (which was to last for several months) in Germany. Mr. Kanjoos decided to take his family with him. He persuaded the delegation to employ his wife as a Secretary. He could also manage to pass-off his younger child, a boy of fifteen, as under twelve and so travel at half-rates. At the conference, they attended several receptions and cocktails to pick up new contacts for the future conferences. During the course of the conference Mrs. Kanjoos comes across one Mr. Buddhu Sen, an I.A.S. in Indian Embassy and decides to get her daughter, Bhooki,[6] a girl of 18 married to him. She consults her astrologer (whom she could even find in Bonn). Mr. Buddhu and Miss Bhooki must be married on 15th August, the Independence Day of India, at 3.00 p.m. at the Indian Embassy. The marriage takes place at the expense of Indian Ambassador in Germany. Perhaps, the writer zeros in on covetous nature of Indians. No matter where they are, for them a daughter's marriage is the most important issue at the expense of others.

Sex and male understanding of sex are issues of major significance;' Singh writes about the vast complexities as well as superficialities. In *Train to Pakistan* (1956) Iqbal Singh thinks, "It was not possible to keep Indians off the subject of sex for long. It obsessed their minds. It came out in their art, literature and religion."[7] Though it is a generalization but it is unadulterated. 'Kusum,' 'The Rape,' and 'The Bottom Pincher' are stories on the subject. Dalip Singh, the protagonist in 'The Rape' is "possessed with a maddening desire" for his uncle's (now his enemy) daughter Bindu and rapes her. Initially she 'fought like a wild cat but then gave up.' Brought to the magistrate, Dalip Singh pleads not guilty. The magistrate asks if she consented. She affirms. Women unnecessarily try to impose all vices related to sex on males but Singh is of the view that sometimes women too are willing. 'The Bottom Pincher' is a story of a perverted old man who seeks pleasure in brushing and pinching bottoms of women. Both the stories gyrate around perversion and abnormality towards the opposite sex.

Khushwant Singh's belief in a kind of political and moral anarchy serves as the material and argument for social criticism. He makes fun of bureaucracy in 'Man How the Government of India Is Run!' and democratic election procedure in 'A Voice of God.' Sunder Singh in 'Man How the Government of India Is Run!' is a Personal Assistant and Stenographer in a government office. He has two colleagues, Sambamurthy and Ghosh. The triumvirate feels that the entire government machinery rested on their shoulders because great decisions behind most policies were initiated by the people like them but no one has ever realized their importance. They also discuss social, political and sports events. Ghosh is more interested in matrimonials read from the newspaper. Then the three go to see and play the volleyball match. They return to their office at 3.45 p.m. to settle down to work. It is time for tea. 'They discuss postings, transfers, promotions and office intrigues.' (101) They conclude that 'the secret in government service is very simple. You only have to get on with the man just above you and forget everyone else. It has nothing to do with work or ability or anything else like that.' (101-2) Sunder Singh represents the creed of a typical Babu in any government office. 'The Voice of God' narrates a story about election campaign and its result. Singh concludes that 'the voice of people is the voice of God' in the present political scenario in India.

III

In the short stories of Khushwant Singh, men and women live and tolerate each other with their natural instincts and weaknesses. Through them, he reveals such truths which often trouble the common man's life. He comprehends human nature with sympathy and ironic humour in his stories like 'Karma,' 'Mr. Kanjoos,' The Great Miracle' and 'The Voice of God.' His main character "I" is present in several stories. The distinction between the author and 'the narrator I' becomes hairline thin. He has a veritable experience that is the reason he socialises with people. He describes and analyses the games people play in their particular milieu. In some instances like 'When a Sikh Meets Sikh' and 'The Red Tie,' the ironies he illustrates have a lot to say about Indians.

Singh is not much concerned about intellectual and situational framework in stories in which the issues of insecurity and other relationships are examined. He takes a definite stand either as an author or through a character on the issues he raises. He also involves his reader to share the society as it appears to be but tangentially he instructs it. In his opinion the short story "can be fantastic and its characters and situations as fanciful as the writer cares to make them—provided they have the ring of truth and a 'message' to convey." (xii) Almost all stories have an element of truth and a 'message.' He is one of the few writers who observe, record and analyse people and place freshly without recourse to hackneyed situations. He uses the genre to reveal comedy of life, which makes him an 'intelligent,' 'shrewd' and 'exciting' short story writer.

The settings of his stories and the choice of his characters are Indian. Few of his stories have their setting in Europe. Everything which occurs in the life of his characters is in a becoming manner. Neither his plots are tense and melodramatic nor his themes are Freudian. Some of the stories can also be read on symbolic level. 'Karma' opens with Sir Mohanlal looking himself in the 'mirror' of a first class waiting room at the railway station. The mirror is an instrument of self-contemplation as well as the reflection of the universe. Sir Mohanlal suffers from the Naricissitic complex just because he lived in Europe for sometime; on his return to India, he behaves like a European, his make-believe world is shattered the moment two British army officers throw out his luggage on the platform. 'Karma' holds up the mirror to all anglicized Indians for their snobberies.

IV

Like Frank O'Connor, Khushwant Singh seems to believe that stories are means for "submerged population groups" to address a dominating community. Though he shifted from short story to journalism, he never gave up writing short story because of his sensitivity to the world around him. He acknowledges that George Orwell and Somerset Maugham became 'the greatest spinners of short stories of all times.' (xiii) Like others, they aided him to improve his understanding about the world around him; in no way does he ever try to imitate them. Among Indian writers, Sadat Hasan Manto and Munshi Premchand fascinated him the most. Singh is an artist of rare calibre. Experiences stimulate his imagination in such a manner that a story emerges giving him an occasion for reading motives of men and women.

N O T E S

1. Khushwant Singh, *The Collected Short Stories of Khushwant Singh* (New Delhi: Ravi Dayal, 1989), p. ix.
2. *Ibid.*
3. Address to Expo 1967 Auditorium, Montreal, Canada 1967. Qtd. V.A. Shahane, "Khushwant Singh: An Artist in Realism," *Critical Essays on Indian Writing in English,* ed. M.K. Naik et al (Dharwad, 1972), p. 333.
4. M.K. Naik, *A History of Indian English Literature* (New Delhi: Sahitya Akademi, 1982, rpt. 1989), p. 248.
5. A similar idea is expressed by Bruce Bennet in his article 'The Short Story,' *Westerly,* No. 3 (1969), pp. 105-45.
6. Almost all the names in the story are allegorical. Mrs. and Mr. Kanjoos—penny pincher, Ms. Bhooki—famished, Mr. Buddhu—simpleton. Perhaps the names enhance comic satire in the story.
7. Khushwant Singh, *Train to Pakistan* (New Delhi: Times Books International 1956, rpt. 1981), p. 107.

Khushwant Singh's Play *Tyger Tyger Burning Bright*: Binarism at the Cross-roads

KRISHNA MOHAN PANDEY

Khushwant Singh ranks among India's distinguished men of letters on account of his achievement as a novelist, journalist, historian, translator, and short-story writer. His publication *Tyger Tyger Burning Bright* (1993)[1] shows his hidden dramatic craftsmanship of some literary magnitude. The drama dilates between action and stillness, illusion and reality, and lays bare before us our utter ideological impasse. The title has possibly been borrowed from William Blake's poem of the same name. It immediately gives the dramatist an advantageous position because he makes the reader interpret the play in the light of Blake's poem which ensues from the binary structure of the tiger and the lamb. In Blake's poetic world the tiger stands for the powerful, symmetrical, active, destructive yet beautiful, whereas the lamb symbolizes the powerless, passive, beautiful and innocent. Blake wants to make a kind of synthesis of the two, especially, he wants to locate the tiger in the lamb. Khushwant Singh's play is written against the background of a real tiger who has become a man-eater. But the tiger/lamb binarism continues and gives a meaning to the whole play, the summation of which is the victory of instinct over intellect, of feeling over thought.

The play consists of three Acts. Act I has three scenes. The opening scene shows the assembling of the major characters in a new hotel situated in the midst of jungle. The second scene shows these characters in interpersonal relationship. They intend to see the wild life during the night, but the news of the lifting of a village woman by a tiger reaches them and they are advised not to go outside the hotel. The third scene shows the love/lust relationship between Conran-Smith and Yasmeen Ahmad. Conran-Smith reveals his hippy nature by talking of love and trying his best to do love against the background of the immediate death of the village woman. Act II, consisting of only one scene, shows the characters talking to one another as their plan to see the wild life has been postponed for the time being because of the tiger's reported presence within the vicinity of the hotel. Act III has two scenes. Scene I shows Yasmeen Ahmad and Conran-Smith talking together in which Yasmeen tells him that only Sardool Singh had the nerve to go to the villagers' help. Sardool Singh arrives with some villagers to take help from "the big sahibs." The last scene shows Mathur asking Conran-Smith to read *The Gita* so that he may learn the *Nishkama Karmayoga*, but he rejects it because he has his own philosophy of life and he does not want to change it for any religion, dogma, or book. All the characters are worried about their safety. The villagers are asked to wait. All the characters take wine, hear music and go to sleep except Conran-Smith who remembers the monkey-god Hanuman; though he is an areligious person, and goes out of the trellis gate of the hotel and kills the tiger.

Tyger Tyger Burning Bright is remarkable for the neat observation of the three unities of time, place and action. The dramatic principle of the unity of time demands that the action of the play should not take much longer time than does its representation on the stage and should certainly not extend over "a single revolution of the sun." The events of the play are supposed to happen between the evening and the beginning of the following night. The unity of place is strictly observed as the whole of the action takes place in the hotel without any change of scene. The unity of action requires that a play should contain one main and central interest or motive. The play's action ensues from the presence of the tiger near the hotel and ends with his supposed killing by Conran-Smith. Thus, it is remarkable for the skilful manipulation of the plot and dramatic construction of incidents.

The play consists of seven characters and the tiger whose

presence is felt throughout the play. It is significant that they belong to different nations and religions. One is reminded of the plays of Aurobindo where he adopts the scheme of country-wise situations by choosing different countries as the scene of action in different dramas.[2] Khushwant Singh, on the other hand, makes different nationals coexist in the realm of his play. The receptionist Yasmeen Ahmad is a young Muslim girl of twenty-two who has earlier been an air-hostess. Sardool Singh, aged sixty, is the commissionaire. A Sikh by religion, he is a retired soldier and a *shikari.* A.N. Mathur, 35, is the Joint Secretary, Director of Tourism, Government of India H.H. Maharaja of Shamnagar, aged 30, is a maharaja for namesake, having no regal powers in the democratic India. Jack Conran-Smith, 25, hails from England and is a hippy by appearance as well as behaviour. Alf and Babette Schneiderman, 60 and 55 respectively, are American tourists.

Aristotle says that the characters should be true to human types and to life. They should also be self-consistent. By this he meant that characters of different ages and sexes should exhibit the virtues or vices traditionally associated with them. The characters of Khushwant Singh are true to this dictum. Yasmeen Ahmad is a young receptionist and she knows how to entertain different types of guests in the hotel. Conran-Smith is a hippy whose only aim is to get pleasure at any cost. He is not bound by the laws of the so-called civilized society. His conversation with Yasmeen is replete with sensual remarks as well as action. He likes catching the roaring of the wild animals. When told by Yasmeen that the villagers expect the guests' support in killing the tiger, he, like all others, outrightly rejects the idea. But when everybody sleeps and he hears the tiger's roar near the hotel, he catches the roaring and also kills him. Mathur represents the Indian bureaucracy with all the negative connotations it is known for—showiness, lethargy, and maintenance of law and order at least at the surface level. He goes on telling the American pair about India's Five-Year plans, its new temples (by which he means the steel plants) and the prospect of its becoming a powerful nation even when they do not show much interest in his talk. The Maharaja has lost all his power and uses only the valour of his tongue to criticize the Indian bureaucracy. Mr. and Mrs. Schneiderman, who hail from America, the country which feeds half of the dying humanity, expect and get respect from the Indians.

The superb stage-craft of the play is also remarkable. Khushwant Singh's stage directions are complete to the minutest detail. The following description, for example, is a part of how he wants the stage set for the first scene:

> (Scene: Foyer of a hotel in a national game preserve. On one side there is a reception desk with cubby-holes for keys and letters and a telephone switchboard. On the desk there is a large guest-book, a notice saying "Dry Day" a figure of the Air-India Maharaja, and other bric-a-brac typical of small hotels.
>
> The foyer is also the hotel lobby. Facing the reception desk are a sofa, three armchairs and a table. Potted palms, flowers, vases decorate the room.)

The stage-direction is enough to give the reader the feel of the hotel. Likewise, the stage-direction given at the end of the play is very evocative:

> Receptionist lowers the light of the lamps and finds herself an easy chair. Guests drop off to sleep one by one. The jungle sounds are more distinct. Maintain scene for a minute or more. Conran-Smith gets up, makes sure everyone is asleep. He tiptoes towards the commissionaire, slowly extricates the gun out of his grasp and goes out of the trellis gate. After another minute, the roar of the tiger becomes louder and closer. Guests begin to wake in alarm and look around. There is a loud roar as when a tiger springs to attack, and then the report of a gun.

Dialogue is the soul of a play and Khushwant Singh makes very apt use of this dramatic device. He lets the reader think about the tiger from the dialogue between Sardool Singh and Yasmeen Ahmad just at the commencement of the play. Sardool

Singh is irritated because he has killed dozens of tigers and now been given a *bandook* to look at. He asks Yasmeen what to do if there is a man-eater before him. The dialogue shows an aged, retired army personnel's play with words:

Receptionist:	Sardool Singh, you will see how many people will come here. All you have to do is set a few man-eaters to pose for them when they have their cameras ready. You will see how many people will want to take pictures of man-eaters. You see everyone in the world is interested in that kind of animal.
Commissionaire:	Do you know what a man-eater is, Miss Sahib?
Receptionist:	A man-eater is a man-eater. Eats man.
Commissionaire:	Eats women too.
Receptionist:	And children.
Commissionaire:	Accha bhai, he eats men, women and children. He eats human beings.
Receptionist:	He is not always a he, Miss Sahib. A she-tiger often eats more humans than a he tiger.
Commissionaire:	Oh, does she?
Receptionist:	She does. And older she gets, the more man-hungry. (370-71)

The positioning of the hotel in the forest gives a kind of hint to the presence of the tiger which appears as an idea through the dialogue of the receptionist and the Commissionaire. The tiger becomes real when at the end of the scene the roaring of a tiger is heard. The lifting of the village woman by the tiger turns him from the romantic presence to a dangerous reality which continues to remain the same throughout the play. Its presence within the vicinity of the hotel further heightens the horrifying effect. However, the tiger is supposed to be killed when the curtain falls.

The introduction of characters from different strata of society and nations gives Khushwant Singh the freedom to throw light on different aspects of human relationship. Thus, in free India, the power has shifted into the hands of the bureaucracy, though the *maharajas* still possess words of honour like "H.H.," showing their power which no longer is with them. When the receptionist tells the I.A.S. Mathur that the suite has been reserved for him and she hopes that His Highness the Maharaja will not be offended, Mathur retorts, "Why should he be offended?"

It is time these *Maharajas* learnt "who the real rulers of the country are." (375) The receptionist later tells the Commissionaire, "Sardool Singh, the rulers of today are people like our Burra Sahib and Americans. The Maharaja and the Englishman were rulers of yesterday." (376)

Khushwant Singh is the master artist of dialogue writing. Take, for example, the following dialogue which aptly suggests the power-structure within India and also outside it:

Mr. Schneiderman:	And our cigars. (Taking tubes out of his pocket) Anyone care for a genuine Havana? Can't get them back home—thanks to Comrade Fidel Castro. You sir, Maharaja of whatever-it-is?
Maharaja:	No, thank you, Mr. Singh. I do not smoke.
Mr. Schneiderman:	Hey what land of Maharaja are you? You don't drink, you don't smoke. Next you'll be telling us you don't have a harem. How many wives do you have anyway?
Maharaja:	Only one, Mr. Schneiderman. By Maharaja's standards I am almost a bachelor. (All laugh).
Mathur:	You see, the days of Maharajas with many wives are over. In new India . . .
Maharaja:	It's the days of ministers, industrialists, and civil servants with many mistresses. (383-84)

This shows that the freedom of the country from the British imperialism and breaking the vessel of local regal power-structure has simply created new power-structures. The evils of the society have not been eradicated, only their shape has changed. The love/lust of Conran for Yasmeen is well-represented by the playwright through the dialogue. Since he has to prove that love and physical desire are the same, the dialogues spoken by him naturally become a bit longer. The hippy nature of Conran is obvious from the following dialogue:

Conran: Your voice is as beautiful as your face. I expect under your sari your body is more beautiful than either.

Receptionist: Lecherous bastard! I wonder how the legend of the English being cold-blooded was generated! You are the randiest nation on earth.

Conran: How true! For further proof of British randiness come to Room Nine. (Takes her hand) Please! (391)

It is significant that she accepts the compliments of Conran and rather welcomes his advances, but the dramatist also shows the human touch in her character. In this dramatic realm it is only she who shows her concern for the dead village woman:

> In any case how pointless it all is in the face of death. That dead woman with her bones crunched by the tiger is real. The sobbing of her children is real. Being in love or making love to someone you love and who loves you is trivial and unimportant. (389)

The imagery of the play is very effective. The images are born of the emotions of the theme and are subtle, complex and varied. They are intensely vivid and revealing. The central image is that of the tiger—imaginary as well as real, invoking, by implication, the lamb. This is the "floating image" of the play. Conran-Smith wants to "make the world's first recording of a man-eater eating a woman." (386) Forbidden by the receptionist to do so, he says, "If I cannot record a woman-eating tiger, I'll settle for a man-eating tigress." (390) In doing so, he treats himself as a lion, "I especially recommend the mating call of the British lion." (392) Later he calls the receptionist "a lonely luscious bait for the ravenously hungry British lion." (412) The bombs produced by different countries of the world are seen by the Maharaja as man-eating tigers. The receptionist says that "It's like getting tiger cubs from a zoo, training them to be killers and letting them loose in the city." (396) The word "Maharaja" implies that he should be a killer of tigers, but the *Maharaja* in the play is not a tiger (*purushsingh* as the king is often referred to in the Sanskrit plays). He is rather a lamb "scared of the over-sized pussy cats." (394) The reference to the Chinese attack of 1962 again brings the tiger/lamb binarism into focus. Mrs. Schneiderman rightly says, "Somebody is always stabbing somebody else in the back. It's like your man-eating tiger. Crawl up from behind, crouch, then spring to make the kill." (407)

The American pair and the I.A.S. Mathur symbolize the tiger in the socio-political world of the play. The villagers, the *Maharaja*, the receptionist, and Conran-Smith symbolize the lamb. But the presence of the tiger converts all these characters into lamb. However, two of these 'lambs' are able to see the "tiger" in them. The first of these is the commissionaire—the illiterate retired sepoy—who has the nerve to try in helping the villagers. The second character is Conran-Smith who is an indecent, irresponsible hippy in the eyes of the so-called civilized, polished people. He shows the courage to "venture forth into the jaws of the man-eater." (413) It is only Conran who goes not only to record the roar of the tiger but also to kill him. Through the portrayal of Conran, Khushwant Singh suggests the essential humanism and the heroic dimension of his character. In his own way, he succeeds in doing what Blake wanted to do, that is, seeing the tiger in the lamb.

The play has the Khushwantian touch as far as its language is concerned. Khushwant Singh is known for frequent use of the four-letter words. The following dialogue is one such instance:

Conran-Smith:	I can tell you why we are in a mood to get drunk. We are in a bloody funk.
Mr. Schneiderman:	A bloody what?
Conran-Smith:	Funk. Don't you know what it means to be in a blue funk. We are plain scared. (422)

Khushwant Singh creates the Indian idiom through the commissionaire and Mathur. The commissionaire says to the receptionist, "One day you will say Sardool Singh told me something worth a hundred thousand rupees." (377) Such an expression as *lakh take ki bat* is quite common in the Hindi/Punjabi belt of India. When Mathur is irritated by the criticism of the functioning of the government machinery by Conran-Smith and the Maharaja, he says, "For people like you and Mr. Conran-Smith, nothing is right with this country. That is because neither your kind, the princess, nor his, the British, count for a copper *naya paisa.*" (408-9) The same expression—"sixteenth anna of the rupee"[3]—was used by Meet Singh in *Train to Pakistan* which indicates Meet Singh's acceptance of the fullness of truth. Words such as "rich Sahib log," "Miss Sahibji," "Burra Sahib," "accha bhai," "chowkidar," "namaskar," "bahut accha," etc. further add up to create the Indian atmosphere. The notice saying "Dry Day" arouses much laughter indeed. Mrs. Schneiderman thinks that Indians are very clever because "they know when it's going to rain and when it's going to be dry." Immediately she is told by the receptionist that the notice simply means that alcoholic beverages will not be served that day.

The characters speak language true to their selves. Thus, language functions as a register of the characters' social and class position, as well as a tool for measuring their self-consciousness. Khushwant Singh is able to show through the use of his language how ideology intervenes in the consciousness of certain characters and prevents them from understanding the implication of their own statements. Thus, Mathur's words on the *Karma Yoga* leave no impact on anyone because there is a vast chasm between what he professes and what he really does. However, Conran-Smith interprets it in the light of his own socio-cultural background, "(*Nishkama Kamna*) sounds like 'some kind of birth control device—do all you can without worrying about the results.'" (419) Thus, Khushwant Singh has attempted to show an image of the time, employing for that purpose "language such as men do use."

The tiger and the lamb not only denote shifting loyalties on the changing sands of time; they are multiple perspectives which exchange colours and textures as per the situational contexts within a temporal-spatial framework. The tiger and the lamb could also be understood as the bourgeois and proletariat. The lamb is too poor and innocent to be a Marxist and the tiger or tigress would not democratize things on their own. That is what places binarism in trouble. The killing of the tiger by Conran-Smith (a hippy and not an Indian) from the gun of an Indian not only presents a haphazard picture of Indian idealism but also emphasizes how one can become a tiger from the position of a lamb (and *vice versa*) even when one does not know it.

NOTES

1. Khushwant Singh, *Not a Nice Man to Know* (New Delhi: Penguin, 1993), pp, 367-426.
2. The action in *Perseus the Deliverer* and *Rodogune* takes place in Syria. *Eric* has Norway as its locale. *Vasavadutta* and *The Viziers* have ancient India and Persia respectively for their action.
3. Khushwant Singh, *Train to Pakistan* (New York: Grove Press, 1976), p. 49.

Contributors

SUBHASH CHANDRA	Shaheed Bhagat Singh College University of Delhi
R.K. DHAWAN	Shaheed Bhagat Singh College University of Delhi
GILLIAN DOOLEY	Flinders University South Australia
V.T. GIRDHARI	People's College Nanded
R.K. JACOB	St. John's College Palayamkottai
NOVY KAPADIA	S.G.T.B. Khalsa College University of Delhi
P.S. KASTURE	R.D.G. College for Women Akola
C.L. KHATRI	Rajendra College Chapra
MALASHRI LAL	Department of English University of Delhi
O.P. MATHUR	B.H.U. Varanasi
ALESSANDRO MONTI	University of Torino Italy
BASAVARAJ NAIKAR	Karnatak University Dharwad
RANGANATH NANDYAL	IGNOU New Delhi
BHAGABAT NAYAK	Kandarpur College Cuttack

PRAMOD K. NAYAR	Kuvempu University Shimoga
D.K. PABBY	Ram Lal Anand College University of Delhi
KRISHNA MOHAN PANDEY	Kashi Vidyapeeth Varanasi
D. PREMPATI	Delhi College of Arts & Commerce University of Delhi
HARISH RAIZADA	A.M.U. Aligarh
S. RAVINDRANATHAN	M.S. University Tirunelveli
VIJAY K. SHARMA	Ram Lal Anand (Eve.) College University of Delhi
ANITA SINGH	Vasanta College Varanasi
JAGDEV SINGH	Punjab Agricultural University Ludhiana
KHUSHWANT SINGH	Eminent Writer New Delhi
K.V. SURENDRAN	Kannur University Palayad
S.P. SWAIN	Municipal College Rourkela
G.R. TANEJA	Ram Lal Anand College University of Delhi
PRADEEP TRIKHA	Dayanand College Ajmer
HAYDN MOORE WILLIAMS	Flinders University Adelaide